I0796517

THE **SCRIPPS** SCHOOL

SCHOONOVER CENTER FOR COMMUNICATION

THE SCRIPPS SCHOOL

Its Stories, People, and Legacy

Edited by Ralph Izard

Ohio University Press
Athens

Ohio University Press, Athens, Ohio 45701
ohioswallow.com

Printed in the United States of America
Ohio University Press books are printed on acid-free paper ∞ ™

28 27 26 25 24 23 22 21 20 19 18   5 4 3 2 1

Frontispiece: Schoonover Center for Communication, home of the school, 2013–present. *(Photo courtesy of Ohio University)*

Photographs, pages xiv, xx, 402, and 428: Scripps Hall, home of the school, 1986–2013. *(Photo courtesy of Ohio University)*

Hardcover ISBN: 978-0-8214-2315-8
Electronic ISBN: 978-0-8214-4630-0

Library of Congress Control Number: 2018945765

The E.W. Scripps School of Journalism is indebted to G. Kenner Bush for funding this project through the Gordon K. Bush Memorial Fund. The fund honors a longtime publisher of *The Athens Messenger* who was a special friend to the school.

CONTENTS

Scripps Hall
College Green

A NOTE FROM THE DIRECTOR

By Robert Stewart

The E.W. Scripps School of Journalism counts 2023 as the century mark for journalism education at Ohio University, 100 years after the Department of English offered its first newswriting course. Several decades before that, *The New York Times* Managing Editor Carr Van Anda studied science for two years at OU, and by 1912, Ohio students interested in journalism worked on *The Green & White,* the precursor to today's (still) independent student newspaper, *The Post.* But it wasn't until 1923 that an actual journalism curriculum took shape at the first university to be established in the Northwest Territory.

The following year, George Starr Lasher was recruited to create a Department of Journalism, which a decade later became the School of Journalism in the newly formed College of Commerce. The school offered its first High School Journalism Workshop in 1946, and six years later, the department was accredited for the first time by the American Council on Education in Journalism. In the late 1960s, the school became an anchor program in the new College of Communication, founded by school Director John R. Wilhelm.

By the time I joined the faculty in 1987, the school was recognized as one of the top journalism programs in the United States, with nationally regarded faculty members such as Guido H. Stempel III, Hugh Culbertson, Dru Riley Evarts, Russell Baird, and many more. The Associated Press Managing Editors had designated it a "top 10 program" in 1983, and the Scripps Howard Foundation had endowed it shortly before that, a testimony to the school's stature.

I've now been associated with the school for more than a third of its life span, long enough to form a few meaningful opinions about the program. These opinions are offered as prelude to this unique historical treatment of a very special academic unit, the E.W. Scripps School of Journalism at Ohio University.

What attracted me to the school back in the 1980s was its reputation for putting students first—whether it be a doctoral student or an incoming 18-year-old freshman. All of the faculty taught both undergrads and grad students, and whether a faculty member had a PhD mattered little when it came to shaping school affairs.

Over the years, this institutional culture has remained intact, guarded by an affection for a tradition understood as unique, even fundamental to the program. To a great degree, faculty members with the greatest academic research reputations often were the ones proudest of this equilibrium between the "professionals" and the "academics." As a young assistant professor, this deeply impressed me.

Also impressive to me was the degree to which young faculty members like me and my fellow assistant professors were able to carve out leadership roles, which might have been highly protected assignments had the culture been like the more hierarchically structured academic units across the university and across the country.

This book is a collection of stories and reflections about this very special program, the "Scripps School." The authors mostly are the school's alumni. We are collectively indebted to Ralph Izard, my mentor and the director who hired me, for agreeing to take on telling the story of the first 100 years of the program. He has done exactly what I'd hoped he would do: rally our alumni, friends, and faculty to apply their talents to the telling of our tale. The loyalty and talent of these contributors impresses me every day that I'm privileged to serve as director.

Whether you're a friend, an alumnus/alumna, a current or former faculty member, or a prospective student, I think you'll enjoy these stories and, like me, will be inspired by the history of the very special E.W. Scripps School of Journalism.

ACKNOWLEDGMENTS

Credit must be given to Director Robert Stewart, who conceived the idea for this book. We thank him for his confidence and for his consistent contributions during what was a longer-than-anticipated process.

This book belongs primarily to those who provided its content—the information, insight, and photos. That's a long list. They include alumni, faculty, and friends of the School of Journalism. Most are included in the "Contributors" section at the book's end. Their willingness to spend a few hours sharing their memories or writing about topics important to the school is impressive. And that especially is true of those who agreed when asked, "You wanna do another one?" From the standpoint of the editor, the greatest joy was found in regaining contact with former students and colleagues, many of whom I hadn't seen for 40 or more years. They brought back memories of many happy days, and I am especially proud of the success they have achieved.

Among the many who added quality to this book are photographers who kindly allowed us to use their photos. We are particularly indebted to *The Columbus Dispatch* and especially appreciate the kindness and contributions of *Dispatch* Picture Editor Craig Holman. And special kudos are sent to Ken Steinhoff and Joe Vitti.

Our gratitude is expressed to Dr. Dru Riley Evarts, who contributed in many ways, including preparation of a dedicated stylebook.

Throughout the process, we have depended on major contributions from Burton Speakman, first as a graduate assistant, then as a willing volunteer, who wrote several articles, did research, and provided counsel on graphics and photos. We appreciate all that he did to develop and improve the content of this book. We also appreciate Katie Pittman, who went through this book with a careful eye.

Since facts are important, we must say we are indebted for the help of Robin Stock of the Scripps College of Communication and Jessica Cyders of the Southeast Ohio History Center. Likewise, we appreciate the guidance, advice and other contributions of many from the Ohio University Press, with whom it's been a joy to work.

And, finally, thanks to two colleagues from Alden Library: William Kimok, university archivist and records manager; and Janet Carleton, digital initiatives coordinator. Without their contributions of photos from the Ohio University Archives, Mahn Center for Archives and Special Collections, this book would be much less meaningful and, certainly, less interesting.

—*Ralph Izard*

THE **SCRIPPS** SCHOOL

OHIO
E. W. Scripps
School of
Journalism

It takes a community

For nearly 100 years, the success of what is now known as the E.W. Scripps School of Journalism at Ohio University has resulted from the talents, efforts, and contributions of hundreds of faculty, students, and alumni. But they have had help. Certainly, a program that achieves an outstanding national reputation is dependent upon special friends from within and beyond the campus and the Athens community. In this chapter we explore a few of these friends—only a representative sample—as a means of recognizing those who were there when the school needed them.

VIEW FROM THE TOP

By Andrew Alexander

For Ohio University presidents, the E.W. Scripps School of Journalism has been an asset for the institution, even before it gained the Scripps imprimatur. And in some cases, it added an attraction to the job.

When Roderick McDavis became Ohio University president in 2004, he already was "well aware that the Scripps School of Journalism was among the best journalism schools in the nation." McDavis, who received a BA from Ohio University in 1970 before starting a long career in higher education, recalled that the school's "reputation for excellence was one of many pride points that drew me home" to become the university's 20th president.

His predecessor, Robert Glidden (1994–2004), recalled learning about the journalism school shortly after a search firm approached him about Ohio University's top job while he was provost and vice president for academic affairs at Florida State University. "I realized immediately that Scripps was considered to be one of the 'jewels in the crown' of Ohio University," he said.

Charles Ping knew little about the journalism school when, in 1975, he left his job as provost at Central Michigan University to become president of Ohio University. But soon after his arrival, and during a tenure that lasted nearly two decades, Ping recognized that "journalism was the one program that had a national draw" because its reputation attracted talented students and instructors from around the country and the world.

Facing page: (clockwise) Charles J. Ping, Vernon R. Alden, Roderick J. McDavis, and Robert Glidden. *Photos of Presidents Alden, Ping, and Glidden are courtesy of Ohio University Archives, Mahn Center for Archives and Special Collections. The photo of President McDavis is included with the permission of Ohio University Photography Supervisor Ben Siegel.*

In search of global recognition

Achieving global recognition was a key goal of President Vernon Alden's (1962–69) when he hired John Wilhelm to head the journalism school in 1968. Alden had gotten to know Wilhelm while serving on the board of directors of the New York–based McGraw-Hill Publishing Company, a leading news and book publisher. Alden recalled that he had developed a "good relationship" with Wilhelm as head of the McGraw-Hill World News division and knew he had "far-reaching and influential connections in the industry all around the world."

Ohio University was about to receive capital funding for a new complex that would include journalism, television, radio, and speech and hearing. Alden's plan was to eventually pull together all these entities and create a college of communication. Also, he needed someone to head the journalism school because its longtime director, L.J. Hortin, had retired in 1967. Alden's plan: find someone who could fill Hortin's position and, soon after, become dean of the new College of Communication.

"I needed someone with an outstanding reputation, who was really a part of the emerging world of modern communications," Alden recalled, adding that he wanted an industry professional "who also had the skills to assume the leadership of journalism and this start-up endeavor."

Wilhelm was reticent, arguing that he lacked academic credentials because he didn't have a PhD. "But that was exactly why I wanted him," Alden said. "With his contacts, he could help arrange internships for our students and give them truly 'world-class' exposure and experience.

"I persisted," Alden remembered, "and invited John and his wife to come to campus. After further discussion, John agreed to join us, and he certainly fulfilled all my expectations." Wilhelm soon became dean of the new College of Communication and was named dean emeritus in 1981. He died in 1994.

Given the stature and importance of journalism within Ohio University, the four university presidents recalled having a necessarily close involvement with the school.

Ping said he was "very much involved" with Wilhelm and former school Director Cortland Anderson in negotiating the original endowment from the Scripps Howard Foundation in 1982. It included renaming the program the E.W. Scripps School of Journalism.

"I got to know all the faculty and all the directors," Ping recalled. "I was also involved in tenure disputes, freedom of speech issues, and other issues. There's no point in being a faculty member if you can't be contrary," he joked.

Achieving a "delicate balance"

Glidden said he felt the journalism school "projected an appropriate balance between theory and practice—something that's not always easily achieved in a professional school."

McDavis, who retired as president in 2017, said that combining all five Scripps College of Communication schools in the new Steven L. Schoonover Center for Communication would strengthen the journalism school. "By housing all of our aspiring communicators under one roof, we are better preparing students for the media convergence and cross-collaboration that has transformed journalism in the 21st century," he said.

Each of the four presidents also experienced moments of tension with *The Post,* the editorially independent student newspaper that is not part of the journalism school.

"*The Post* is the bane of every president's existence," said Ping. "But it is also a great student newspaper."

Glidden said he had good relations with *The Post* "for at least eight of the ten years I served as president." And "even in the other years, my relationship was not poor," he recalled. "It was just nonexistent because the editors at the time thought it unprofessional or unethical" to have social dealings with those in university leadership.

Early in his presidency, Glidden said, a member of *The Post*'s editorial staff invited him and his wife to a spaghetti dinner at the student's apartment. Glidden sensed a "trap," but he said, "We had a delightful time."

The Gliddens reciprocated, inviting a handful of *Post* staffers to the president's Park Place residence for pizza before they all descended to the basement to play pocket billiards. "The agreement was no university business questions from them and no lobbying from us, and it worked great," Glidden said, adding that it became an annual tradition for most of his time as president.

Glidden said he made a point of making himself available for interviews by student journalists from *The Post* or WOUB, the university's public broadcasting station. "Often, I was quite certain that the questions had been prompted by a Scripps faculty member, so I would sometimes ask about that," he said. "But I seldom got an admission."

—Dwight Woodward contributed to this story.

A TRIP WORTH TAKING—REPEATEDLY

By Sue Porter

Those who've regularly traveled the 155 miles from The E.W. Scripps Company's headquarters in Cincinnati to Ohio University's Athens campus know the road to a friend's house is never long.

For more than 30 years, State Route 32 has connected one of the nation's oldest and most successful media companies with one of the top journalism schools in the country. The journey has brought more than $20 million to OU's coffers from the company's philanthropic division, the Scripps Howard Foundation, and forged a deep and mutually beneficial partnership.

The first trips were made in the mid-1970s.

The foundation had just marked its 10th anniversary, and board members thought it was time for more-strategic expenditures. Until then, grants were in the form of scholarships to several dozen journalism schools—including OU—and rarely was there feedback. A nationwide search committee was charged with identifying a journalism school that could become a significant partner.

Ohio University easily made the short list. But it was the strong recommendation of mutual friend Richard R. Campbell, then editor of Scripps' *Columbus Citizen-Journal* and a diehard Bobcat (BSJ '47), that made OU the favorite candidate.

As a news professional, Campbell was well aware of the extraordinary education OU journalism students were receiving and hired as many alumni as possible. But as a confidant of several OU administrators, he knew maintaining that excellence would be difficult without a new facility and more financial support.

Ohio Governor James A. Rhodes presides over a June 10, 1982, ceremony that affirmed the partnership between the Scripps Howard Foundation and Ohio University. Participants, from the left, included the governor; Charles E. Scripps, chairman of the E.W. Scripps Company; OU President Charles J. Ping; Jacques A. Caldwell, president of the foundation; and OU journalism alumnus Richard R. Campbell. *(Reprinted with permission from the E.W. Scripps Company)*

A visit by the chairman

The most significant trip of all was made in 1980 by Charles E. Scripps, chairman of The E.W. Scripps Company.

He was impressed with the glowing reports he'd read about OU journalism, but he wanted to personally see results before endorsing a commitment. So on a beautiful spring day, in his tan Mercedes that bore the bumper sticker "to err is human," the grandson of company founder E.W. Scripps drove east on SR 32 to attend the annual journalism awards banquet.

So warm was the welcome, so outstanding were the students and faculty, foundation plans for a major gift to Ohio University moved quickly after that. And when Cortland Anderson arrived on campus in 1981 as the school's new director, he made cementing a deal with Scripps—and a capital allocation from the State of Ohio—top priorities.

Thus, June 10, 1982, was a proud day in Columbus, Cincinnati, and Athens.

Ohio Governor James A. Rhodes presided over a ceremony in his office that affirmed the Scripps-OU partnership. Charles Scripps and Jacques A. Caldwell, president of the foundation, presented OU President Charles Ping with a check for $375,000, the first installment of a $1.5 million endowment gift to the journalism school. The funds were earmarked for "innovative journalism programs," with a portion allocated for architectural plans to convert Carnegie Hall to new journalism quarters. A $3 million capital improvement bill to renovate the 27,000-square-foot building—thereby doubling the school's space—was on schedule for legislative approval.

A living memorial to E.W. Scripps

Charles Scripps called the endowment a "living memorial" to his grandfather's name because it would make more highly trained journalists available to the profession in perpetuity.

Caldwell offered perspective, saying the named school should be at OU because E.W. Scripps published his first newspaper in Cleveland, and Ohio is home to Scripps headquarters and several of its operating units.

Ping accurately predicted, "Generations of Ohio University students will show their gratitude by what they do better than any words I can say."

Days after the announcement, OU trustees approved naming the school the E.W. Scripps School of Journalism, and on September 12, 1984, ground was broken for the $3.5 million renovation of the Carnegie building now known as E.W. Scripps Hall.

Charles Scripps again made the trip to Athens, this time with his daughters Marilyn and Julie, who joined the lineup of shovel-wielding celebrants. Lawrence A. Leser, president of The E.W. Scripps Company, accompanied them to present an additional gift of $250,000 to help furnish Scripps Hall. Director Anderson used the occasion to announce the more rigorous admission standards and curriculum that would accompany the relocation. "We're not looking to be bigger," he said. "We are looking to be better."

Charles Scripps and his daughters were back on campus 20 months later with dozens of representatives from the company and foundation to dedicate Scripps Hall. This time Leser came bearing a $25,000 check for the Cortland Anderson Memorial Endowment, a fund that would provide an annual award to the school's outstanding student or students.

Anderson, who had died from cancer the previous December, had become a friend, Leser said, and the Scripps "Cincinnati connection" didn't want his contribution to the new building and the benefits it would bring to OU and the profession forgotten.

As the school's new director, Ralph Izard made sure the friendship between the two Scripps entities continued to flourish. He hosted a Jobs in Journalism workshop and invited Scripps professionals to work with students; in addition, working with the foundation's new president, Albert J. Schottelkotte, Izard appointed a journalism advisory board with major representation from the Scripps organizations.

Schottelkotte frequently visited the school and accumulated a handful of speeding tickets from Ohio State Highway Patrol troopers to prove it. "It seems I'm in a hurry to get there to find out what's new," he'd say, "and I'm always in a hurry to get back to Cincinnati to share the good news."

Izard and others stayed in close touch with the Scripps family, and in 1988 Charles Scripps donated his grandfather's papers to Ohio University. The historically valuable collection, which spans the period 1868 to 1926, includes personal correspondence with U.S. presidents and priceless memorabilia.

In 1990, the collection was featured in a display at Alden Library, and the school invited Scripps family members and company representatives to a conference titled "Celebration of the Legacies of E.W. Scripps" on May 2–3. The program featured both academic presentations and more-informal discussions.

But it also was a social success for school, corporate, and family members. Scripps cousins had such a good time at what was the family's first reunion in nearly 100 years that they decided to get together annually ever after. And Maggie Scripps Klenzing, who lived in Fredericksburg, Texas, at the time, was so favorably impressed with the school that she returned as a full-time student.

Scripps Visiting Professional Chair

Foundation trustees liked what they saw, too, and later that year approved a $1 million endowment for a Scripps Visiting Professional Chair to bring noted working journalists to the school as resources for students and faculty.

In recent years, Izard's successors Michael Real, Thomas Hodson, and Robert Stewart have continued to build the relationship through annual Scripps Days that bring more than a dozen Scripps professionals to campus for classroom presentations and recruitment for internships and jobs; inclusion in curriculum reviews to ensure that students receive the education and practical experience necessary to meet industry needs; and partnership in the presentation of an annual $20,000 Ursula and Gilbert Farfel Prize for excellence in investigative journalism as part of the foundation's Scripps Howard Awards for professionals.

As partners in education, Schottelkotte's successors Judith G. Clabes and Mike Philipps have offered Scripps students special opportunities at the foundation's Semester in Washington program, funding for creation of a research center, support for the school's Statehouse Bureau in Columbus, internship stipends for more than 200 students, scholarships for more than 500 students, and a diversity fund that has increased minority student participation in the school's High School Journalism Workshop.

The list could go on, but an event that took place April 4, 2006, heralded a new peak as testament to the university's enduring friendship with the Scripps company. That was the day the Scripps Howard Foundation announced its $15 million gift to Ohio University for the College of Communication, which led OU trustees to create the Scripps College of Communication.

"My father would definitely be pleased with the way our friendship with the school has evolved," said Julie Scripps-Heidt, who as a longtime member of the school's advisory board knows that the road to Athens is always a trip worth taking.

SOCIETY OF ALUMNI AND FRIENDS

By Ron Iori

The E.W. Scripps School of Journalism arguably has the most loyal alumni base of any college or school at Ohio University. By the mid-1990s, the thousands of Scripps alumni also were among some of the most successful Ohio University graduates in their disciplines.

It seemed certain that the loyalty of these successful graduates could be organized to help the school in its programs and future development.

So, in 1995, school Director Ralph Izard formed an exploratory committee of about a dozen Athens-area alumni to consider establishing a Society of Alumni and Friends to help boost the engagement of this successful alumni base. The most notable member of the committee was Mary Elizabeth Lasher Meyers (BSJ '42), daughter of long-time school Director George Starr Lasher.

A Scripps student interning for the school was enlisted to research other alumni societies at the university. After months of interviews and coordination with the alumni association, a draft constitution and bylaws were developed.

At that point, Izard and the committee decided to move forward to establish a more formal and lasting organization. On March 7, 1997, the Journalism School's Society of Alumni and Friends was officially chartered by OU's Alumni Association.

The society's first officers

Later that spring, Izard tapped his strong network of alumni to find four who would serve as the society's first officers. In addition to Mary Elizabeth Lasher Meyers, I was one of those, along with Melody (Lawrence) Snure

Ron Iori. *(Photo provided by Ron Iori)*

(BSJ '72); Angela (Hazlett) Krile (BSJ '97), the intern referenced previously; and Kori (Wisniewski) Gassaway (BSJ '97).

We met one weekend in Athens in the summer of 1997, trying to determine the society's focus and how it could best help the school. We eventually examined several types of programming and ideas, ranging from establishing scholarships to helping with Communication Week.

To codify the new society's goals, the officers wrote and adopted a mission statement: "The Society of Alumni and Friends is an organization dedicated to enhancing the relationships among alumni, faculty, staff and students of the School of Journalism. The society provides programming to encourage the development of those relationships."

As the society evolved, the officers began to form committees to distribute the workload and become more effective. Among the many initial ideas and programs were a speakers' bureau, a quarterly e-newsletter for current students with job tips and career information, a key contact guide, a website, and participation (along with faculty) in the organization of Journalism Day during Communication Week.

The beginning of Senior Saturday

After eliminating some ideas, the officers began determining the gaps in programming for students and the activities that would attract alumni back to campus to help students. Out of that effort emerged Senior Saturday, the most enduring and perhaps the signature program of the society.

Senior Saturday is a one-day event for journalism school seniors in which alumni come to campus, offer career-guidance workshops, conduct mock interviews and résumé reviews, and interact with seniors. The ultimate goal: provide the seniors with the information and tools needed to land jobs and be successful in them.

The inaugural Senior Saturday was held in February 2003. Since its inception, Senior Saturday has become an award-winning program that has helped guide hundreds of seniors in launching their careers.

Today, the society continues its work. In addition to Senior Saturday, it raises money for scholarships, maintains a speakers' bureau, hosts a LinkedIn page to encourage alumni networking, and publishes a newsletter. But the work isn't complete and will continue to evolve. For all of those involved in the early days, the original vision has succeeded in ways they couldn't possibly have imagined.

A SPECIAL FRIEND

By Jack G. Ellis

It all began with an urgent telephone call from J. Warren McClure (BS '40).

McClure was not a graduate of Ohio's School of Journalism, but his career was in the newspaper business, as publisher for the McClure Newspaper Group, which included as its anchor publication the *Burlington Free Press* in Vermont.

When McClure sold his company to the Gannett Company Inc. in 1971, he became Gannett's first vice president/marketing, as well as Gannett's largest individual stockholder. He retired in 1975.

"Mac" telephoned me, saying, "We've some trouble brewing with Gannett's relationship with Ohio University, and our recruiter just returned to Rochester [New York] requesting that Ohio State University replace Ohio University on the recruiting schedule." Evidently, for some reason, the recruiter did not see his most recent trip to Ohio University as a good experience and was offended by the lack of attention and the small number of students with whom he met.

"Mac" said OU needed to do something quickly.

As the university's vice president for development, I met immediately with Dean John Wilhelm and explained the problem; we flew off to Rochester the next day to meet with the executive staff of Gannett, including McClure. We were graciously received and given the opportunity to present our "case" to assure them of the importance of continuing our relationship with Gannett and of the care that would be given to future recruiting visits.

The Gannett officials agreed to continue the relationship and to keep the J-School on their recruiting schedule. McClure was instrumental in helping maintain the relationship through his early notification of a potential problem and by speaking strongly on behalf of Ohio University and the J-School.

As a result of the meeting in Rochester, we learned of a Gannett "Technology on Wheels" demonstration bus that was on tour to demonstrate the changes in newspaper publishing techniques. The bus visited Ohio University for several days, exposing the faculty and students to "what was coming" in newspaper reporting and printing.

Further, and again with thanks to McClure and the quick visit to Gannett by Ohio University officials, a substantial grant was made to the Ohio University Foundation for the School of Journalism, specifically for the purchase of the school's first computers, launching the school into the first phase of 20th-century newspaper technology and helping continue its reputation among the nation's leading schools of journalism.

What began as a potential disaster in a relationship with one of the premier national newspaper companies developed into an even stronger bond between the Gannett Company and Ohio University. And it was the concern and loyalty of Ohio University's alumnus J. Warren McClure that made it happen.

McClure later visited Ohio University and, at a small luncheon in his honor, presented a prototype of a new publication Gannett planned to introduce in the near future. It was to be a daily newspaper with national distribution, a feature thought by some at the luncheon as a near impossibility. The newspaper was to be called *USA Today.*

Later, "Mac" also personally provided funds to help create, in the Scripps College of Communication, the J. Warren McClure School of Information and Technology Systems, one of only a few such academic programs in the nation.

Leadership

It is undeniable that the school's directors do not deserve exclusive credit for the school's success over the years. The nine individuals who have held that title have witnessed growth and improvement through the impressive thought and support of faculty, alumni, university administrators, and students. Nevertheless, leadership is important. Directors and associate/assistant directors make contributions of substance. Thus, those who have served administratively merit special attention.

Facing page: Ellis Hall, home of the school, 1923–36. *(Photo courtesy of the Ohio University Archives, Mahn Center for Archives and Special Collections)*

George Starr Lasher.
(Photo courtesy of the Ohio University Archives, Mahn Center for Archives and Special Collections)

FOUNDER AND MOTIVATOR: GEORGE STARR LASHER

By Ralph E. Kliesch and Dru Riley Evarts

"GEORGE STARR LASHER. . . . It was always that. George STARR Lasher . . . or simply Lasher.

"Nobody would think of calling him George Lasher or G.L. or even George S. Lasher. Those would be lesser names for lesser folk. This was a special one. You could see it in the way he walked across the campus. Strolled, really, and it was as if Cutler Walk were Broadway. Or when he looked at you from under those bushy eyebrows, his eyes dark, not questioning, waiting; jaws set, lips tight beneath that gray smudge of a mustache that seemed to fade into his pink skin."

Thus did Ralph Brem (BSJ '55), who at the time was managing editor of *The Pittsburgh Press,* highlight the prevailing view of the School of Journalism's founder and first director.

George Starr Lasher stimulated fear combined with respect and even adoration among his students. From the perspective of Ohio University, he effectively laid the foundation of what was to become the School of Journalism. Lasher was the program's first administrator and founder of it as a school, and he guided the school to one of its special building blocks—a longstanding emphasis on writing and proper language usage.

It was nearly a century ago, in 1924, when university President E.B. Bryan engaged the remarkably well prepared Lasher to develop a journalism program on the elm-laden Athens campus. Bryan, who the previous year had obtained Board of Trustees approval to establish a Department of Journalism, had no way of knowing the academic and professional dividends his choice was to pay, but his selection bore obvious promise.

As part of the College of Arts and Sciences, the journalism program was first located in Ellis Hall, near the English Department. When journalism became a school in 1936, it was moved to the ground floor of Ewing Hall, the only nonconforming yellow-brick building on campus (no longer there but then located near the top of the present John Wilhelm Amphitheater in front of Scripps Hall).

During the late '40s and early '50s, Lasher lived in an apartment at the corner of Court and Union streets, above what is now the College Bookstore. He subscribed to many newspapers that he picked up daily at the Post Office, the Union Street building now called Haning Hall. His daily journeys from home base to Ewing Hall to the Post Office and back to either home or Ewing, then, beat a regular triangle along which he had many greeters. His two daughters were by then pursuing careers or studying for them. Both are Ohio University graduates who received degrees in Lasher's two loves—journalism and theater—Mary Elizabeth (BSJ '42), the first female editor of *The Post;* and Dorothy (BFA '50), heavily involved in the university theater.

He always had time for students

He served as the program's administrator from 1924 until his administrative retirement in 1951, still the longest term of any among the school's leaders. (He retired from teaching in 1956.)

Lasher had begun his professional career at the age of 12 by working for editors who did not know his age as a correspondent from his hometown for *The Gazette* in Kalamazoo, Michigan, a city of some 40,000. In close succession during and after high school, he organized the first newspaper and magazine subscription service in his hometown of Plainwell, bought the semiweekly *Plainwell News,* and covered the St. Louis Exposition and the Democratic national convention as a freelancer for a string of Indiana and Michigan newspapers. Eventually, he worked as sports editor of *The Grand Rapids* (Michigan) *Press* and then moved to the opposition newspaper, *The Grand Rapids Post,* as sports editor and drama critic.

He earned his bachelor's and master's degrees at the University of Michigan, the latter in 1917. While there, where his education was financed by his profits from the *Plainwell News,* he participated in collegiate theatricals. More significant to his future as an educator, however, were his work on the campus newspaper, *The Michigan Daily,* and his efforts to found a local fraternity, later to become a chapter of Theta Chi. After postgraduate work at Columbia University and the University of Chicago, he taught high school and college English for several years. At the time he moved to Ohio, he was teaching rhetoric and English at the University of Michigan.

Lasher's on-campus presence, as teacher, adviser, friend, or friendly foe, made indelible impressions and inspired reminiscences. Certainly, he performed his administrative duties with distinction—including an innovative program that sent students to work at *The Athens Messenger* for course credit, thought to be the first such program in the country. But clearly it was his classroom work that most inspired students.

"Why, the man looked and talked and acted more like a college professor than any man I've ever known!" Saul Bennett (BSJ '57) said. "That silver mane, that vest and watch chain laced with what must have been all the right academic ornaments, that somewhat rumpled yet perfectly-in-keeping professorial air. He was all class and dignity, but we didn't seem to appreciate it then. I, for one, was too busy trying to wriggle out of taking his basic journalism course because I knew it was a chamber of sentence-diagramming horrors certain to generate a failing grade from the Lasher red pencil."

The infamous Introduction to News Writing

It probably goes without contradiction that no two Lasher students will ever get together without rehashing fond, sometimes even bittersweet, memories. The tartest of the latter undoubtedly stem from Lasher's infamous Journalism 103, Introduction to News Writing, the dreaded sophomore gantlet that initiated the school's continuing emphasis on proper and grammatically correct language usage.

Perhaps among his students it was now-retired journalism faculty member Dru Riley Evarts (BSJ '51, MSJ '73, PhD '77) who knew Lasher best, through her service as his undergraduate grader for more than three years. Years later, she continued in his footsteps with her course Precision Language, perhaps not the same as Lasher's class but certainly one, like that of her mentor, that inspired fear, respect, and, yes, grammar and usage knowledge in the minds and hearts of her students.

Frank Bowers (BSJ '57), however, gained his fondest memories from Lasher's class in reviewing.

"In George Starr Lasher's bill o' fare, if 103 was the meat and potatoes, Reviewing and Criticism was the dessert—a light, fluffy confection served up as a welcome departure from the strict regimen usually proffered by journalism's master," he said. "Reviewing and Criticism revealed the truer, instinctive side of George Starr Lasher. . . . I think of George Starr Lasher as a successful teacher because he made you want to know the things he knew because you felt the things he knew were worth knowing."

Lasher's love of culture—and his teaching—went well beyond his classroom. During his years at Ohio University, he organized bus trips to the Hartman Theater in Columbus and occasionally to New York, sometimes five or six times a year. Among the first to experience these trips was Ludel Sauvageot (BSJ '27), the first woman graduate of the program. For her, the recollections went beyond the cultural experiences.

"I was impressed from the first with his sincere interest in students, their work, and their futures," she said. "Mr. Lasher was what novelists sometimes refer to as a 'gentleman of the old school.' Accompanying his innate dignity were his friendliness, a unique sense of humor, and his almost fanatical regard for the ethics of journalism. He was a great teacher and a true friend."

But whether people remember Lasher for what he was, what he did, or how he looked or acted, there is no question that he was remembered wherever he went.

In the future, students and faculty who didn't know the man will have reminders given by those who did know him. Many students will be reminded of the school's first director when they are awarded the George Starr

Lasher Scholarship. Or perhaps it will be because they gained special cultural experiences through the George Starr Lasher Living Legacy Award. Or maybe it will be as they walk past or have classes in Lasher Hall, built in 1925, appropriately for *The Athens Messenger,* but the home of the school from 1975 through part of 1986. These have been provided through the generosity of Lasher's daughters and the support of his many admirers.

—Excerpts from a booklet, "George Starr Lasher: Founder and First Director, the Ohio University School of Journalism," by Ralph E. Kliesch and Dru Riley Evarts, May 1975

REFLECTIONS ON A JOURNALISM LIFE: L.J. HORTIN

By Sid Davis

> So Enter That Daily Thou Mayest Grow
> In Knowledge Wisdom and Love

Nearly every day of the 1948 school year, 5,611 students passed under or near that inscription on the main gateway to the Ohio University campus—simple but meaningful words, a gift left by the class of 1915 commemorating the hundredth anniversary of the university's first graduating class. (The Athens campus today has 22,000 students.)

The year 1948 was no ordinary school year. Like most other colleges in America, Ohio University was experiencing the stampede, begun in 1946, of World War II veterans toward a college education paid for by the United States government. The gift of a four-year college education was a part of federal law that came to be known as "The GI Bill of Rights," considered one of the greatest endeavors in social legislation in the nation's history.

I had spent two years with the United States Navy, serving aboard the USS *Toledo* as part of the American Occupation Forces in Japan. Now, I was

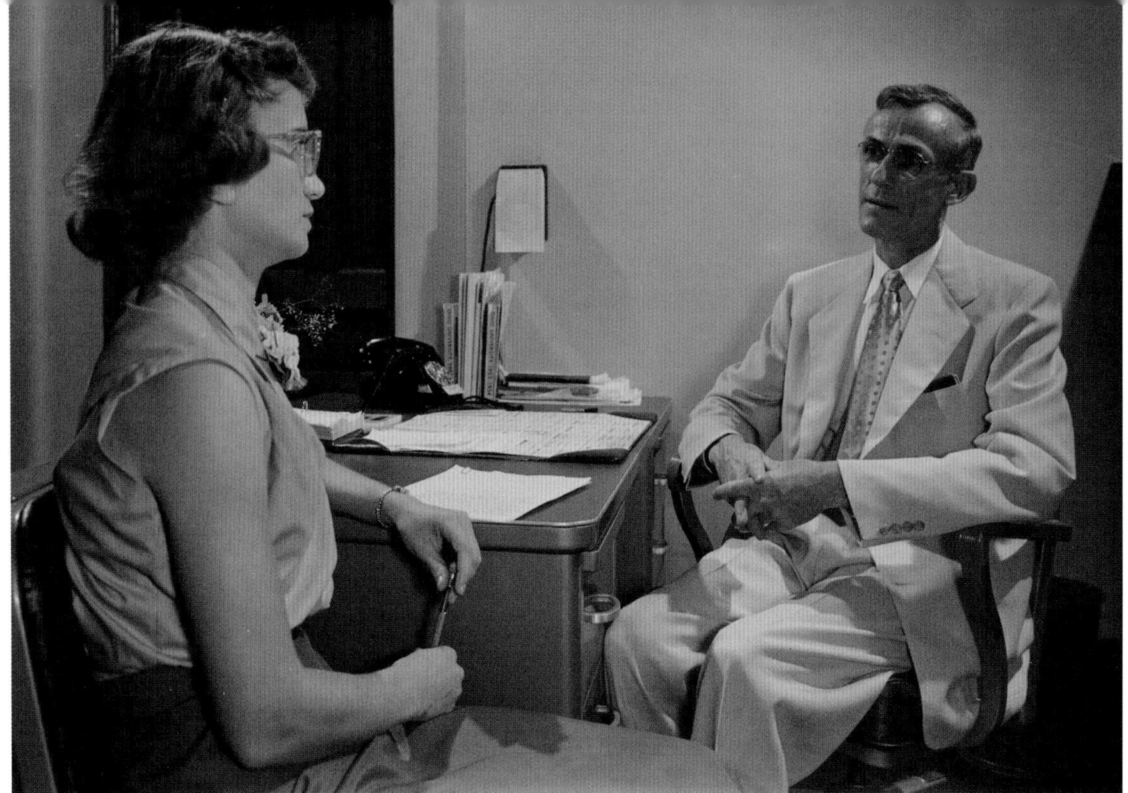

L.J. Hortin. *(Photo courtesy of the Ohio University Archives, Mahn Center for Archives and Special Collections)*

a college freshman in the Class of 1952. It was generally believed that the vets took college more seriously. They were in a hurry. That was so in my case.

The influx of students swamped the university. The campus was spotted with military-style Quonset Huts for overflow classes or administration.

Into that swelling of the campus and the stretch pains that ensued marched Loren Joseph Hortin, a former high school teacher, reporter for the *St. Louis Post-Dispatch,* and wire service guy, a stringer for 17 years for The Associated Press.

L.J. joined the faculty in 1947, one year before my class arrived. Later, in 1951, he became director, following in the big footsteps of George Starr Lasher, a nationally recognized journalism educator. L.J.'s classes leaned to the folksier side. His hands-on background provided many anecdotes, and his colorful stories made his points. A thin, tall man, he had only one mood: cheerful, blessed with a warm grin. If ever he was glum or angry, I never saw it. In his classes, as I recall, his teaching style was something on the order of a city editor addressing the staff in the "bullpen," going over the assignments, praising a good piece of journalism, or admonishing sloppy writing. I remember laughter.

We students were in the pen, so to speak, sharing L.J.'s teachings together, all at once.

Straightforward and straightlaced

L.J. was straightforward with students and pretty straightlaced, I think, a religious person. He did show deference to the GI Bill folks, recognizing that we were a bit older and perhaps a bit slower too.

L.J. also had broad stints in public service and business, having been on a committee of the Tennessee Valley Authority, the Lower Tennessee Valley Association, and a manager of the City Chamber of Commerce in Murray, Kentucky. He held a Master of Arts degree from Murray State College and after his tour at Ohio University returned to Murray State as head of the journalism program, serving in that position until he retired in 1974.

Professor Hortin's teaching was strengthened by the personal interest he took in his students. After I had spent seven years at WKBN Radio/TV in Youngstown, my first job, he suggested that it was time to try for Washington. I had brashly confided to him earlier that something on the order of the White House beat was my ultimate goal. Within a month and quite by surprise, there was an opening for a White House correspondent in the Westinghouse Broadcasting Company Washington News Bureau. I got the job.

Professor Hortin held an additional role as faculty adviser to OU's Sigma Delta Chi chapter of the men's professional journalism fraternity (now the Society of Professional Journalists). As with everything else, he took that job seriously. When we held events, such as passing out large desk blotters free to thousands of students, typically, L.J. showed up on Saturday mornings to help. The popular blotters carried paid advertisements of Athens merchants

PERSONAL FRIENDSHIPS

Joan Herrold Wood. (*Scripps College of Communication photograph*)

I HAVE A SENSE that L.J. Hortin mentored many of his students long after they graduated. I know I received a note or two from him. Joan Herrold Wood (BSJ '52), a J-School pal from Lancaster, Ohio, remained close to OU. We have been in touch, lo, these several decades. With her BSJ in hand, Joan launched into daily journalism, choosing Pittsburgh, a gritty yet great newspaper town, working for Scripps Howard's *Pittsburgh Press.* She later joined the powerful communications giant J. Walter Thompson.

Joan lent her skills to Ohio University's future too. She's remained an energetic, generous, most dedicated alumna. (Much of her energy came from professional ballroom dance competitions.) With great affection, here's what Joan emailed about our mentor, L.J. Hortin. Note that Joan mentions Mrs. Hortin. Many of us got to know her.

"Loren J. Hortin—what memories that name generates. When we met I was a very new freshman and he, my adviser. I walked into his office not knowing what to expect. He jumped up from his desk. Right hand extended. Big, big smile. That was his trademark. Always a big smile. It was the beginning of a friendship that lasted long after I graduated. Christmas cards. Nuggets of advice. News of Mellie and himself. Later I wondered if his wonderful Mellie decorated a Christmas tree in his classroom in Kentucky as she did in Ohio."

–Sid Davis

and paid for travel to SDX events. They were the brainchild of my roommates, Gerry Davis (BSJ '52) and Ivan Weinstock (BSJ '52) of Cleveland, both of whom were in L.J.'s classes as well.

Personal interest in his students

"I remember well the lessons learned in the School of Journalism, especially Mr. Hortin's impact. His personal interest in us impresses me to this day," Gerry said. "Mr. Hortin impressed me with his stature, his knowledge, and his warmth of feelings. He was a quiet talker, but you had to listen. It may have been there that I first heard of the two axioms of journalism that I have carried with me through life. I share these with my associates in our work and especially with my grandchildren when they ask for help."

Surely, like Gerry Davis, all of my classmates must remember the first of these axioms, a refrain taken by L.J. from French literature: "What did Flaubert teach his protégé, Guy de Maupassant?" he'd ask. Then, quickly, L.J. would point a finger and declare, "For everything there is to be said, there is but one noun to name it, one adjective to describe it, and one verb to give it life." The second axiom—well known by journalism students and professionals everywhere—is "the story always starts with the five Ws: Who, What, Where, Why, and When."

That Professor Hortin loved his classroom and teaching, there is no doubt. That he was well liked? Without question. He had the gift. Period. He was sincere, humorous. His classes were learning experiences. But under his leadership, there was his larger role, and the School of Journalism prospered.

I do wonder what L.J. would think about today's journalism. If there is a single, lasting reflection his students hold of Professor Hortin, it is his patience as a teacher. The lure of the classroom was a thrill for him, as was his devotion to journalistic integrity. He emphasized a lesson that remains: "First, get it right." I am certain I recalled those words on November 22, 1963, as I reported the assassination of President John F. Kennedy from Dallas. Despite the chaos, the confusion, the wild rumors, and the enormity of the crime that terrible, sad day, I somehow held to the truth as I saw it.

"HORTINISMS"

DIRECTOR L.J. HORTIN had his own manner of speaking and frequently produced what *The Post* staff referred to as "Hortinisms." Many of these were compiled and published. With thanks to *The Post,* here are some examples:

> February 4, 1966: "The electric chair is period furniture. It ends the sentence."
>
> April 6, 1967: "There are two types of people in this world—the good and the bad. The good determine which is which."
>
> April 10, 1967: "Every man must have a seed of hope, however small, in order to live a fruitful life."

—Compiled by Katie Pittman

EXPANDING THE HORIZON: JOHN R. WILHELM

By Brendon Butler

In 1944, John Wilhelm was working in New York as a news editor with United Press on the overnight cable desk, rewriting international reports for the afternoon papers. He later said these cables from distinguished reporters made him "feel a need to become a war correspondent." So he jumped at a chance for a job in London when Reuters called seeking correspondents to cover the upcoming invasion of Europe.

He didn't know it at the time, but this war experience would lead him to a successful career in international journalism and, later, a major leadership role in journalism education at Ohio University.

Wilhelm joined OU in 1968 as the School of Journalism's third director, but within a year, he was named by President Vernon R. Alden as dean of the university's new College of Communication. It was in this position that he merged his professional background, journalism friends, administrative experience, confidence, and energy into leadership that resulted in major growth and national prominence for the school and the new college.

John R. Wilhelm. *(Photo courtesy of the Ohio University Archives, Mahn Center for Archives and Special Collections)*

His experience as a war correspondent began with a tank landing ship, or LST, crossing of the English Channel to the beachhead known as "Easy Red," Omaha Sector, on D-Day plus one. For the next 11 months spanning June 1944 through April 1945, Wilhelm filed stories for Reuters and the *Chicago Tribune* as the Allies advanced toward Berlin. He also became the European correspondent for the *Chicago Sun*.

During these times, Wilhelm met many of the friends with whom he would later share a strong professional camaraderie, including Walter Cronkite, Edward R. Murrow, and noted journalist and historian Cornelius Ryan. Wilhelm and Ryan traveled and lived together for a time while covering the Allied push at the Battle of the Bulge.

An emotional and memorable experience

Among Wilhelm's most compelling memories was of the day he walked with Edward R. Murrow into Buchenwald just after the first American reconnaissance troops liberated the concentration camp on April 12, 1945. Wilhelm later wrote of the experience in a personal history now held by his son, Larry Wilhelm:

"We arrived at Buchenwald near Weimar and came to an area surrounded by a steel fence. Behind the fence were several brick structures with a courtyard. Two of the jeeps pulled in with eight American soldiers, accepting the surrender of 24 Gestapo officers with their arms held high and their weapons at their feet. It was obvious they preferred to be taken by the U.S. troops rather than the Soviets approaching from the east. . . . The German soldiers refused to go into a much larger area behind the barbed wire fencing. There we found a mass of at least 16,000 emaciated people, who were delighted to see Murrow and me in U.S. uniforms. They had no idea that the Allies were so close. I spoke with an obviously cultured and educated prisoner who turned out to be the former director of the Bibliotheque Francaise in Paris, Julian Cain."

Famed CBS journalist Walter Cronkite, historically considered the nation's most trusted television anchor, was among the early recipients of the Carr Van Anda Award. *(Photo courtesy of the Ohio University Archives, Mahn Center for Archives and Special Collections)*

It was Cornelius Ryan who introduced Wilhelm to the woman who would become his wife. In late 1944, while Wilhelm and Ryan shared a room at the front in Verdun, Ryan introduced a Red Cross doughnut girl (and former small-town newspaper journalist) named Margaret "Peggy" Maslin. In January 1945, after a whirlwind romance, John and Peggy were married at a church in Maastricht, Holland. Many soldiers and journalists attached to the press camp were in attendance, including *Life* photographer George Silk, who captured the event. A two-page photo spread subsequently appeared in *Life* magazine.

After the war, the young couple moved to London, where their first son, Richard, was born. Wilhelm worked for Reuters of London on Fleet Street until 1947. After two years, the young family moved to Buenos Aires, Argentina, where he began a business reporting job for McGraw-Hill World News, the internal news gathering agency for McGraw-Hill Publishing. Wilhelm was promoted after a couple of years to chief of the Mexico City news bureau for McGraw-Hill. In 1958, he moved to New York, where he was promoted to head of McGraw-Hill's World News Service.

Arrival at Ohio University

It was from the job in New York at McGraw-Hill that Wilhelm was recruited, through his connection with an Ohio University faculty member, Ralph Kliesch, who had been writing his PhD dissertation on the news service. Kliesch later became the school's assistant director when Wilhelm assumed double duties as school director and college dean.

Wilhelm proved himself to be an implementer of good ideas, and he wasn't always picky about where a good idea came from. Many of the programs he instituted were suggestions from colleagues or adapted from successful programs he'd witnessed at other universities. Among these was Journalism Week, renamed Communication Week two years later and redesigned to include the whole college.

That first year, 1968, in an effort to attract prominent speakers—often Wilhelm's friends—to Ohio University, he created an award for "enduring contributions to journalism." The award was named after Carr Van Anda, the famed managing editor of *The New York Times* who gained special prominence for that paper's coverage of the sinking of the *Titanic*. Van Anda hailed from Ohio and briefly attended Ohio University, though he left without earning a degree. Kliesch had learned about Van Anda in his graduate program at the University of Minnesota, and he shared this information with Wilhelm.

In 2018, the school and the college will celebrate the 50th anniversary of both Communication Week and the Carr Van Anda Award.

Work with the Scripps Howard Foundation

The beginning of a major legacy of Wilhelm's tenure was the initial wooing of financial support from the Scripps Howard Foundation. Kliesch had suggested the prospect of the school developing a relationship under the name of famed Ohio publisher E.W. Scripps. Wilhelm and Kliesch worked with then-President Charles Ping and Jack Ellis, vice president for development, on a proposal. The whole process took several years to complete, and Wilhelm had retired by the time the deal was finished under Cortland Anderson's leadership, resulting in the school being named after Scripps and a major foundation grant of $1.5 million.

Many of Wilhelm's fund-raising abilities were dedicated to the search for an endowment to support student internships overseas, an idea that grew from his background as a foreign correspondent. The result was development of a foreign-correspondence internship program through which several students each year would spend up to three months in another country as reporters and writers for world-class news organizations. In recent decades, this program has been named the John R. Wilhelm Foreign Correspondence Program.

To raise the initial grant for an internship, Wilhelm leveraged his friendship with legendary author Cornelius Ryan, who had gone on to publish several books about World War II, including the best seller *The Longest Day.* An initial $50,000 endowment was raised for the scholarship. As a result of that success, along with Wilhelm's friendship, Mrs. Ryan donated many of her husband's papers after his death to the Ohio University library, where they now reside in a special collection.

Over the years, to support the students' foreign internships, other scholarship endowments were created. These included a Robert Considine Foreign Correspondence Internship, to honor Wilhelm's friendship with another famed journalist; the William and Shirley Fleischer Foreign Correspondence Internship in Israel; the Maxine Stewart Foreign Correspondence Internship for Coverage of Culture and Religion; and a student travel program in honor of former faculty member Mark Leff.

Wilhelm's tenure in Athens was marked by a strong social sense that he and Peggy exhibited in their day-to-day lives. Many faculty members and students will remember parties at the home the Wilhelms built on a hill overlooking the city. There they met the Wilhelm family, which included three who graduated from Ohio University: Larry (AB '72), Charles "Skip" (BSJ '75), and Martha (BSJ '80). Their oldest son, Richard, had already begun his career when the family came to Ohio and so didn't graduate from Ohio University, but he currently lives in Athens.

During his tenure, Wilhelm presided over a major expansion of the school's national reputation and the financial growth of its endowment. In the decades before Wilhelm served, Ohio University's School of Journalism had developed a reputation among many as the best in Ohio. As one of his colleagues put it, "What Wilhelm did was expand the horizon."

DRESSING A DEAN

One of the problems that may have plagued John Wilhelm as he adjusted to life as an academic administrator in the School of Journalism and College of Communication was that he possessed only a bachelor's degree.

That credential carried with it an implication that had nothing to do with Wilhelm's qualifications for the job. It dictated how he dressed during formal university functions such as graduation.

Wilhelm's friend, Jack Ellis, then the university's vice president for development, recalled that during the first university graduation commencement in which Wilhelm participated, the gown Wilhelm wore lacked the insignias displayed by professors with advanced degrees: "I can remember sitting there with [Wilhelm's wife,] Peggy, and, of course, they had the deans up on the platform greeting people . . . and John . . . he looked so nude up there—all he'd got was this black outline, no hoods or anything."

Eventually, in 1979, Wilhelm was awarded an honorary doctorate of humanities by the Universidad de los Americas in Mexico City.

"From that year forth," Ellis said, "he had a very fancy, very colorful gown and hood, so that's how he went about it thereafter. He did what he always did, and well, but he was better dressed for his role as dean."

–Brendon Butler

TEACHER AND SCHOLAR: GUIDO H. STEMPEL III

By Nicholas Hirshon

Guido H. Stempel III didn't think much of himself as a hitter. In his own words, he was only "halfway decent" when the Ohio University journalism faculty played softball against the undergraduates in the 1970s.

"We had these long-ball hitters," said Stempel, a sports editor at the *Frankfort* (Indiana) *Morning Times* before a 45-year career at the E.W. Scripps School of Journalism. "I was not a long-ball hitter."

Stempel wasn't flashy, even when he was cranking out proverbial home runs in his day job. As director of one of the nation's top journalism schools from 1972 to 1979 and again in 1986, Stempel churned out well-regarded research, edited a top academic journal, and launched the school's doctoral program.

Until 2016, only one faculty member from the College of Communication had been named a distinguished professor, Ohio University's top faculty honor. And that person doesn't think he's a long-ball hitter.

"By and large the journalism school has been fortunate in having the right person be director at the right time in history," Stempel said. "We've all been different, and we were all in different circumstances." The right person at the right time. That's about as close as Stempel comes to bragging.

But in the school's long history, few figures loom as large as Stempel, who began teaching at Scripps in 1965. He is recognized nationally as among the most prominent figures in journalism education. His CV lists nine awards, including the prestigious Deutschmann Award for Excellence in Research and recognition from the Newspaper Division of the Association for Education in Journalism and Mass Communication for a Lifetime of Exemplary Contributions to Journalism and Journalism Education.

A champion of academic productivity

It was his continued productivity that earned some of his highest accolades. For nearly two decades, he was editor of *Journalism Quarterly,* the nation's most prominent academic journal in journalism and mass communication. He could, but he won't, boast of coauthorship of six books and dozens of journal articles and book chapters. He was coauthor and coeditor of a textbook on research methods that for years was dominant. Even after his retirement, he was cofounder and coeditor of the *Web Journal of Mass Communication Research* and senior research editor of *Newspaper Research Journal.* In recognition of his prolific career, the school in 2014 inaugurated the Guido H. Stempel III Award for Journalism and Mass Communication Research.

"Guido had the stature and experience and credibility with his peers to keep everything going in a good, positive direction," said Frank Deaner, a 1967 Scripps graduate who went on to become the longtime executive director of the Ohio Newspaper Association and professional adviser to the campus chapter of the Public Relations Student Society of America.

Stempel got not only the job but also the frustrations that came with it. He opposed the dean's proposal to make a laboratory newspaper out of the student-run *Post.* He dealt with outsiders who confused Ohio University with "that one in Columbus." And, of course, he had to wade into periodic faculty disputes. But Stempel recalled the tone among professors as mostly collegial.

Guido H. Stempel III. *(Photo courtesy of the Ohio University Archives, Mahn Center for Archives and Special Collections)*

Mentor of younger instructors

Besides building camaraderie as director, Stempel proposed new courses and mentored younger instructors. J.W. Click (MS '59), who taught at Scripps from 1965 to 1983, described Stempel as a "man of integrity" who avoided playing politics and maintained a stunning research pace.

"Some people marveled that he could edit an academic journal and still do the duties of a director," Click said. "He's very fast, and he doesn't usually go back and go over things. He does it right the first time. I think he amazed everyone with his productivity."

For all his research accolades, Stempel took pride in his teaching and continued to teach a full load, with special focus on research, editing, and communication law, despite his administrative duties. He especially forged personal connections with students. A third-generation college faculty member, Stempel believed in the importance of teaching.

In a publish-or-perish climate, tenure-track professors at times may be tempted to neglect teaching to clear time for research. But Stempel recognized the fallacy of placing scholarship before students. "That's important, but it's secondary," he said in an interview posted on the Scripps website. "It's what the faculty member does with students that matters, and it matters to people in this program. And I think any student has seen this. And if that doesn't happen to be happening for you, maybe you need to look up another faculty member."

Stempel recognized that the search for relatable faculty members frustrated many students at the time he became director. No matter how much they looked, they would not find a woman or a black person on the Scripps faculty. As director, Stempel acknowledged the restrictions of a bunch of white male professors, himself included, trying to reach a growing base of minority students.

"I can be a role model for a woman student in some respects," Stempel said. "But there are limits there, and a woman can do that to a greater extent than I can. You come to the point of a woman journalism student saying, 'Well, yeah, but I don't know that I can go and do what you did.'"

During his time as director, he hired the first African American and the first woman to hold a long-term permanent position on the Scripps faculty. "He was forward thinking and had the foresight to put those things into action," Deaner said.

Appropriately, the first recipient of Stempel's namesake award for journalism research was his former student Pamela Shoemaker (BSJ and MSJ '72), who launched an impressive career that brought her to an endowed chair position at Syracuse University. "I would not be doing any of the work that I'm doing if not for Guido," Shoemaker said. "He has changed my life and made me the person I am today."

Guido H. Stempel III passed away in June 2016.

HIGH-ENERGY, SMART, FUNNY: CORTLAND ANDERSON

By Laralyn Sasaki Dearing

"With Cortland, you knew where you stood."

But that was only one of the reasons remembered by Associate Professor Emeritus Tom Peters for his respect for Cortland Anderson, who served as the fifth director of the School of Journalism from 1981 to 1985.

"A. He was always in a hurry. B. He always had a plan and purpose. C. He was very sharp," said Peters, the school's first associate director. "You might have thought you got ahead of him, but he was ready to checkmate you."

Peters added, "I would describe him as high-energy, smart, funny. He always knew where he was going. He had a plan. He wouldn't run you over to do it. He would marshal his forces. Eventually you would climb on board. He was both aggressive and considerate."

Remembered primarily for putting the finishing touches on the private endowment that named the journalism school for the founder of the E.W. Scripps Company, Anderson was renowned for a "booming voice that rattled

Cortland Anderson. *(Photo courtesy of the Ohio University Archives, Mahn Center for Archives and Special Collections)*

the windows," his charismatic personality, and his fast pace—in thinking, talking, and moving.

Impressive professional background

Anderson's journalism career began in 1959 at *The St. Petersburg Times* in Florida, following his graduation from Florida Southern College with a bachelor's degree in English. He was city editor and later managing editor when the newspaper was awarded the Pulitzer Prize for Public Service. In 1966 he helped found the *Suffolk Sun* in New York, serving as the paper's editor and vice president until 1969. Anderson worked as assistant vice president for public relations at the New York Telephone Company and later as executive vice president for the Corporation for Public Broadcasting in Washington, D.C. Before coming to OU, he served The Washington Post Company as vice president of corporate affairs.

Professor Emeritus Guido Stempel, who also served as director, said there was a question at the time of Anderson's appointment whether someone without a background in academia could successfully lead the journalism school.

"He didn't come in with a notion of what a journalism school should be. What made it work was we had a good faculty with good reputations. They didn't need to be bossed from the director's office," Stempel said. "At his memorial service, it was said, 'The great thing about Cortland was he didn't try to make outfielders out of second basemen.'"

Peters said the school was looking for a fund-raiser and someone to generate outside support—plus someone with terrific journalistic credentials, adding, "It was an easy decision to invite him. He was so interesting, so dynamic, so well-spoken. You could hear him picking up speed as we were talking."

Peters continued, "His view of the faculty was, 'These people are very good. My job is to support them and get out of their way.'"

The respect of faculty members

Two faculty members hired during Anderson's term as director were Patrick Washburn and Anne Cooper-Chen, both now retired.

"I was leery of him because he did not have a doctorate, and I did not know whether he would truly appreciate those who had one," remembered now–Professor Emeritus Washburn. "But immediately I found out that there was no cause for concern. Cortland was equally comfortable around PhDs and non-PhDs, and he treated both fairly. No matter what degree or what type of background people had, he simply wanted them to be good teachers and to be productive. I admired him a lot for that."

Professor Emerita Cooper-Chen said she came to Ohio University largely because of Anderson, whose daughter Laura was her student at the University of North Carolina at Chapel Hill.

"On his 50th birthday, Cortland was out of the hospital for one or two days," she said. "Dru [Evarts] organized Don Lambert with his baritone, Ralph Izard with his trombone, and the rest of us had kazoos. We parked far away and walked up the street singing, playing badly, and making a lot of noise. We gave him a birthday concert, and he laughed a lot."

One of Anderson's enhancements of the journalism school was creating the position of associate director, which Peters ultimately filled for 18 years. As he recounts, Peters was flattered but at first declined Anderson's initial two job offers.

"He made the third pitch in person. Cortland was good at telling you things that were sweet to your ears," he said with a laugh. "Cortland realized that as much as he enjoyed campus life, he didn't know how academia worked. He needed a 'Mr. Inside' so he could focus on external relationships, fundraising, making more professional contacts for the school." Peters continued, "I had my role, and he had his, but we didn't get in each other's way."

Wooing the foundation bucks

Anderson picked up on an effort begun by former Director John Wilhelm and solidified the school's relationship that led to a $1.5 million grant from the Scripps Howard Foundation in Cincinnati. That endowment, in addition to state appropriations, allowed the renovation of Carnegie Hall into Scripps Hall to occur at least 10 years ahead of schedule.

Before the renovation was complete, however, Anderson died of esophageal cancer on December 24, 1985. He was 50 years old.

During his memorial service, led by then–OU President Charles Ping, Anderson was remembered as someone who truly enjoyed working with college students. "He was sort of a father-figure," said then–public relations senior Bill Mason (BSJ '86), an Anderson advisee quoted in *The Post* coverage of the event.

Considering what Anderson achieved in fewer than five years as director, Peters mused, "You can only imagine what he could have accomplished" had he lived longer.

A worthy footnote to Anderson's legacy was written in a Father's Day blog post by his daughter Laura Mercer in May 2010 in the blog "Laura's Diary" (*https://lauramercer.wordpress.com*). She described her father as "fun and full of life" and said he once gathered the family in their first-floor living room and declared to them in his booming baritone voice from the second-floor balcony, "Today is the first day of the rest of my life!"

Mercer noted that she continued to receive letters from annual recipients of the Ohio University scholarship endowed in her father's name, citing one thank-you letter that spoke of how great it felt to receive a scholarship and, specifically, one honoring Anderson: "The privilege of putting his name on my resume one day, and be associated with his name, is awesome."

NEVER A BYSTANDER: RALPH IZARD

By Susan DeFord

When Ralph Izard was a fresh-faced reporter, he knew that he wanted to teach in a college classroom. After Izard achieved his goal of becoming a professor, he felt a constant tug to go back to the world of deadlines and headlines.

Izard never resolved his conflicting urges. Instead, he threaded his scholarly career at Ohio University with stints of professional journalism that broadened his outlook, sharpened his teaching, and cultivated a deep network of professional contacts. Izard made good use of it all when he became

Ralph Izard. *(Photo courtesy of the Ohio University Archives, Mahn Center for Archives and Special Collections)*

director of the E.W. Scripps School of Journalism in 1986. During his 12 years in the position, Izard extended the school's reach and burnished its heavyweight reputation at a time when traditional forms of journalism still dominated on campus and in the profession.

It was not love at first sight when Izard visited Ohio University to interview for a teaching job in 1966. Two years earlier, he had left a newspaper reporting job in his native West Virginia to study for a doctorate in communication at the University of Illinois in Urbana-Champaign. He was just shy of his dissertation when he received an invitation from then-Director L.J. Hortin. Izard returned from Athens with a job offer, telling his wife, Janet, "It's a dumpy little town, but we'll be there five years, and we'll move on."

Four years later, Izard not only had his doctorate, he also had published, along with colleagues Donald Lambert and Hugh Culbertson, *Fundamentals of News Reporting*. The textbook became a primer for aspiring journalists at more than a hundred universities around the country and went through six editions by 1994.

He could be a nag

Izard was a joiner and a doer, publishing regularly in scholarly journals and serving as a longtime campus adviser and well-known national office holder with the Society of Professional Journalists. He was Riz to his students, an affable, familiar figure who wielded a green felt-tip marker on their writing and who espoused the role of the diligent, ever-inquiring journalist. His calm, deliberate demeanor seemed to take everything in, with a steady gaze and the hint of a smile. He could be a nag, former students recalled gratefully.

Izard zeroed in on former *Post* editor Andy Alexander (BSJ '72) after Alexander left Ohio University in 1970 with job prospects but no journalism degree. Alexander had led the independent student newspaper through a tumultuous spring when campus riots closed the university. Izard helped him with an independent study project so that two years later, Alexander had his OU degree as he pursued a news career that brought him increasing prominence.

Laralyn Sasaki Dearing (BSJ '86) said Izard was a guiding presence from her first days on campus through her studies as an Honors Tutorial College student and during her years of work as a member of the Society of Professional Journalists. In her senior year as editor of *The Post* in 1985–86, Izard was at her side to add his criticism of the university administration's idea to end *The Post*'s independence and make it a lab paper.

"It seems I can't remember a time when I did not know Ralph Izard," she said.

In the spring of 1986, Izard had a dream sabbatical, working for The Associated Press in Honolulu, as his colleagues in Athens sought candidates to become the next director of the E.W. Scripps School of Journalism. He thought twice about his usual aversion to administration. "It seemed to be a way to be in the thick of things," he said. On the day before the deadline for applications, he faxed in his paperwork. Some weeks later, Izard returned to Athens from Hawaii, apparently said the right things during his interview, and was named director.

Focus on expanding the school's reach

Izard had his agenda ready. "I said we have to spread our wings and fly," he recalled. He wanted faculty members publishing, joining professional

INTIMIDATION DEFINED

WHAT IS THE DEFINITION of "intimidation"?

Here's one: The professor who wrote the textbook *Fundamentals of News Reporting* that you used in your freshman class telephoning years later to ask you for a job.

Double the intimidation because, to make matters more fear-inducing, you will be his supervisor. What a horror scenario!

Ralph Izard relished this. Every now and then while Izard taught at OU, he would dial one of his former students or friends at The Associated Press. He wanted to hone his skills in the summer before returning to the classroom in the fall.

In the summer of 1975, Izard contacted me, as news editor of the AP in Columbus, with a request for employment. Six years earlier I had sat in Izard's Journalism 101 class praying for praise for my 100- to 150-word practice news reports on local fires.

The conversation went something like this:

Izard: How about I come to work at the AP this summer? It's important for me to keep in touch with the profession.

Heilbrunn: Here? Really? With me? Me giving you assignments? Me editing your copy? You, the professor who taught me?

Izard: Don't worry. We'll make this work.

He did. From his first day on rewrite sitting across the desk from me as I handed him press releases to convert to acceptable wire service style to his final days on night broadcast, Izard was the professional himself and demonstrated the reason he successfully helped launch thousands of careers in journalism.

Izard had practice before the stint with me in Columbus. He had performed a similar role earlier at the AP bureau in Miami for Dick Carelli (BSJ '68), who as day editor was Izard's direct supervisor.

—Henry Heilbrunn

societies, and attending conventions to promote their work and the school. He also wanted to get a lot more people of color teaching in the classrooms.

The Scripps Howard Foundation, which had recently bestowed a $1.5 million endowment on the school in a partnership forged with Izard's predecessor, liked the new director's approach.

"His vision was beyond Ohio and the region," said Sue Porter, vice president of programs with the Scripps Howard Foundation in Cincinnati.

"My impression is he wanted students to see a much larger world. He raised their aspirations."

One of Izard's key administrative moves was to consolidate the school's existing international initiatives, which included study tours and foreign correspondence internships. In 1991, the university's Board of Trustees approved the school's new Center for International Journalism.

The next year, university administrators asked the journalism school to help the University of Leipzig in former East Germany build a journalism program. Izard secured an $80,000 grant to send 10 journalism professors to Leipzig, launching a partnership between the two universities that has grown into one of OU's most successful efforts.

As international journalism developed new initiatives, Izard contemplated larger quarters for the center. He learned that one of his faculty members had been a mentor to Sally Aw Sian, chairwoman of Sing Tao Holdings Ltd., of Hong Kong. Sing Tao Holdings published Chinese-language newspapers in cities with large Chinese populations. Izard traveled to Hong Kong repeatedly to make his pitch. Sally Aw Sian became one of the school's major donors, giving $125,000 to help build Sing Tao Center for what is now called the Institute for International Journalism and giving another $500,000 for an endowed chair. The new building was dedicated in 1997 on the site of a former university fraternity house.

Retirement was a shifting of gears

For Izard, his retirement as director in 1998 was more of a shifting of gears as he entered another career phase. For two years he worked at the Media Studies Center in New York City, and then he accepted an offer in 2001 to teach and build a graduate program at Louisiana State University for what he thought would be a short stretch. He ended up staying 10 years, eventually serving as interim dean of LSU's Manship School of Mass Communication. In 2014, Izard was named to the LSU communication school's Hall of Fame, the latest in his collection of university and professional honors. He was named an honorary alumnus by Ohio University in 2000 and received the L.J. Hortin Faculty Mentor Award from OU's Scripps College of Communication in 2007.

It was at LSU that Izard took an action that he considers among his proudest—founding the Media Diversity Forum, a website dedicated to providing information about diversity in the media and higher education. The forum now has a staff of 14, all volunteers from around the country, in its search for meaningful academic and professional materials.

At one point Baton Rouge may have beckoned as a new home, but the little burg of Athens long ago sealed its hold on Izard and his wife, Janet. These days, Izard works on projects for OU and LSU, and he has professor emeritus status at both institutions. Although the Internet and social media have transformed journalism in ways that Izard never contemplated, he is not content to be a bystander.

He summed it up in his matter-of-fact way: "What's important to me is that I'm doing something worthwhile."

A PEACEFUL SPIRIT: MICHAEL REAL

By Nicholas Hirshon

GRADUATE STUDENTS TALK. They complain about professors who push their own research interests on students and pressure them to think the same way about mass communication.

Michaela Meyer (MSJ '01, PhD in rhetorical criticism '04) heard the talk. Then she took some classes at Ohio University with Michael Real, whose research centered on televised sports, Hollywood movies, and political campaigns. She was more interested in analyzing TV dramas for teenagers, shows such as *Smallville* and *Dawson's Creek*.

Michael Real. *(Photo provided by Michael Real)*

To her delight, Real encouraged Meyer to research what she loved.

"He was really good at encouraging students to follow their own direction," said Meyer, who went on to write her dissertation on relationships depicted on young adult television. "He was, like, 'Decide what you want to do, make your own career,' and that was really refreshing."

Real, director of the E.W. Scripps School of Journalism from 2000 to 2004, was known as a world-class scholar when he came to Ohio. During his tenure, he added to his impressive number of publications but also said he sought to strengthen the High School Journalism Workshop. And, yes, he encouraged his doctoral students to research what they wanted.

Research generated national headlines

In 1975, Real published a seminal study on television coverage of the Super Bowl in the *Journal of Communication,* at a time when little research focused on sports media. His article pointed out that only 3 percent of the 1974 Super Bowl broadcast was dedicated to actual play action, while the majority was consumed by advertisements, pregame and postgame shows, and half-time commentary.

The surprising claim generated national headlines and landed on the cover of *TV Guide.* It also initiated a wave of sports media scholarship. Upon the 40th anniversary of the article's publication in 2015, Real was invited to be the keynote speaker at the conference of a leading sports media research organization, the International Association for Communication and Sport.

But he also had a career as an administrator, and joining the Scripps faculty marked a turning point for him. Before coming to Athens, he had taught for nearly two decades at San Diego State University, including four years as director of its communication school. He enjoyed raising the profile of the program, but Scripps afforded a rare opportunity to teach at an established, highly regarded journalism school.

"Scripps had in place so many of the things that at San Diego State we were in the process of trying to generate," Real said. "It was a real upgrade for me to go from a good but developing journalism school to one that had been operating at a high level for a long period of time."

School's reputation a real advantage

Once Real started as director, he found that the program brought other advantages, too. The Scripps reputation attracted top-notch applicants and allowed for selective admissions. Geographic isolation lent charm to Athens, and the relative proximity to the East Coast let faculty and students hop on short flights to media centers such as New York and Washington. Generous travel budgets attracted elite faculty, and the Scripps endowment allowed Real to fund student events.

Still, there was drama unfolding in Scripps Hall. The turn of the century marked a transitional period in journalism education. Some faculty thought the curriculum should continue to reinforce reporting and writing, the foundation of the Scripps School's education for decades. Others saw newspapers dying and thought classes should focus more on broadcast and the Internet.

Wading into some difficult ideological battles, Real won over his associate director, Eddith Dashiell.

"He had a peaceful spirit about him," Dashiell said. "I really enjoyed his quiet, calming influence."

With money to spend, Real set his eyes on the High School Journalism Workshop, a key recruiting tool for Scripps, seeking to get multiple faculty members involved.

"I wanted to enhance what I considered to be the strongest asset of the Scripps School, which was its regional and national reputation as a top J-School," Real said. "My focus was to continue the programs and activities that had gotten Scripps there."

He also enjoyed the perks of the job.

He chatted with Helen Thomas, the grand dame of the White House press corps, at an alumni gathering in Washington. He presented the Carr Van Anda Award for enduring contributions in journalism to famed CNN correspondent Christiane Amanpour.

Real also traveled to connect with alumni. On a trip to an alumni event in Dayton, Real flew in the university plane with then-President Robert Glidden and Barbara Ross-Lee, dean of the College of Osteopathic Medicine. Stormy weather made for a bumpy, nerve-wracking flight. But the journey became even more memorable when Ross-Lee shared childhood anecdotes about her sister, singer Diana Ross.

"We were bouncing around in this plane with lightning and thunder and getting the most amazing stories," Real said.

Impressed with his colleagues

Real also was impressed with colleagues such as Bernhard Debatin, who brought a European perspective to the program, and Patricia Cambridge (MA in international affairs '88, PhD '92), who gave a concert piano performance in the university chapel. While he was fascinated by the varied perspectives and talents of his colleagues, Real's graduate students were drawn to his charisma.

"He just had this sort of vibrancy about him," said Meyer, who went on to teach at Christopher Newport University in Virginia. "He was really interested in helping students engage and learn."

Impressed by Real's research, Karen Nava, a 2007 PhD recipient in telecommunication, thought about approaching him for help on her dissertation about communication technologies in Bolivian households in Washington, D.C. But she worried that Real might turn her down because he had never met her.

"He was open to collaborate, and that is not typical," said Nava, who later became director of graphics and publications for the National Council of La Raza, the largest national Hispanic civil rights and advocacy organization in the United States. "He was incredibly friendly, helpful, collaborative. He was always ready to meet."

Real left the Scripps School in 2004 to join the faculty at Royal Roads University in Victoria, British Columbia, in Canada. But his mark was left on alumni such as Meyer and Nava.

"The sense of contribution from Scripps to people's lives was very satisfying. I was glad to feel I had been a part of it," he said.

MULTITALENTED: THOMAS HODSON

By Susan DeFord

Thomas Hodson hadn't worked as a full-time reporter before becoming director of the E.W. Scripps School of Journalism in 2003. This irony, however, paled against his credentials as a lawyer, judge, lecturer, writer, Supreme Court fellow, broadcaster, teacher, and administrator, all of which convinced university officials that he was the right person for the school at a crucial time.

Hodson (BSJ '70), the first undergrad alumnus to become the school's director, used his wide-ranging skills to pursue a sweeping modernization. He also felt the heat of intense university politics near the end of his seven-year directorship.

He was confident as he embarked on refashioning Ohio University's nationally known school while it struggled with dissension among faculty members and what some considered a dated curriculum.

"I knew my experience as a judge and lawyer would bring some order to a chaotic situation," he said.

Athens long ago had become Hodson's springboard for a far-reaching career. The Ohio native enrolled at OU during the 1960s, and in his senior year he was associate editor of *The Post,* covering anti–Vietnam War protests that engulfed the campus. A photograph from that tumultuous spring shows a youthful, intent Hodson, dressed in a button-down shirt and with a shock of blond hair falling across his forehead, as he readied the next day's edition of *The Post.* Despite riots that forced the university to close early, Hodson graduated on time and started law school that fall at Ohio State University. A law degree, he reasoned, would help him become a more astute reporter.

Attorney and judge

Thomas Hodson, 1968. *(© Ken Steinhoff, all rights reserved, reproduced with permission)*

After graduation, Hodson decided that working as an attorney for a few years would pay better than reporting, and he accepted an offer to join an established Athens law firm. In 1979, he ran for a local judgeship and defeated a longtime incumbent, becoming the youngest judge in Ohio at 31.

During his years as a judge, he wrote and lectured around the country on court, community, and media relations and taught as an adjunct professor at OU. In 1986, he was one of two people selected from a national pool of applicants to serve a one-year fellowship with the U.S. Supreme Court. He clerked for the new chief justice, William Rehnquist, and made valuable Washington contacts for OU.

He returned to private practice in Athens and in 1989 was appointed by the Ohio governor to OU's Board of Trustees. As a trustee he assisted in the search to select a new university president, which resulted in Robert B. Glidden's selection, and in 1999, he became Glidden's special assistant. True to his multitasking ways, Hodson continued to serve Glidden while adding a new assignment as chair of the Mass Media Department at nearby Marietta College in 2001.

In 2003, OU's former dean of the College of Communication, Kathy Krendl, asked Hodson if he was interested in a big job: directing the School of Journalism. Absolutely, he replied.

"Tom was exactly what we needed at the time," said Mary Rogus, associate professor. "Everyone felt they were being treated fairly, and resources were allocated fairly."

A focus on the curriculum

Hodson took a hard look at the faculty and pushed retirement for some to facilitate hiring younger, tech-savvy educators with fresh experience in the professions. He shared the opinion that the journalism curriculum needed an overhaul to reflect the digital age.

A fundamental question, he said, was "How were we going to teach in this new world? How can we be more nimble with the curriculum?" Starting in 2008, Hodson and Associate Director Bob Stewart shepherded the merger of the school's five sequences into two main tracks: news and information for the reporting profession, and strategic communication for disciplines such as advertising and public relations. The switch took place in 2012, along with the university's adoption of a new semester schedule. Even amid the refurbishing, enrollment at the Scripps School grew to a yearly average of more than 900 undergraduates.

Thomas Hodson. *(Photo by Megan Westervelt used with permission from the Scripps College of Communication)*

Throughout the rebuilding, Hodson continued to teach and pursue his longtime passion for sports, doing radio play-by-play for local teams and university sports. His avocation became a valuable mentoring tool. As he announced play-by-play for the OU women's basketball team, he advised player Allie LaForce to try broadcasting. LaForce, a 2011 OU journalism graduate, recalled that it seemed "a crazy idea at first because of my love for playing, but that is the exact path I ended up taking. Tom Hodson is the reason I pursued a career in broadcast journalism." LaForce currently is a CBS sports reporter.

On another occasion, Hodson took advantage of a chance meeting on campus to ask Brian Boesch (BSJ '12), a bright, shy student with an interest in sports, whether he had considered broadcasting. Boesch found the school director intimidating, but he was intrigued.

"That conversation started it. He saw something in me," said Boesch, who now does broadcasting and related media work for a minor league baseball team in North Carolina. "He used whatever connections he had to help me."

Though Hodson deftly operated in many arenas, he became mired in a faculty tenure case that churned for more than a year in 2009–10. Hodson took the unusual step of recommending against tenure for a journalism faculty member, overturning a faculty committee's 7–5 vote in favor of both tenure and promotion. The appeal of the negative recommendations by Hodson and Greg Shepherd, then College of Communication dean, sparked sharp debate across campus and generated national media reports. In March 2010, Ohio University President Roderick McDavis went against the recommendation by Hodson and the college and awarded tenure.

"Would I do anything differently? Probably not," Hodson said, noting that as a local judge, his rulings sometimes were overturned on appeal. "I respected the process. The process worked."

Passing the torch

Hodson resigned as the school's director in 2010 after seven years in the position, citing major family health concerns and a sense of professional accomplishment.

"I felt that I had stabilized the school, got us through accreditation, brought in new resources, brought in new faculty, raised enrollments, and had accomplished what I set out to do," he said. "So, professionally, I thought it was a great time to pass the torch and return to the faculty."

But in less than a year, the dean of the College of Communication appointed him interim director and general manager of the WOUB Center for Public Media. Hodson was charged by the dean to revitalize the struggling university-owned broadcast operation, and in 2011, he became its full-time director.

Hodson saw the assignment as his chance, finally, to delve deeply into the craft of journalism. Within months, he integrated the WOUB Center as a nonacademic unit within the Scripps College of Communication, where students work as volunteers alongside radio and television professionals. Under Hodson, the station's finances stabilized, and new funding sources were cultivated. The PBS affiliate produced documentaries and developed a social media presence.

Hodson intends to go further, helping the college expand its resources for storytelling and social impact beyond the traditional documentary. "People who are decrying the downturn of the media, they're decrying what was, but there's so many exciting things going on right now," he said. "There's so many different ways of telling stories."

ALWAYS READY FOR CHANGE: ROBERT STEWART

By Susan DeFord

LONG AGO, ROBERT STEWART, current director of the E.W. Scripps School of Journalism, learned that being a second-round choice still offered first-rate opportunities. More than once in his career, he got to the top only after being No. 2. So Stewart kept saying yes to assignments when others had declined.

Through 23 years at OU (before being named director), Stewart had left his mark on some of the school's most important initiatives in international studies and curriculum reform. He advanced steadily through the school's ranks and in 2010 accepted a new set of challenges by becoming its director.

As the school's top administrator, Stewart daily addresses a sweeping challenge: to position the school and its students to succeed in an unsettled industry in which traditional forms of print and broadcast media have faded. Students, he says, must develop the skills and confidence to shape new media, even if the media haven't fully emerged.

With an air of equanimity, Stewart advises, "There is no master game plan except to be ready for change."

Robert Stewart. *(E.W. Scripps School of Journalism photo)*

Stewart is a gregarious, familiar figure roaming classroom hallways and campus offices, modeling his approachable style after the man who hired him, former Director Ralph Izard. In group shots, he's the tall guy on the end, sporting a wide, engaging smile. Students sometimes discover their school's director playing acoustic guitar and singing with his folk blues band at local bars or on the campus green.

"I felt like I was home"

When Stewart moved to Athens in 1987 at the age of 30, as a husband and father of young children, he recalled, "I felt like I was home in America for the first time."

Stewart spent his childhood and youth in Thailand as the child of Southern Baptist missionaries. They settled in a small Thai village, where Stewart wandered freely on his bike. The Stewart family lived in a house with a cook, a washperson, and a gardener but no telephone. It was idyllic and isolating.

Stewart knew that when he turned 18, his family expected him to study at a university in the United States. The 12,000-mile relocation was jarring. He enrolled at Samford University in Birmingham, Alabama, as a music major. Then he relocated to Hunter College in New York City and switched his major from music to communications. When he was held up at knifepoint in a street robbery, Stewart lost his appetite for the Big Apple and moved across the country to Seattle.

He did a stint teaching at a small business college and discovered that his calling was in the classroom. In graduate work at the University of Washington, he focused on American media history, a topic in which he had little background.

An important German connection

After his studies, Stewart pursued a teaching position at OU in 1987. He was the school's second choice when the top candidate turned down the position. But when Izard offered him the job, he grabbed it. "Cool bean for me," Stewart summed up.

A few years later, Izard turned to Stewart to manage a new international partnership between OU and Leipzig University in the former East Germany, an exchange program designed to bridge knowledge gaps that had developed between West and East during the Cold War decades. Stewart frequently taught at Leipzig, and after more than two decades of partnership, the universities have designed dual master's degree programs in communications, as well as in journalism and global media.

"We're going from dating to marriage," said Stewart, who served as director for the Scripps School's Institute for International Journalism from

2002 to 2008. The first class in the OU-Leipzig dual degree program came in fall 2015.

In 2007, Stewart was named the Scripps School's assistant director, serving under Tom Hodson. Early on, Stewart helped launch an overhaul of the journalism school curriculum, which would take effect as the university moved from a quarter-based academic calendar to semesters. To keep the massive undertaking from becoming unwieldy and divisive, Hodson and Stewart created a collaborative process arising from the work of faculty committees. Course requirements emphasized fundamental skills in writing, reporting, and digital literacy that could be used across media platforms. The new curriculum was phased in from 2010 to 2012.

"I'm extremely proud of what the faculty did," Stewart said. "It's a flexible curriculum that I enjoy talking about with prospective students."

In 2010, when it was clear that Hodson intended to step down as director, Stewart felt that his turn to be No. 1 had arrived. A small faction at the school pressed for a national search and a "marquee director." In a compromise move, Greg Shepherd, former dean of the College of Communication, offered Stewart a three-year term as director. Stewart said yes, and two years later, the journalism faculty voted to add five years to his term.

His door is always open

Faculty members appreciate Stewart's leadership style.

"His door was always open [as associate director], and it's always open now," said Craig Davis, associate professor in advertising and marketing. "There's so much work that gets done by me popping in Bob's office."

Stewart took the helm as the school felt the impact of declining traditional media in print and broadcasting. While the graduate student enrollment at the journalism school has remained steady, the much larger undergrad enrollment had slipped, to a yearly average of 835 students, from 2011 through 2014. The school's average undergrad yearly enrollment had been about 890 in the previous decade.

Looking ahead, the faculty, with Stewart's leadership, has added a focus on the role of social media in journalism.

"It's a sell to the parents [of prospective students] because to a lot of them, journalism means newspapers," said Mary Rogus, an associate professor whose specialty is broadcasting. "We are so far away from journalism equals newspapers. We are storytellers; we are information providers."

Stewart, who daily utilizes social media and can rebuild a website for an iPhone platform, advises students that they must be adept multitaskers in the digital world. Stephanie Cesear (BSJ '13), a media planner in New York City for a global advertising firm, recalled that OU's revamped curriculum required her to take additional classes her senior year. She found it worthwhile to study disciplines such as public relations even as she planned for a career in advertising. "It was more eye-opening and a broader range," Cesear said.

Jim Ryan (BSJ '15), a former editor of *The Post,* the student newspaper in Athens, remembered asking Stewart as a prospective student what OU offered that made it distinctive. Stewart replied that if OU didn't have the right media experience for students, they had permission to create it. That entrepreneurial encouragement, Ryan said, "sealed the deal."

The school's approach to social media has had a direct impact on one set of enrollment numbers that has grown during Stewart's time as director. The school's annual high school publications workshop had suffered from neglect and in 2009 had only 23 participants. Stewart made it a focus of the school's outreach, and in the summer of 2014, the program had 110 students from 11 states attending. The Scripps Howard Foundation provides scholarship money to help bring minority students to the journalism workshop.

When Stewart sees eager looks in a group of visiting 17-year-olds, he feels assured that the E.W. Scripps School of Journalism is on the right path. He tells those curious young visitors on campus, and their equally curious parents, "There will be jobs. They may not exist yet, but they will be there when you graduate."

"The opportunities are greater than ever, the variety is greater than ever, and the uncertainty is greater than ever," he adds. "Prepare yourself in as many ways as you can."

THE J-SCHOOL'S UNSUNG HEROES

By Laralyn Sasaki Dearing

Students don't always know how much of what they do in the E.W. Scripps School of Journalism—perhaps even many of their successes—depends on a corps of often unnoticed engineers, the "unsung heroes" of the school's leadership team: associate and assistant directors and, occasionally, interim directors.

"Being associate director is a hard job with a lot of responsibility," said Jan Slater, who served as associate director for undergraduate studies from 2003 to 2006 and recently stepped down as dean of the College of Media at the University of Illinois. "You're scheduling courses and admitting students and handling the academic pieces of the school, including advising. You deal with a lot of faculty issues as well as student issues."

An associate director for undergraduate studies performs an array of complicated, often time-consuming, tasks that are indispensable in keeping the classes meeting, students flowing, faculty organized—and graduations occurring.

Eddith Dashiell currently schedules all classes—and assigns classrooms—for the school's nearly 1,000 students. "I like solving puzzles, figuring out different strategies and planning A, B, and C—how to reconfigure a schedule with the least disruption," she said.

In addition to constructing that school infrastructure, the associate director works directly with faculty to help keep their advisees on track for graduation by monitoring credits earned and those still required, as well as addressing student and faculty individual concerns.

The goal is to provide support

"An administrator is not a leadership position. You're a support person," said Michael Bugeja, associate director from 2001 to 2003. "When you become an administrator, you have to concentrate more on the people who teach students. If you do that, you give them resources they need, and the students get the best instruction possible."

Dashiell agrees: "I can't boss people around. I can encourage them. I have no authority—other than scheduling them to teach a 7:30 a.m. class."

Most who have served at the school were faculty members who did not set out to become administrators. Dan Riffe (MSJ '76) is among those who contend they were committed to teaching rather than administrating but nevertheless served as associate director.

"It's a very 360-degree kind of thing. It's demanding but also addictive," Riffe said. "It's exhilarating but at the same time a bit burdensome. All those people who were your colleagues, you now know more about them—their student evaluations, complaints about them."

Slater said she thought about it for long periods of time when she was asked to take on the role. "The minute I decided, my stomach would turn. Then a friend told me the only way to make change was to be in the administration."

Slater left Ohio University to lead the advertising program at the University of Illinois' College of Media and served as dean there from 2007 to 2016. Other past associate directors have continued as administrators, including Bugeja, director of the Greenlee School of Journalism and Communication at Iowa State University until 2016. In 2015, he was named the national journalism and mass communication administrator of the year.

Robert Stewart, the school's current director, has this perception of the associate director's job: "In a way, you're kind of the vice president. You realize you have a lot of influence over how the school functions and the student experience."

Thomas Peters, on the right. *(Photo courtesy of the Ohio University Archives, Mahn Center for Archives and Special Collections)*

Stewart is only the second director of the J-School who arrived with the operational experience of having been associate director (2006–10) or assistant director. Ralph Izard, assistant director in 1971, is the other.

The first associate director

The first to carve out what would become the permanent role of associate director for the school was Thomas Peters, now associate professor emeritus. Peters came on as associate director to run day-to-day operations at the school—at first mostly scheduling and budgeting—while the final steps were taken to secure the school's $1.5 million endowment from the Scripps Howard Foundation. That donation triggered the renovation of Carnegie Hall into Scripps Hall in 1985, and Peters quickly assumed the primary logistical role of supervising the building's transformation, as well as the mammoth job of relocating students, faculty, staff, and equipment during the school year.

"Tom Peters was instrumental in designing the Scripps Hall facility," said Ralph Kliesch (BSJ '56, MS '62), a member of the journalism faculty since 1965 and himself a former assistant director. "That place was our happy home for many years because of what Peters made it."

During his term, 1981–98, long after the journalism school first nested in Scripps Hall, Peters molded the position of associate director into what it has become today, with the school's operations demanding even more puzzle-master skills.

"It's a complicated Rubik's Cube every single time," said Stewart. "You learn rhythms and patterns, but it's new every time."

Working with students and parents

While past associate directors view their contributions to their faculty colleagues as paramount, their work with students—recruiting, admitting, tracking credits for graduation—is cited by many as the most enjoyable part of the job, especially because they got to know many more students than they did while teaching.

Riffe remembers meeting with prospective undergraduate students as a highlight of his term. "I loved those sessions. I really loved telling those students and their parents what a good choice they were making."

That connection to students continues through advising and answering parent questions and complaints, tasks often requiring some measure of finesse.

"Most parents are wonderful, but we used to have a term for some, 'helicopter parents,'" Dashiell said. "But now they are taking it to the next level.

Eddith Dashiell.
(E.W. Scripps School of Journalism photo)

Now I call them 'drones.' They speak in the first-person plural—'What classes do *we* need to take?' It's extremely annoying. They need to let their children take responsibility."

Patrick Washburn. *(Photo courtesy of the Ohio University Archives, Mahn Center for Archives and Special Collections)*

But current Director Stewart, who also handled those calls as associate director, said, "If you look at it from a purely economic rationale, the cost of tuition is so high that parents look at a failure as an expense."

While the majority of journalism students are undergraduates, graduate students have their own unique experiences, and they have had their own assistant or associate director at the school since 1987, when Patrick Washburn, now professor emeritus, took up the task. Prior to his appointment, the program was in the hands of a graduate coordinator.

"The journalism program got a lot of attention nationally. The undergraduate program was so good," Washburn said. "My point was that the graduate program contributed just as much to the school's reputation as the undergraduate program. Undergraduates would go out and get good jobs and raise the reputation of the school that way. The graduate students were equally important because they went out to professional jobs or to teaching, and people would take note of that."

Over time, raising English proficiency requirements resulted in the acceptance of international students with greater knowledge of English and, surprisingly, more applications for both the master's and the doctoral programs. Now the school's graduate program is recognized as one of the top 10 in the country, Washburn said.

Michael Sweeney, who benefited as a 1996 PhD graduate, is now shepherding graduate students through the school, helping recruit 3–5 doctoral students and 10–12 master's students annually.

"Like many professors of graduate studies, what faculty members are most excited and proud of is seeing their students succeed and get jobs and teach and publish," he said. "It's almost like they are your children, perhaps children of your mind."

He said that for many years faculty and students have forged and renewed bonds each year during a "welcome picnic" at the home of a faculty member or at a local park. "We introduce Chinese students to Frisbee and football," he said. "They start to bond together as people who support each other. They grow very close. And grad students are friends for life."

Maintaining a nurturing environment

"Students are under a great deal of stress, and [the Scripps School has] a very nurturing environment," Sweeney said. "That's my job: to maintain that nurturing environment."

And although the associate director position has been as infused with technology as other administrative offices, there are still "layers and layers, lots and lots of process and paperwork. Massive paper files have become massive digital files," Sweeney said with a laugh.

"When I started, we had lots of applications from professionals in traditional media who wanted to learn to teach," he added. "The application pool has changed. It has gotten smaller, more focused, more interested in digital stuff. They are older, more international, more focused on the new world of social media and digital media."

Ellen Gerl (MSJ '75) became associate director for undergraduate studies in 2012 during the university's transition from quarters to semesters. Having been chair of the curriculum committee and coordinator of the "Q2S"—quarter to semester—transition, she held the needed tools for the job at that time.

"It was bad enough we went to semesters, but we changed the whole curriculum," she said, adding that she learned "a good associate director has to have patience. You have to be really patient with faculty."

Another key player in the Q2S transition was Dashiell, who, before serving as associate director for undergraduate studies, served the Scripps College of Communication as assistant dean for undergraduate services and programs, and for a time she was the university's associate provost for minority graduate student recruitment.

Gerl and Dashiell are among those who said being proactive is an important attribute for the job.

"The helpful attitude is important so faculty feel free to come in and ask questions or for help," Gerl said. "Better than to correct an error later. You don't want them scared of you. You have to have an open office."

"Being proactive is important," Dashiell agreed. "If you can prevent problems, that's an improvement. I like to identify a potential problem and figure it out and nip it in the bud."

Other challenges are less tangible.

"I think one of the greatest opportunities and challenges was being in a named program," Slater said, thinking back to her term. "Having the E.W. Scripps name on the school was incredibly advantageous. That speaks volumes for the school. Students refer to themselves as part of the Scripps School of Journalism."

She continued, "The burden is, you walk into that school every day with the responsibility of holding up that standard and that name. Looking at E.W. Scripps' [statue] every day as we walked into that building was something. The students rubbed his nose for luck. I looked at it and said to myself, 'I'm going to do right by you today.'"

The role of interim director

A small number of faculty members have been called to uphold the school's standard in a unique way, as acting or interim directors. Serving as pinch hitters, they are charged with maintaining the school's operations and reputation during critical periods of transition, and the need for their expertise can occur without much warning because of illness, resignation, or retirement.

"During my brief stint, the most I can say is that nobody got hurt. No faculty or students were harmed in this administration," Riffe joked. He served the school as interim director as well as associate director.

"When you're an interim director, you usually just tread water. I'm not the 'treading water' type," said Guido Stempel, who served in a multitude of roles including being the school's permanent director, graduate coordinator, faculty, and many related roles. Stempel said he made clear when appointed interim director in 1985 that his first commitment was to the faculty. "I was not going to have the dean tell me to do something to the faculty that wasn't a good idea."

Ralph Kliesch, interim director in 1980, previously served as assistant director in 1968–71, long before the position became a permanent part of the school's administration. He covered operations while the director, John Wilhelm, held the post of the first dean of the College of Communication. "I was running the school 100 percent," Kliesch said. "I didn't have the title or the 'do re mi' that should have been there. As assistant, I did everything. I assigned people to classes, recommended raises, everything."

At times, Kliesch added, the assistant/associate director comes up with an idea that the director turns into a hallmark of the school. In his graduate history class at the University of Minnesota, Kliesch learned about the Ohio connections of noted journalists E.W. Scripps and Carr Van Anda. Based on his suggestions, Wilhelm, then director/dean, initiated the Carr Van Anda Award and development of the school's relationship with the Scripps Howard Foundation.

Most agree that those who serve in these roles, whether associate director or interim director, must be calm, consistent, and organized. Stewart said an associate director should be someone who isn't afraid of detail, someone who doesn't mind interacting with students, faculty, and parents.

"It's like they're giving you the steering wheel, pushing on the gas pedal, and applying the brakes, letting you drive the bus for a while. There's something about it that's very fulfilling," he said.

Bugeja sees a parallel between an administrator's tasks and the roles of journalism.

"A lot of this is being a good journalist or what's defined as a good journalist—be objective, fair, and observant," he said. "If you're a good journalist and apply those tenets and add zeal to that, you will ultimately create a good culture. When you work with alumni you share these values. Anyone who falls into trouble as a director just needs to call upon the alumni, their secret weapon."

Whatever role they play, past associate, assistant, and interim directors all say they are glad to have served a key role in a special school.

"The School of Journalism here is special," said Hugh Martin, remembering his term as associate director for undergraduate studies from 2010 to 2012. "One night when I was first doing the job, I walked into the building. No classes were being taught that night, and I thought I would get some work done."

He observed, "The hallway was packed! At night the building filled up with students doing student organizations, student publications, all kinds of things. There were no faculty members around. Bob [Stewart] called it 'Scripps after Dark.' At night all of the students are doing a lot of things, and a lot of it they are figuring out themselves."

"This is what makes the Scripps School special," he said. "It's not just a place where people go to class; it's a place where students are trying things out for themselves."

EXIT

Teachers, teaching, and service

From the beginning, good teaching has been revered in Ohio University's School of Journalism. The school's first director, George Starr Lasher, was respected by his students more for his work in the classroom than for his administrative skills. That set the stage for what has continued to be defined as the school's most important quality, a tradition that has been maintained by a long list of faculty members. While many qualify for inclusion, here, from the perspective of former students, are a few selected examples of outstanding classroom work and service to the school.

Facing page: Scripps Howard Visiting Professional Andrew Alexander shares his expertise with journalism students. *(E.W. Scripps School of Journalism photo)*

LESSONS IMPARTED, NEVER FORGOTTEN

By Peter King

It's been 40 years since I enrolled at Ohio University, but I have many vivid memories. Funny the things you remember. I was managing editor of *The Post* as a senior, and I'll never forget one autumn night putting the paper to bed and someone ordering a pizza. Turns out the pizza was a nightmare: whole wheat with veggies only. The smell of it was offensive. The look was offensive.

Well, the pizza-orderer got ridiculed, and as the power-mad managing editor, I decreed that the offending pizza would not be eaten. No, the pizza would sit and dry, and then we would nail it to the wall in the editorial offices at Pilcher House, the little house on Union Street, until the university moved *The Post* out of it a few years later. We loved that darned pizza on the wall. I remember my father saw the well-molded wall ornament later in the year and shook his head sadly. As would any responsible person.

Well, enough of the tomfoolery. I loved my time at Ohio University. What a perfect place to go to college. *The Post* is the biggest single reason why I was able to make my love of journalism a career. The practical experience and pressure of putting out a daily paper with fairly prehistoric resources was vital to overcoming any reporting obstacles I encountered later in my real-world jobs.

Impact of the automatic F

My journalism and English classes helped too. One particular piece of advice I got my freshman year was vital. I had a professor, Dru Riley Evarts, who was exacting and demanded the same of her students. On the first day of her class in old Lasher Hall, she issued her most important instruction for papers we would write that quarter. I am certainly messing up a word or two from her class-opening directive, but Evarts told us her expectations in words to this effect:

If you hand in an assignment with a spelling error, or a grammatical error, or a capitalization error, your grade will be a zero. Not an F. A zero.

Peter King. *(Photo provided by Peter King)*

Hmmm. Ten assignments in the quarter. One zero and . . . well, the math was daunting. I just knew it wouldn't be good to make a single error on a reporting assignment that term. I wish I could remember whether I ever blew a paper; I can't. And I don't recall my grade. But I do recall the impact. I read every paper three times before I submitted it. When I left school, I had an internship at The Associated Press in Amsterdam, The Netherlands, and midway through it, the bureau chief said to me one day, "Your copy's so clean for a college kid."

Later, the crush of deadlines at *The Cincinnati Enquirer* and *Newsday* made me much less than perfect. At the *Enquirer,* as backup beat writer covering the Reds, I had three stories plus a massage on the third to do between 7 and midnight for a night game—a "Reds Notebook" that lasted all editions, then a story for the early edition to the outlying 'burbs by 10 p.m., then a story for the Kentucky edition by 11 p.m., then a final final, with quotes and a rewritten lead by 11:45 p.m. It was hard to be perfect night after night in banging out so much copy, but I tried. I hope my editors on the rim at the *Enquirer* noticed.

Then, and in years to follow, I've always recalled Evarts' golden rule. When I was hired by *Sports Illustrated* in 1989, it got reinforced. I was told by the managing editor, Mark Mulvoy, "The editors have to work hard enough. Don't make their jobs any harder. Turn in your copy clean."

That's a great lesson for a writer. Or, in fact, for anyone: Don't turn in work so messy that someone else has to clean it up.

Carrying the message forward

In 2013, Time Inc. and the editors at *SI* gave me a chance to found a new football-centric microsite under the magazine's umbrella. We christened it *The MMQB* (naming it after "Monday Morning Quarterback," a Monday column I'd started when the Internet was a pup), and I got to hire a small staff. I'd be editor-in-chief.

In our second year, a young and talented reporter, Emily Kaplan, came to us from Penn State University and quickly established herself as a writer who could handle tough assignments and turn around quality work quickly. She was a bulldog. No amount of work was too much. Emails came in time-stamped in the middle of the night. Emily wanted it and wanted it bad.

But she was a little sloppy. A lot sloppy, sometimes. After one assignment came in with, by my count, seven spelling or grammar or capitalization errors, we talked. I told her about Dru Evarts' class and her rules I still remembered as gospel four decades later. It's not like a lightbulb went off over her head or anything. I just said, "You're better than this. Don't make your editors work harder than they have to. Why is your time more important than their time? There's no reason you can't finish a story, walk away from it for a half hour, then go back and line-edit it yourself before filing it."

Her copy got cleaner. I had no idea whether I would need to keep reminding Emily of this. I have no idea whether she remembers it today. But I remember it, and as long as I stay in the business I'll pass it on. It's one of the best pieces of formative-years teaching I got—from my parents or from any teacher, any editor, any peer.

Advice about clean copy at Ohio University in 1975, reinforced at *Sports Illustrated* in 1989 with a warning, has stuck with me. Isn't that what college is supposed to be about—lessons imparted, never forgotten? And for those with a love of the journalism tradition at Ohio University, aren't you glad something other than the memory of the nailed-to-the-wall pizza sticks with me all these years later?

DARE WE SAY IT? CONAN THE GRAMMARIAN

By B. DaVida Plummer

Dru Riley as grader for George Starr Lasher, 1948–51. *(E.W. Scripps School of Journalism photo from* The Athena)

It was a fall afternoon in 1982 when I first stepped onto the Ohio University campus as a transfer student. I was anxious and apprehensive. I didn't know anyone, and I was entering the Athens population without the comfort of having already bonded with an entering freshman class. I fought through my fear and found my center after the first week or so. Actually, I pledged to prove that I was just as prepared as my peers, if not more so. After all, I hailed from Hampton University, among the most prestigious of historically black colleges and universities. I was destined to excel to the letter of the promise detailed in my scholarship award from the McGraw-Hill Publishing Company. I was ready.

Enter Dr. Dru Riley Evarts. Academic life as I knew it was about to change drastically.

She crossed the threshold of the classroom toting canvas bags lined and stuffed with pens, pencils, highlighters, articles, texts, reference journals, and the much-needed energy substances of the '80s—candy, nuts, and crackers. My classmates and I exchanged knowing glances. This was the professor we'd all heard about. Dr. Evarts' reputation for being one of the toughest teachers in the program preceded her.

She greeted us with "Hello. If you're here, make sure you're supposed to be, so we can get started." I'll never forget that salutation because it signaled her unapologetic demand for accuracy. So, realizing I was holding my breath, I exhaled and immediately dissolved into a soupy, syrupy mess. This professor meant business. She eyeballed the class, and I tell you, with one sniff she could smell the fuming fear in the room. She wasn't after us. She was after the writing weakness simmering in each and every form in front of her.

Armed with a syllabus, she began her first lecture, which essentially outlined her expectations for the class. Rule number one: There were no shortcuts in her class. With those words, Dr. Evarts began the delicate process of transforming us from enrolled students to scholars. We were about to get what we paid for on our journey through the science of journalism. At the time, of course, we had no clue about what was about to happen. Little did we know that Dr. Dru Riley Evarts' razor-sharp eye for detail was surpassed only by her skill with the quill.

A passion for the written word

I guess the best way to share the experience in hindsight is to paraphrase Carole King: "The earth moved under our feet and the sky came tumbling down," as did our poor grammar. Dr. Evarts was on a mission to rid us of our run-on sentences, subject and verb disagreement, muddy construction, missing attribution, and weak leads. She made it her business to prepare us for the news business. She infused her students with her unparalleled passion for the written word. There have been many days during my professional career, spanning more than three decades now, that I have channeled her passion.

Life lessons were attached to the coursework under Dr. Evarts' leadership. She allowed us to stretch and grow. She had the uncanny capacity to

Dru Riley Evarts, right, joined those who shared firsthand memories of the School of Journalism's history during a memorial service in Athens for Mary Elizabeth Lasher Barnette, daughter of the school's founder, George Starr Lasher. Here, with Dr. Evarts, from the left, are Kathy Watt and Melanie Caldwell, Lasher granddaughters, and Milena Miller of the Athens County Visiting Nurses Association, who worked with Mary Elizabeth. *(E.W. Scripps School of Journalism photo)*

foresee how high and wide we needed to expand cerebrally to peak as storytellers. The construction of a narrative for publication is a journalistic science complete with word and headline count. Dr. Evarts made sure we understood how to color inside the lines with solid copy. What was extraordinary about her special dose of pedagogy was how she encouraged us to respect and adhere to those lines and to file copy that was not just solid but compelling and engaging.

Class was intense. Some heated moments served to draw us closer to her linguistic fire instinctively, like moths. We couldn't get enough. We would get to class early and stay as long as she would allow an audience. We would spill out of her class and stream down the hallway, talking with her as she walked to her office. She would allow us to sit in her crammed office for a postclass session. We had to move the stacks of books, journals, and newspapers to sit down. Dr. Evarts has an insatiable appetite for reading.

The importance of reading

I remember being both stunned and challenged by how much she read. It made me want to read more. She would hand you something to read, and if you were engrossed in it, she would leave you and say, "I have to go to class

Three journalism graduates visit with a favored faculty member, Dru Riley Evarts, during the 2016 Black Alumni Reunion. The graduates, from the left, are Cleveland-based attorney Marlon A. Primes (BSJ '86); Byron P. White (BSJ '87), executive director of Strive Partnership in Cincinnati; and Tony Pugh (BSJ '83), national correspondent for McClatchy Newspapers Washington bureau. *(E.W. Scripps School of Journalism photo)*

or run an errand. Stay where you are." She was sincerely interested in hearing what you thought about the work in your hands. Time in her office was memorable. If you were a ready sponge, she would test your capacity for absorption and just pour it on.

Just recently, I reconnected with a dear friend who was in the graduate program at OU while I was an undergrad. I mentioned Dr. Evarts, and a big, bright smile filled my friend's face. Within seconds that infectious smile hit me, and we laughed together without sharing a word. We are both in academe these days teaching journalism. That colleague, Dr. Sonja Williams (MS '84), is a tenured professor at Howard University. We enjoyed vivid memories of Dr. Evarts editing everything, everywhere, every day. She would come to class with a picture of some pitiful expression of information on a billboard or in a headline and ask, "Can you believe this? It never ceases to amaze me how people who clearly can't write get hired. It's awful."

She hated carelessness. She would encourage each of us to "look it up" if we were unclear about a word or a grammar rule. She would go on to say professional writers use tools to protect the integrity of their work. "The written word lasts forever, people," she'd say. "When in doubt, pick up a dictionary or thesaurus. That's what reference materials are for."

And then she'd quip, "Good grief."

Somewhere between Journalism 333, News Editing, and Journalism 792, Precision Language, my journalistic foundation was set. Six Emmy awards later, this journalist attributes the skill to write, the confidence to place hands on the home keys in top market newsrooms, and the drive to develop and grow in the craft to Ohio University and its crownworthy professor emerita, Dr. Dru Riley Evarts.

PLAYING IMPORTANT WORD GAMES

Alumnus Ralph Brem (BSJ '55) admired George Starr Lasher's love of words and how he managed to convey that love as a method of teaching his students. The following passage is from the booklet "George Starr Lasher" by Dru Riley Evarts and Ralph E. Kliesch:

> [H]e loved words and played with them as a boy plays with marbles, arranging them, clicking one off against another, flicking this one around to become a modifier or knocking that one aside because it was redundant.
>
> "Make the verbs tell the story," he'd say. Then he'd play a game with the students.
>
> "Take 'walk,'" he'd say, leaning back in his chair. "Now, how many ways can one say 'walk' and make the reader see the man walking?" Mostly he'd get a few synonyms from his fledging writers. Then he'd start.
>
> "Well, he doesn't just walk. He strolls, staggers, limps, rolls.
>
> "He can march, don't you know, tramp, pace, stomp, swagger, shuffle, drag, drip, dance. . . ." (He could dance, too. He was always the first one on the floor at just about every dance held on campus, rarely missing a tune or a step.)
>
> And he'd talk about other words, precise words. . . .

"Miss Christner, what does the word 'house' mean to you?"

"Mr. Brem, what does 'home' suggest?"

And slowly his students would get a feeling for the shading, the nuances, that subtle shift of emphasis that comes with knowing that one word doesn't quite mean the same as another.

ONE BEST WORD: REMEMBERING RUSS BAIRD

By Tom Price

Russell N. Baird was my favorite teacher during my early years as an OU journalism student. He was an effective, knowledgeable instructor. He had a quirky sense of humor and a bit of mischievous innocence about him.

One time, in a journalism history class, he was lecturing about an itinerant printer who employed a donkey to carry his equipment from town to town. According to Baird, this guy would set up shop somewhere, then inevitably would print something so offensive that he would have to look for a new place to do business.

The printer would pack his equipment on his donkey, Baird said, and "haul his ass out of town." As the classroom groaned, Baird let out a bit of a giggle. Then he blushed.

More seriously, before Dru Riley Evarts organized the precision language class, Baird preached that there is one best word for every circumstance. "The plural of 'person' is 'persons,'" he lectured. "Use 'people' for groups such as 'the American people.' Don't be afraid of repetition if you're repeating the right word. Use 'said' unless there's a specific reason to use a different verb of attribution. A person 'states' when making a formal statement, for instance."

I thought of Baird years later when reading a column by James J. Kilpatrick, one of my favorite writers on writing. Don't be afraid of repetition when you're repeating the right word, Kirkpatrick wrote under the headline "A Banana Is Not an Elongated Yellow Fruit."

WHEN FAILURE IS A TEACHING TOOL

By Leah Fightmaster

Donald A. Lambert. *(Photo provided by Joyce Lambert)*

"How could I have gotten an F?"

That was my question as I looked at my first failing grade in college. All because I had written an obituary in less than 10 minutes and misspelled the most difficult name I had ever heard: Stephan Wasielewski.

It was Donald A. Lambert's infamous Polish obituary.

I wasn't alone. Hundreds of students who took Lambert's newswriting class still remember their fear of the automatic F if they misspelled a proper name. Of course, at first some of us—students in their second year of journalism as I was, with a self-identified skill in spelling—believed getting names right in articles should be a piece of cake.

Wrong. Lambert gleefully assigned names that were impossible for normal students.

With each class, the names got a little harder and stories more entwined. Students listened the best they could to hear Lambert spell each name and call out each detail, attempting to write them down correctly before he moved on to another fact. It was the classroom, but it was an experience shared daily by professionals.

Lambert was old-school. He began his career in 1958 at the *Erie Morning News* in Pennsylvania after earning bachelor's and master's degrees from Pennsylvania State University and serving an 18-month stint in the United States Army. He spent 10 years in Erie, starting as a general-assignment reporter, then moving to city government and finishing up as the editorial editor, where he especially enjoyed writing columns.

He always had an opinion

Typical Lambert—relishing a chance to express his opinion. He had lots of those, and some were not always conventional.

He joined the Ohio University faculty in 1967 and, for the next 30 years, taught young journalists newswriting, editorial writing, column writing, and journalism ethics. That old-school style and attitude that he brought to the newswriting class is what taught his students some of the most fundamental and important skills they would need to make it as journalists.

Robert Stewart, director of the E.W. Scripps School of Journalism, remembers Lambert similarly. He first met him in 1987 when Stewart came to OU as an assistant professor. In Lambert's book, Stewart had a few strikes against him—he was working on his PhD, the kind of academics Lambert insisted he didn't think much of. He was tasked to develop the first web journalism course, which included two things of which Lambert was not a fan—computers and the Internet. Lambert also said he didn't much like broadcast journalism. That was among Stewart's main assignments.

But it all was typical Don Lambert interaction. You knew he meant it, but the small grin took away the sting. So the story of their professional and personal relationship ends well. Stewart said those fundamental differences never altered his opinion of Lambert as a colleague and person.

"Don was a gentleman, though he may never have thought of himself as such," he said.

Students likewise experienced Lambert's straightforward and at times acidic manner.

As the daughter of an OU journalism professor, Martha Izard (BSC '97) knew Lambert differently than did most of his other students. As a student with a minor in journalism, when she enrolled in news writing, her choices were between Lambert and her father, Ralph Izard. She chose Lambert.

Martha already knew Lambert because of her father's association with him, and this gave her a special incentive to keep from slipping up and getting the dreaded F. She was successful until the last day of speed week. When she returned to class the next day, Lambert was standing outside the classroom door flashing that special grin. And she knew immediately she finally had misspelled a proper noun.

"He wanted to catch me. He wanted me to miss one," she said. "Lesson learned, and now as a fourth-grade teacher, I teach my students the importance of capitalization and spelling. He taught dedication, instilled hard work, and enforced paying careful attention."

That automatic F sounded intimidating and harsh in the beginning, especially to a young college student with little or no real experience in journalism.

HOW DO YOU SPELL YOUR NAME?

"MARSHALL MCLUHAN, what are you doin'?" was a popular phrase heard on the *Rowan and Martin's Laugh-In* television show during the late 1960s.

McLuhan, renowned Canadian media philosopher, during a guest speaking appearance for Communication Week himself silenced some laughter from a capacity crowd in Memorial Auditorium as he prepared to answer an OU journalism student's question.

The question that caused the laughter? The student, first in the question line, asked, "How do you spell your name?"

When order had been restored, McLuhan said something to the effect "That was the best question I have ever been asked." He then inquired, "Why did you ask the question?"

The young man replied, "I arrived late at the auditorium and did not receive a program. I need to know how to spell your name because I am going to write a class assignment. Professor Donald Lambert has an automatic F rule. You misspell a proper noun, and you get an F on that assignment."

McLuhan spelled his name and went on with answers to other questions.

At the conclusion of the program, McLuhan kept an eye on the young student and invited him to come to the stage. Because of having the conviction to ask an elementary question, the young man became McLuhan's driver during his Athens stay and for the trip to Port Columbus Airport for his return flight to Canada.

And upon graduation, that student was hired by McLuhan's company.

–Roger Bennett

But under the surface was the real lesson. Names are important. And it wasn't that the consequences of carelessness were always dire, although for some they could be. It was that the smallest details are sometimes the most important, and the practice of writing accurately while double-checking your work helps to build a good reputation as a smart journalist.

Great professors are hard on students

"He was hard on us, but great professors are," Martha said. "You could tell he cared about his students. As an educator and person, he was great on both accounts. He had our best interests at heart."

Nicole Franz (BSJ '09), who took the class as a sophomore, remembers Lambert as someone who came off with a gruff demeanor but had a kind heart. She had made it to speed week without an F until she came to class terribly sick one day. Before she could get through her third assignment, he told her to go home; she clearly was unable to finish it. They would work it out later when she was better. When she received her grades the next week, she learned that because of her condition he never graded her third assignment.

"It was very unexpected," she said. "And it was a nice moment. I definitely got a zero at some point, but it's all part of the learning process. He taught us the basics of how to write quickly and efficiently."

That's a lesson Franz took into her professional career as an editor and copy editor. Breaking news happens, and the paper is on a deadline, but being right supersedes being first.

"Those are practical skills that will never go out of fashion, even in the digital world," she said.

Today, I take solace in the fact that the name I spelled wrong to earn me my first F in college was a Polish name that a lot of my classmates got wrong as well. However, I know I should have double-checked my obit before turning it in to make certain it was correct. That was one of the lessons Lambert wanted me to learn in his class. Thank you—it worked.

PERSISTENTLY INSISTENT

By Ralph Izard

James E. Alsbrook. *(Photo courtesy of the Ohio University Archives, Mahn Center for Archives and Special Collections)*

James E. Alsbrook carried the fact that he was the first African American faculty member in the School of Journalism with pride and distinction, but perhaps he was best remembered in Scripps Hall for his legendary insistence on proper grammar and word choice.

In the classroom, in faculty meetings, and in the hallways, he persistently reminded students and colleagues of the importance of correct language usage. On some occasions, he used late-night telephone conversations with faculty colleagues to advance his message. He was known as a strict and effective classroom teacher.

Alsbrook, who taught in the school from 1978 until his retirement in 1984, had previously worked for the *Kansas City Plaindealer,* the *St. Louis Call,* the *Kansas City Call,* the *Afro-American Newspapers* in Baltimore, and *The Courier-Journal* in Louisville, Kentucky. He came to Ohio University from Central State University, where he chaired the communications program.

A native of Kansas, he earned his bachelor's degree in journalism from the University of Kansas in 1963, a master's degree in journalism from the University of Iowa in 1964, and a doctorate in mass communication from Iowa in 1968.

A QUICK QUIP AND A GENTLE HAND

By P.J. Bednarski

When Roger Bennett (BSJ '69, MSJ '70) was leaving the Scripps School in 1979, the *Ohio Journalist* newsletter said the journalism school was losing its "resident character," and the phrase was bracketed in those quotes as the author searched for an umbrella term to explain him.

And that's not easy.

Journalism students in the late '60s and '70s know Bennett wore a lot of hats: He was a respected teacher—and a classmate pal—a husband, mentor, editor, father figure, and to a few, even a landlord. Later on, he could add director, fib-catcher, and mayor to his résumé.

In 1967, Bennett was city editor at *The Athens Messenger* and became the point person for student reporters in the university's professional practice program there. It should have been awkward. After all, although he had about a decade of experience at newspapers, he had no college degree and, in fact, only one year of college at Ohio University. "I majored in saloons and girls, in that order," the Portsmouth, Ohio, native says now about his few moments as a college student back in 1956, after a five-year stint in the U.S. Navy.

But it turned out he was good at teaching college students, in the newsroom and elsewhere. Soon he was thrust into a role as an instructor in Copeland Hall, where journalism classes were held back then, and was urged by the faculty to finish his degree on the fly.

He ended up taking courses at the same time he was teaching them. "I would go to a psych class and say 'Yes, sir" to the prof and then go over to Copeland Hall and begin teaching the guy I was just sitting next to," he recalls, with a laugh that, even at 81, still sounds a little like a war whoop from an old cowboys-and-Indians film. When one of his charges was a no-show for an early-morning philosophy course they were both taking, he says, he called the student's dorm and said, "Hey, you'd better wake up in time for my class."

By 1969, he had his bachelor's degree and shortly thereafter his master's. He was on his way. By 1978, he was so admired and respected by his students that he was voted a University Professor, one of only six professors so honored from throughout the university that year.

A mix of experience and humility

What students admired about Bennett was a mix of real experience and humorous humility. "I tried to bring real-life things into the class. I could tell my reporting classes about dumb things in the newsroom. You know, I told them I'd be a pretty good teacher for them because I made every mistake in the world. I said, 'Now you don't have to make them because I already did.'"

Bob Stern (BSJ '75), now retired from the *Brockton* (Massachusetts) *Enterprise,* says, "Other than my father, he probably had the biggest influence on my life." Bennett befriended Stern and encouraged his interest in journalism and once invited him to a Super Bowl party with some sports reporters for *The Post.* Surprising himself, Stern remembers he held his own and began working for the school daily, where he had previously thought he wasn't cool enough to be in the newsroom.

Later, in Bennett's newswriting class, Stern finished a test about 20 minutes before everybody else. He remembers that as he walked out of the classroom, where others were still slaving away, he said to himself, "I think I've found what I want to do with my life."

With Bennett's help, Halina Czerniejewski (BSJ '72) became the first woman president of Ohio University's student chapter of the Society of Professional Journalists (SPJ), at the time considered among the nation's outstanding chapters. She went on to have an executive position at SPJ's magazine, *Quill.*

Like Stern, Czerniejewski remembers Bennett's insistence on AP style and punctuation in class and his warning that a misspelled name earned an automatic F. With a name like hers, she was happy to find an ally, but, she recalls, Bennett always just referred to her as "Hal." She also remembers the personal touches. Once, when she was really ill, he seemingly bought out a drugstore's supply of over-the-counter remedies and brought them to the student housing apartment she shared with a roommate.

"What kind of guy does that?" she asks from her current home in Scottsdale, Arizona.

Mark Roth (BSJ '69), a longtime reporter on special projects for the *Pittsburgh Post-Gazette,* was one of Bennett's first interns. Bennett thought he needed to spend time diving deeper into subjects—which now is what Roth does for a living. Back then, Bennett assigned him to look into housing discrimination among landlords who rented to students. "That was my first lame attempt at enterprise reporting," he recalls. "I don't think it ever got published."

Oddly enough, Roth ended up renting a room from Bennett and his wife, Barbara.

In time, Bennett rose in the ranks at Ohio University and knew he also had to pursue a higher degree to get ahead. He entered a PhD program at the University of Texas, where his doctorate research was an attention-grabber: Bennett claimed a method to train journalists to spot when someone was lying by noticing minuscule changes in a person's expressions. He still swears by it.

"That was my dissertation," he says, "on deception, on tics that people emit when they deceive. I thought it might be a tool for journalists in the interview process. They might not necessarily get the truth from an interview subject, but at least they would know if they were being lied to. There had been very little research on it. I took it from the journalistic approach. That had never been tried before."

He came back to Ohio University later, and his University Professor award gave him the chance to teach a course on deciphering the secret behind what is technically called "micro-momentary facial expressions."

In the Woodward and Bernstein/post-Watergate era, Bennett's technique was hot news, and stories about it were published in newspapers and magazines all over the country.

But he also says it brought him some unwanted attention from government agencies in this country and others, which pestered him for information. "That kind of stopped my clock for a while," he says, and not long after all of that Bennett headed back to the Lone Star State to Southwest Texas University (now called Texas State University) to become chairman of its small journalism department. He got busy with the growth of the school, and his facial expression exploration ceased.

He says, "There was a small journalism department when I got there in 1979, with about 150 majors. When I left in 1995 there was a large Mass Comm program with nearly 2,000 majors and 16 full-time professors and a handful of adjunct pros. I was busy."

From teacher to mayor

Since retiring, Bennett and his wife have resided in a small Florida town of slightly more than 600 people called Briny Breezes, located in an oceanside spot in Palm Beach County. The place is a little bit famous. It is one of only two trailer parks in Florida that have officially incorporated as a town.

Bennett was its mayor for seven years, until 2013. During that time a developer offered more than $500 million to buy the entire place and replace it with a condo project, but that deal fell apart when the economy did.

A heart scare while on vacation overseas gave Bennett enough of a reason to step down, and really retire, a few years ago. When he did, a regional paper lauded him for guiding the little town "with a quick quip and a gentle hand."

That's probably what his former students would say about his teaching style, too. Just as he did with the good people of Briny Breezes, he'd surely get their vote.

YOUR DISSERTATION IS GARBAGE

On a hot July day in 1976, I became a garbage expert.

But I had a lot of help extracting my lost dissertation data from a huge landfill (garbage dump) in the western part of Washington County (west of Marietta, Ohio). And the digging ended when my 13-year-old son yelled, "Dad, here is that book with your name on it."

Here's what happened.

I reported to my office on a Monday morning after a July 4 trip, sat down at my desk and reached for the large cardboard box that held all the research documents for my dissertation. I had been studying at the University of Texas for several years to establish whether a journalist could read facial expressions to determine lying behavior.

The box was gone.

For people of the modern era who don't know what that means, the box contained original paper questionnaires, hundreds of computer punch cards, and floppy discs. In today's technology, everything would have been on a hard or thumb drive or in the Cloud.

I learned a lesson that day. Don't put anything of value on top of a large trash can. Not realizing that the box contained anything of value, a janitor did what he was supposed to do. He tossed the box in the dumpster. As a result, I knew my work toward a dissertation and eventual PhD was over.

Ralph Izard had a different idea when he learned I was about to give up. He encouraged me and helped track down the garbage truck driver to learn the location of the landfill where my dissertation load had been dumped.

The garbage dump was a huge operation about 30 miles east of Athens. It was also the dump site for Parkersburg, West Virginia; Marietta, Ohio; and all points in between. So to say it was a "large, stinky garbage dump" was not an exaggeration.

I really didn't want to pursue a search, but Ralph persisted.

Ralph, Hugh Culbertson, and a few students armed with tools, jugs of water, and disinfectant joined in as we set off for the dump. My son, Roger, and (if my memory serves me right) his friends Fred Bush and Steve Culbertson also tagged along.

Somehow we picked up a Columbus TV station crew, so the whole episode was recorded.

We started digging. There must have been a dozen or more with shovels, hoes, and other tools plowing through the muck.

After about two hours of digging, swatting flies, and waving off a huge hog, we all were about ready to quit. Then we started finding items in the dump from buildings surrounding Lasher Hall (then the journalism building).

Again, after several minutes of digging, there was nothing until my son yelled about the discovery he and his buddies had made. They had gotten tired of digging and wandered off.

They had spotted some colorful electrical wiring sticking out of the ground. Hoping for material to play with, they pulled the wire free. Out popped my master's thesis. It had my name on it. I had been using the thesis as a guide for footnoting and style.

We dug down at the "colorful wire spot" and located the entire box of material. Some of the material was wet and some muddy, but we retrieved everything.

Back at the university, faculty colleague Chuck Scott helped me dry out the material. We used a large drum dryer for the wet punch cards and the large floppy discs. To my surprise everything worked when loaded into a computer or a card reader. The dissertation could proceed as planned.

The best line of the whole episode occurred a couple of days later when Professor Guido Stempel passed me in the hall. "That was the first time a dissertation was garbage before it was completed," Stempel commented in his usual deadpan manner.

–Roger Bennett

Chuck Scott. *(Courtesy of* The Columbus Dispatch)

PHOTOJOURNALISM EDITOR AND TEACHER

By Stan Alost

Standing over six feet tall with a booming voice from his barrel chest, Charles "Chuck" Scott cannot be ignored. Combine that with his distinguished careers as a photojournalism practitioner, industry innovator, and educator, and the result is a powerful influence on visual communication on campus and in newsrooms nationally.

He could tell a story like no one else. And he had a lifetime of championing photojournalism stories to tell.

When Scott (MSJ '70) walked through the doors of Ohio University's newly formed College of Communication in 1969, he had already spent 29 years in the photojournalism world.

He began his teaching career in the School of Journalism by creating picture editing and photojournalism classes, and within four years he had risen from lecturer to associate professor before leaving to return to the industry as picture editor for the *Chicago Tribune.* When he departed, the program he started was dropped.

After returning to Ohio University in 1976, Scott within two years had teamed with his son-in-law, School of Art Assistant Professor Terry Eiler, to form the Institute of Visual Communication. Under his leadership, the institute won two statewide awards of excellence before, in 1986, becoming the School of Visual Communication, a program at the time jointly managed by the College of Fine Arts and the College of Communication.

The School of Visual Communication in 1994 was moved completely into what is now known as the Scripps College of Communication.

Scott retired from Ohio University in 1994. His lasting legacy is his impact on the news industry as well as an army of students who became world-recognized photojournalists—their work shaping how we see the world and history. Chuck Scott's students have earned every major photojournalism award; have worked for many of the most important newspapers, news services, and magazines; and have become educators enriching or starting visual communication programs across the country.

A much-honored photographer and editor

Scott's professional career started in high school as a stringer in his hometown of Lincoln, Illinois, for the *Decatur Herald-Review,* and he continued his photography as a U.S. Navy combat photographer in the Pacific theater during World War II.

In 1951 Scott went to work for Acme Newspictures (an early incarnation of United Press International). He was hired later that year as a staff photographer for the *Binghamton Press* in New York before moving to the *Champaign-Urbana Courier* as chief photographer. He was hired in 1956 as assistant picture editor by the renowned Robert Gilka at the *Milwaukee Journal,* was soon promoted to picture editor, and in 1966 moved to the *Chicago Daily News* as graphics director.

Scott earned his Bachelor of Science degree in journalism from the University of Illinois in 1948 and his Master of Science from Ohio University in 1970. He received more than 100 industry awards through the years, including the Grand Prize in 1952 from the National Press Photographers Association and the first Illinois News Photographer of the Year award in 1956.

The 1966 Pictures of the Year recognized Scott as Editor of the Year. In 1975 NPPA recognized his work at the *Chicago Tribune* for the best use of pictures. That same year, his work garnered the Overseas Press Club award for the best daily newspaper or wire reporting and the Grand Prize from the World Press Photo competition. At the *Tribune,* Scott led the photojournalists and picture editors to an unprecedented number of awards, including the 1975 Pulitzer in International Reporting for the work of writer William Mullen and photojournalist Ovie Carter.

He also has been lauded for his teaching, including the Ohio University College of Communication's L.J. Hortin Faculty Mentor Award in 2006 for his teaching and mentoring. In 1970, the NPPA presented Scott with the Kenneth P. McLaughlin Award of Merit, in 1975 the Joseph Sprague Memorial Award, and in 1979 the Robin Galand Photojournalism Educator award.

Forward-thinking and innovative

Along the way Scott always was an innovator. He was part of a team that drew international acclaim for innovative use and reproduction of color photography at the *Milwaukee Journal.* In the 1950s, both AP and UPI adopted his modification of the existing wire service photo transmission system.

Under Scott's leadership, faculty and students of the School of Visual Communication were among the first to use digital photography. In the early 1980s Scott collaborated with Canon USA to use the newly developed still video camera. OU faculty members Chris Carr (BSJ '82), Ed Pieratt, Gary Kirksey, and Terry Eiler produced the first digital images transmitted in color during the Kentucky Derby.

When he died in 2015 at the age of 91, Scott was recognized by Scripps College of Communication Dean Scott Titsworth as "the most influential academic in shaping the modern pedagogy of visual communication" and as one who "helped frame the importance of visual images in storytelling."

HER HIGHNESS, DEBBIE DEPEEL

By Maggie Scaggs Bonecutter

Steno 1. Steno 2. Secretary. Senior Secretary. Administrative Associate. Administrative Coordinator. Administrative Services Specialist. And, in the eyes of students, queen of the E.W. Scripps School of Journalism.

They all work, but the last title best suits Debbie DePeel.

From 1977 to her retirement in 2016, under a bevy of titles, Debbie DePeel's mission remained constant: help the journalism school run—and run extremely well. Her demeanor is quiet, pleasant, and even-keeled, but inside is a powerful workhorse who's fast and accurate and, in her 39 years in the School of Journalism, had amassed incredible institutional knowledge.

"Debbie is unique in the sense that she has this wonderful combination of professional competency packaged with a personality that's warm, understanding, and impressive," said Ralph Izard, past director of the school. "She is totally unselfish. If you need something, she will drop what she's doing and do it for you. That's unusual—not just in this business, but in human life."

Debbie DePeel.
(Photo by Ralph Izard)

Started just out of high school

Debbie was 18 years old—barely out of high school—when she started working in Scripps as a Steno 1. The modes of her work were shorthand and typing. "When I started [at Scripps] I got an IBM Selectric that did corrections," Debbie said. "That was really exciting." She started her career assisting J.W. Click, now professor emeritus, with the details of what was then the nation's largest high school publications workshop.

"Her work ethic is outstanding, she's very efficient, and she works hard," Click said. "I bet Debbie doesn't know this, but after I hired her I learned from my neighbor that she had a 4.25 GPA in secretarial studies in high school. The fact that she's still there and has won numerous awards speaks to her ability."

Click is referring to several high-profile awards Debbie has earned. In 2001 she was named one of six Outstanding Classified Employees for the entire university. In summer 2002 she and a colleague were dubbed College of Communication Employees of the Quarter, and in April 2005 she was crowned Employee of the Year for the college. Impressive, to be sure.

"Your relationship with Debbie tends to always be the same," Izard reflected. "Whether you approach her in a relaxed mode or in a sense of crisis, Debbie simply deals with you in her way. She treats everyone—students, faculty, administrators—the same. They're all just people to Debbie."

And she saw quite a few people in her 39 years at the school. She served—and in her case that's an appropriate word—10 individuals who occupied the director's seat, outlasting all the other full-time faculty and staff members and seeing thousands of students come through the halls of the Scripps School.

Many memories

All of this has contributed to quite a memory bank of experiences. She reflected on a few:

- Most significant change in how she does her job: "Having a computer. No carbon paper, dittos, or copy machines."
- Most significant change in students in her time at Scripps: "They keep getting younger. When I started here, I was younger than most of the students. Now I'm older than their parents."
- Most significant change in OU overall: "The kids are a lot busier. I wonder when they sleep."
- Exciting change in her career: "The move from Lasher Hall to Scripps Hall. I never thought about Lasher being horrible, but the thought of something new was great! That was really exciting."
- Interesting memory: "When we were in Lasher Hall, my office was at the end of the hallway near a reporting class. The professor was teaching, and suddenly a secretary from the dean's office came to the classroom door and shouted, 'You said you'd never see her again!' There was a gunshot. That caused quite a commotion. Then the professor said to the students, 'Write a story.' It was all fake—he had the secretary come over—but it was quite a hook for a good story."
- Most influential coworker in her career: "I worked with Phyllis Cross for a long time. She was another mother figure—not only with work things, but everything: how to get a spot out, how to bake whatever. Phyllis was technology resistant. And now I don't 'tweet,' I have a cell phone that just calls and a text would take a half hour. Oh, my gosh! I've turned into Phyllis!"

Outside of work, Debbie enjoys scouring yard sales for hidden treasures. She's a lifelong Hocking Valley resident, born in Athens as the next-to-youngest of six children. In elementary school she frequently visited the library that was then located in what is now Chubb Hall, and in high school, she went to Alden Library. She now lives in Albany with her husband, Kirk, and their two children, both OU students: Jason, in electrical engineering, and Jessica, in accounting.

"They were Bobcats before they were born," she said.

When asked to predict the Scripps School 20 years from now, she said, "There'll be a lot of new faces, several folks getting ready for retirement, and hopefully I won't be here." She said it jokingly but in 2016 made it official with a retirement that was unexpected by everyone. That marked some upcoming tough times for the School of Journalism, the College of Communication, and Ohio University.

THANKS FOR THE MEMORIES

By Mohamed Najib El Sarayrah

It is often difficult to go back in memory more than 25 years ago, but beautiful memories are easily recalled because they are associated with joy and great moments of accomplishment.

I graduated from E.W. Scripps School of Journalism, Ohio University, in 1987. I still remember when I used to walk through the streets of Ohio University, reflecting on its gorgeous buildings and its old trees. I remember I could feel and smell a history of significant contribution to knowledge and scholarship. History, of course, is crucial in our lives as individuals and institutions. It tells who we are.

Studying journalism and mass communication in the E.W. Scripps School of Journalism had a different feel because of its international reputation. There, you meet and learn from distinguished scholars who have contributed significantly to the discipline. I am honored to be one of the MSJ and PhD graduates of this school and this university. Here I am obliged to mention three important professors with whom I had close contact.

Guido H. Stempel III was well-known in communication research for his field research as a method of teaching. He was a great, firm, and nice scholar. I owe him so much respect. The only problem I had with him was his way of talking. As a foreigner it was quite difficult for me to follow him because he used to speak fast without moving his lips.

The second is Hugh M. Culbertson, who was one of the best in teaching mass communication theories. He had a strong voice that grabs your attention. During his lectures, he would introduce concepts and theories in a way that would help you to think and criticize. Every student in his class used to expect to be forced to respond to Culbertson's famous question: "What do you think about this?"

The third is Ralph Izard, my supervisor on both my MS and my PhD. I learned much from Professor Izard. In my work now, I am using different teaching techniques that I learned from him. I remember he told me in one of our meetings to discuss my PhD dissertation, "Mohamed, I want to learn new ideas and new concepts from your work. This is what will convince me that your work is acceptable."

Professor Izard was close and very helpful to his students; he was friendly, and he always gave you the feeling that you were important. In fact, he had a huge impact on my academic development and on my personality, and I always speak about him to my colleagues and my students. One of the many things I learned from him is that if you want to know something, you need to dig it out from different sources. This will give you profound and multifaceted knowledge. In his class on freedom of the press, we had excellent debates on various issues, and he led the discussions in a very professional way.

OPELAND HA

Journalism in a time of turmoil

THE LATE YEARS of the 1960s and the early years of the following decade were times of momentous social upheaval throughout the county. They were years of assassinations, of campus protests, of demands for equality, and of notable unrest. In the words of one of our writers, it was "a world that seemed on fire." The impact was felt strongly on the Ohio University campus. As is often the case, however, those years posed unusually potent opportunities for journalism and for learning journalism.

Facing page: Copeland Hall, home of the school, 1955–69. *(Photo by Ralph Izard)*

Tom Price. *(Photo provided by Tom Price)*

THE POST IN A WORLD THAT SEEMED ON FIRE

By Tom Price

Ohio University and Athens reacted calmly to the assassination of Martin Luther King Jr. on April 4, 1968.

As we scrambled to put out *The Post* that night—melding wire news of America's many burning cities with our reporting in Athens—small groups of students, mostly black, wandered through our offices to read the reports ticking from our UPI machine. Unlike the thousands of people who rioted in cities from Brooklyn to Oakland, OU's black students seemed mostly stunned and saddened.

The next day, some 4,000 people—mostly white on a campus with only 600 or 700 black students—gathered for a memorial service in front of Baker Center, the student union, which stood where Schoonover Center does now. Much of the crowd then marched to Court and Union streets, where about 200 sat in the intersection.

Athens Police Captain Charles Cochran tried to pull a demonstrator from the street, an act that could have provoked a violent response. But university Vice President James Whalen confronted Cochran, and the captain backed off.

Then James Steele—OU's most prominent black student activist—waded into the middle of the intersection. Called "The Prophet" for his extraordinary speaking skill, Steele raised the demonstrators to a high pitch of anger, then calmed them down with a passionate plea for nonviolent action.

The assassination and aftermath presented special challenges to *The Post.* The memorial service and demonstration occurred Friday, and in those pre-Internet days, we couldn't report them until Monday. And we had much other news to squeeze into the paper those days.

A time of significant news

The April 4 front page was dominated by stories of student government attempts to seize more influence in university decision-making. The story beneath assassination coverage the next day reported a nonacademic employees union pledge to honor picket lines should students strike. Monday's coverage of nationwide riots and memorials shared space with Athens' response to the assassination, more reports of student government activism, and a story about the singing group Peter, Paul & Mary—on campus for a remarkable two-and-a-half-hour concert Friday night—reminiscing about their appearances with King during the 1963 demonstration at the Lincoln Memorial and the 1965 march to Selma.

It's impossible to imagine a more exciting time to work for a college newspaper than the 1967–68 school year. Journalism classes taught us skills we needed to report and edit a newspaper. But we became real journalists on the job, trying to cover and make sense of the ferment boiling around us.

We witnessed the assassinations of King and Democratic presidential candidate Robert Kennedy (after we stopped publishing in June), President Lyndon Johnson's decision to abandon his reelection campaign as the Vietnam War and antiwar protests escalated in tandem, the rise of the black power and student power movements, the first glimmers of the modern women's movement, and a general sense of unending unrest.

Clearly, we were witnessing the earliest moments of campus turmoil that erupted in the spring of 1970.

Locally, students attacked racial discrimination in off-campus housing and worked in projects designed to help the Appalachian poor who lived just beyond Athens' borders. The university seemed under perpetual threat of student and nonacademic employee strikes, which didn't materialize. Undergraduate women campaigned to end the requirement that they be inside their residences before midnight. Women staffers at *The Post* obtained permission to work beyond the witching hour, but we had to summon campus police to escort them home.

This also was a time of profound change for *The Post.* Two years earlier —printed slowly on a flatbed press at an Athens job shop—the newspaper was a five-days-a-week tabloid with morning newspaper deadlines but evening delivery. In 1966–67 it became a five-days-a-week broadsheet, but we still filed final copy at about 1 a.m. for a paper that hit campus at dinnertime. After moving to *The Athens Messenger*'s rotary presses in September 1967, we finally could adopt a real morning-newspaper schedule, going to bed after midnight and watching our work become a staple at breakfast.

The need for African American perspectives

Stylebooks told us that dark-skinned people of African descent were "Negroes." But the black power movement propelled black activists to our offices with demands that we call them "black." Steele and his compatriots also complained that our nearly all-white staff didn't adequately reflect black perspectives in our writing.

We responded by creating the "Black Perspective" column, through which black students and faculty could place their thoughts before the campus. We already had an "In Perspective" column open to anyone, and we later added an "International Perspective" for international students. We never got our arms around the Negro/black conundrum, however, and both terms appeared interchangeably throughout the school year, including sometimes in "Black Perspective" itself.

We also flirted with bankruptcy, learning some painful lessons about the business side of journalism in the process. Vastly overestimating our ability to increase ad sales in a small city, we began the year with an expanded staff producing an eight-page paper, twice the size of the year before. We quickly found ourselves spending faster than we could earn. In less than three weeks we dropped to six pages, then four, then bounced between four and eight depending on our ad staff's productivity.

In early January, we went public with our financial problems and launched a "Save *The Post*" fund-raising drive. The response was amazing. Students, faculty, administrators, nonacademic employees, townspeople, and professional journalists from around Ohio sent us donations. Student organizations—from Student Congress to the Bobcat Cycle Club—chipped in. The WOUB news staff passed the hat. Dormitories and Greek houses sponsored fund-raising dances. The Ohio University Mothers Club of Cleveland sent a check. Even those who had felt the wrath of our editorial page said they didn't like our opinions but believed we were an essential campus institution.

By the end of February, we had raised more than $5,500, and contributions were still rolling in. We were hoping to earn several thousand dollars from a Glenn Yarbrough concert we sponsored in March. And the university administration announced—because of the broad support shown for *The Post*—that it would raise our subsidy to make sure we could publish until the end of the school year.

Strong student support

Grapevine, a student-run polling organization, uncovered reasons for the support. A February survey found that 90 percent of students read us at least three times a week, and half read us every day. Eighty percent rated us at least "average" for covering campus news, while half termed us "good" or "excellent."

Most also understood the dual roles of newspaper as reporter and commentator. Eighty percent said they read editorials most of the time. Just 30 percent thought editorials should reflect the predominant student opinion. Just 10 percent said *The Post* should print only what most students wanted to read.

The Post's quality was confirmed later by the professional journalists who judged the Ohio College Newspaper Association's annual contest. They named us best daily newspaper and gave us 21 additional awards, more than any other paper.

The Post was honored for best public service campaign (race relations), best educational service campaign (education at Ohio University), and best use of photography. Ken Steinhoff (BFA '70), one of our photo editors, won for best feature photo. Walt Harrison (BFA '68), the other photo editor, won for best portrait.

For years, I bragged that, as editor, I had had the best *Post* staff in history. Watching later *Post* grads do great journalism around the world forced me to reconsider that conceit. But we did have quite the crew, and most went on to impressive careers.

The best-known Postie is Clarence Page (BSJ '69), a two-time Pulitzer Prize winner, nationally syndicated columnist for the *Chicago Tribune,* and fixture on national TV talk shows.

To mention just a handful of others: Andy Alexander (BSJ '72) ran the Cox Newspapers Washington Bureau, then became *Washington Post* ombudsman, and now serves his alma mater in several capacities, including as visiting professional in the Scripps College of Communication. Rudy Maxa (BSJ '71) accomplished the unusual feat of being both an investigative reporter and a gossip columnist for *The Washington Post,* then became a nationally broadcast travel journalist. June Kronholz (BSJ '69) was a foreign correspondent for *The Wall Street Journal.* John Felton (BSJ '75) covered foreign affairs for *Congressional Quarterly* before becoming a foreign editor at National Public Radio. Tom Hodson (BSJ '70) directed the OU J-School from 2003 to 2010 and now is director and general manager of the WOUB Center for Public Media.

Others went on to report, edit, or photograph for various media—better professionals for the challenges they met as student journalists when the world seemed to be on fire.

COVERING THE CAMPUS RIOTS OF 1970

By Burton Speakman

THE SCENE ON CAMPUS was chaotic in the spring of 1970, but few would have predicted the rancor and escalation of the situation that occurred after students in Athens learned the National Guard had shot and killed four students and wounded nine others at Kent State University.

Andrew Alexander (BSJ '72), now visiting professional with the Scripps College of Communication, who was editor of *The Post* at the time, said he found out about the Kent State shootings when colleague Tom Hodson (BSJ '70), now director/general manager of the WOUB Center for Public Media, came running across the campus holding a piece of paper from the wire about the shooting.

The shootings escalated the nightly protests that already were occurring as a result of the war in Vietnam, specifically, the U.S. bombing and invasion of Cambodia. What had been institutional protests, the students felt, had become personal.

What occurred on campus during those weeks was confirmed by *The Post* and in a documentary, *The Sky Has Fallen,* about the protests and eventual closing of the university, produced by journalism faculty member Mark Leff.

The Post of May 5 also included stories about plans to strike at the OU campus to protest the Kent State shootings and a plea from then–university President Claude R. Sowle that those protesting on the campus remain calm to avoid the violence that was occurring on other campuses in the state.

A need to "calm them down"

After May 4, journalism faculty member Hugh Culbertson said, the university asked faculty members to go out to the College Green and talk to students to "try and calm them down."

"I had a group of 15 to 20 around me, and they started complaining about the media. After a while I got mad and asked them how many of them had read *The New York Times* or *The Washington Post* in the past month," Culbertson said.

Only one hand went up, he said.

"I told them at that point they didn't know what the media were doing to cover the antiwar movement," Culbertson said. "I probably did more to fire them up than to calm them down."

Alexander said it was an interesting time as clusters of groups sat on the College Green just talking about the shootings and the broader issues.

"The students were very engaged," Alexander said, and often that engagement surged beyond conversation.

"It seemed like every night right about sunset somebody would pry up a brick from the walkway and toss it through a window of a business, and the battle was on again," he added.

The Post argued against violence because of the belief that some people —often from outside of Athens—wanted the students to get violent for political reasons, he said.

Before they left when the university was closed in spring 1970, students witnessed the occupation of campus by the Ohio National Guard. *(Photo courtesy of the Peter Goss Photograph Collection, Mahn Center for Archives and Special Collections)*

Groups of vigilantes were talking about coming to campus to "take care of the problem," he said. "These are people who couldn't go to college and resented the protests of the students. They couldn't understand why the students would damage businesses. They thought of Athens as their town."

Violence on campus

John Kifner, a reporter at *The New York Times,* told students that Ohio University overall was the most violent campus he had visited in terms of the overall protests, Alexander said. Other campuses had worse incidents, he said, but the activity in Athens was more prolonged.

Kifner wasn't alone in his assessment of the situation in Athens. In fact, James Michener in his book *Kent State* stated that Ohio University was the most violent of any of the four public universities in the state that experienced violence.

At times, *The Post* staffers, located in Pilcher House on Union Street, had to deal with tear gas, and reporters and editors had to work with damp masks over their faces in an effort to offset the effects of tear gas as they worked to produce the paper, Alexander said.

As a result, on May 15, Ohio University was shut down amid what had become nightly violence. The day after the campus was closed, every parking spot on Court and Union streets was filled by members of the Ohio National Guard holding weapons.

"There was an attitude at that time that you just didn't mess with the National Guard," Alexander explained.

The situation was especially intimidating given the students' memory that it was the National Guard that had shot and killed four students at Kent State University. Students were told to get out of town within 24 or 48 hours. Sometimes angrily, sometimes sadly, they responded to the orders, rushing to find transportation to get home. Commencement ceremonies were canceled. The campus became quiet for the first time in weeks, but the memories of those who were involved have lingered to this day.

A JOURNALISM CAREER ERUPTS FROM CHAOS

By Randy Rieland

I'm going to go out on a limb here: The best view on the Ohio University campus is from the front of what is now the Schoonover Center for Communication, across Union Street and up through those mammoth shade trees on the College Green.

OK, not such a long limb. I probably wouldn't get much of an argument from anyone who has gazed southward from that spot. But for me, that sight (from what at that time was Baker Center) carries a particularly deep meaning. It's where my journalism career caught its first spark.

It was the spring of 1970, the home stretch of my freshman year. Except nothing felt like it was winding down. The campus was electrified. At the end of April, President Richard Nixon announced that he had ordered American troops in Vietnam to invade Cambodia. That set off antiwar protests on college campuses all across the country, including at Kent State, three hours north of Athens.

Everything turned crazy

A few days later, on May 4, everything took a turn for the crazy. Four Kent State University students died after being shot by Ohio National Guardsmen during an antiwar protest. Suddenly, the abstraction of news events became very real. By the following week, some OU professors began canceling their regular classes and instead giving talks on the College Green about subjects such as Vietnam. That seemed a lot more relevant to what was happening around us.

As a freshman whose connection with college professors had largely been from 20 rows back in giant lecture halls, I was captivated by those sessions.

Students and faculty held discussions on the College Green in an effort to calm the campus during the turmoil of spring 1970. *(Photo courtesy of the Peter Goss Photograph Collection, Mahn Center for Archives and Special Collections)*

This, I remember thinking at the time, was much closer to my idealized notion of learning—engaged students, passionate teachers, meaningful knowledge. Each day the crowds of students gathered around professors seemed to grow, and I was hopeful that events would take a positive turn, that despite all of the tension on campus, OU would not devolve into the ugliness and riots that had occurred elsewhere.

That positive turn did not happen. By the middle of May, each night brought a new level of nastiness to Court and Union streets, culminating in an intense version of street violence call and response. Students threw rocks and bricks, provoking police to fire pepper spray, and those acts were answered with more rocks and bricks. It was weirdly predictable chaos.

I was paying particularly close attention because it was my first attempt at reporting, albeit in a strictly volunteer capacity. Earlier that spring, I had walked into *The Post* office, which then was in the bowels of the old Baker Center, and told one of the editors that I was interested in working for the paper. He didn't give me an assignment that first day but encouraged me to see if I could help staff writers gather information for their stories.

The beginning of a career in journalism

That was good enough for me, and when things started getting crazy, I made my way up to *The Post*'s office to see what I could do. I spent the night shadowing Bill Choyke (BSJ '71), a reporter for the paper, as he roamed all over downtown Athens, following the chaos. After a while, I began venturing out on my own and then reported back what I had seen. It was a long night, and I'm not sure anything I passed on made it into the paper.

Hours later, in the middle of the night, university President Claude Sowle announced that school was closing. We were told we had 24 hours to leave campus; the next morning, Court Street was lined with armed soldiers from the Ohio National Guard. My freshman year was over.

As intense as that first night of reporting was, though, it's not the image from those times that sticks in my mind. What I remember more vividly were not the nights of May 1970 but the days, the times when I stood on the College Green with hundreds of other kids listening to teachers talk about Vietnam. I even learned some critical reporting lessons during those open-air lectures—the value of bringing context and perspective and history to a story.

Many years later, when my wife, Carol Ryder (BSJ '75), and I returned to Ohio University with our son, Ben, when he was deciding where he wanted to go to school, I was anxious to show him the College Green. As we stood up near Cutler Hall, I waved in front of me.

Randy Rieland. *(Photo provided by Randy Rieland)*

"What do you think?" I asked Ben.

"Nice," he answered, with just a hint of enthusiasm.

I was disappointed with his reaction, but, in fairness, he was just seeing brick sidewalks and tall trees. I was still seeing those kids back in the spring of 1970, standing in circles, listening intently as we tried to make sense of the swirl of events pulling us all together, and I was seeing a young journalist-to-be gathering information to share with newspaper readers.

PR EXEC THOUGHT HE COULD CALM THE STORM

By Hugh M. Culbertson

The mood on campus was tense prior to the 1970 visit to the School of Journalism by Edward L. Bernays, considered by many to be one of the fathers of public relations.

And that was before the news arrived about the shootings at Kent State. Ohio University was one of several colleges across the state where students had been protesting the Vietnam War and U.S. bombings in Cambodia.

So it was not a good time to bring a distinguished visitor to campus. After Bernays arrived on May 4 and we escorted him to campus, students already were pouring onto the College Green. They were listening to a bunch of fiery speeches about police officers as "pigs."

Before we brought Mr. Bernays to campus, we had a couple of students do a reconnaissance mission to see if it was safe, a tactic that may have come from my days in the Marine Corps. When they reported back that it was safe, we brought him into Memorial Auditorium through a side door.

Only about 100–200 students were in the auditorium when it was time for Bernays to give his speech. Most seemed to be there because attendance had been made a classroom assignment. They probably would have preferred to be outside, where the scene was different, with the protests of 3,000 to 4,000 students resounding clearly inside the auditorium.

Bernays, never at a loss for action, had his own ideas.

He wanted to go outside and address the crowd of protesters. Mr. Bernays had a big ego, and he thought he was going to be able to persuade and assuage the students.

His wife, Doris E. Fleischman, nationally well known herself in public relations, was able to talk him out of going outside. She was afraid he would incite a riot.

The Post quotes Bernays on May 5 referencing the protest outside, saying the situation could have been avoided with "better communication" by the government. Otherwise, we had no idea what Bernays thought about Vietnam or the bombings of Cambodia or what he would have said to the students if he had dived into the protests.

Living the mission

Through a blend of professional education, practical experience, and intellectual exploration, we teach journalism in a way that it can be applied to many professions and to a rewarding life in a multicultural and fast changing world. Whether it's telling a story, building a brand, or engaging in research, we prepare students for their chosen professions now and as those professions change in the future.

–From the E.W. Scripps School of Journalism Mission Statement, April 24, 2013

Facing page: Ewing Hall, home of the school, 1936–55. *(Photo courtesy of the Peter Goss Photograph Collection, Mahn Center for Archives and Special Collections)*

Among those who contributed to the school as Scripps Howard Visiting Professionals are, from the left, Andrew Alexander of *The Washington Post,* Julie Agnone of the National Geographic Society, and Robert Benz of Hanley Wood & Ledge Solutions. *(E.W. Scripps School of Journalism photo)*

A PROFESSIONAL EXTRA

By Walter Friedenberg

In 1990 I was one of several members of the Washington Bureau of the Scripps Howard News Service invited by Dru Riley Evarts to come to Ohio University for a week to lecture and attend seminars at the E.W. Scripps School of Journalism. I had an absolutely satisfying time. More than that, I loved it.

I had always hoped to wind up my journalistic career by teaching at a university. So before returning to Washington I hopefully asked then-Director Ralph Izard, "How do you get to come back to the school permanently?" Ralph answered, amiably, "Oh, you have to wait for a professor to die or leave." My follow-up question was "Is there anybody who's likely to die soon?" He told me all faculty members appeared to be in good health. Bummer, I thought, but them's the breaks.

Two years later, when I was executive editor of the *Santa Fe New Mexican,* I received a press release saying that the Scripps Howard Foundation was funding the establishment of a 10-year program to bring visiting professionals to the Scripps School for a whole year. I rushed to send in my application.

It took a year for the fund income to accumulate, but for the 1993–94 academic year, I was chosen as the first Scripps Howard Visiting Professional. And I loved it all over again.

Working in the classroom

I enjoyed being in a classroom with eager young students who were learning how to become journalists. I delighted in answering their questions and imparting purported experience and wisdom. I enjoyed becoming acquainted with professors whose privilege and responsibility it was to scrutinize the profession. I loved walking through that luxuriant College Green and driving down red-brick streets. I loved Athens, the pretty town that is the university and the university that is the town. And so did my wife, Tencha Avila, who earned an OU Master of Fine Arts degree in the equally excellent theatre program.

A year-long visiting professional—what a perceptive, far-sighted idea for helping a journalism school to "improve the breed," so to speak. Originally, the foundation provided funds annually for the visiting professional, but in 1997 it began the process of establishing a fully endowed chair in journalism.

That idea, realized, has given students the services of a diverse roster of professionals fresh from the industry. They include Pulitzer Prize winners, foreign correspondents, a network television reporter, a wire service correspondent, a syndicated columnist, a science writer, a magazine editor, an investigative reporter, a feature writer, a media group executive, and a Washington bureau chief. They have represented some of the world's finest news organizations. Collectively, they have catered to the variety of news media majors. And they have come not just for one lecture, one week, or one month but an entire year. Their add-on presence has given the faculty an extra hand (for free), not just to "take over" a number of courses but also to serve as guest lecturers in their courses.

Benefits for the visiting professional

And what about the benefits for the visiting professional? Unlike me, who was ending a long career, most of the 14 or 15 successive visitors—residents, actually—interrupted their careers to go to Athens and returned to their workplaces not only refreshed and satisfied but also, I trust, enhanced and reinvigorated. For myself, I learned a great deal about the practice of journalism by teaching it, by analyzing and rethinking techniques and principles. I also learned a great deal from my faculty colleagues, through conversations and auditing their courses.

Perhaps I should explain how as the first visitor/resident I came for one year and stayed three. As that first year neared its end, Ralph Izard asked me whether I'd like to return for another. I had been a reporter on four dailies, a stringer in India, a globally traveling correspondent for five years, an editorial writer for three, editor of *The Cincinnati Post* for eight, a European correspondent for two, a Washington-based reporter/analyst for 11, and top editor in Santa Fe for two. At the Scripps School it apparently seemed that there was still more juice to squeeze from the lemon. I said yes. The next spring Ralph asked the same question but added that it definitely had to be the last. I said yes, of course. In three years I taught 12 courses and in bidding a hearty farewell hoped I had gotten the Scripps Visiting Professional program off to a good start.

Long may it continue to give Scripps School students that very special extra.

SCRIPPS HOWARD VISITING PROFESSIONALS

1993–96	Walter Friedenberg, *Santa Fe New Mexican*
1997	Helen Thomas, United Press International
1998	Terry Anderson, The Associated Press
1999	Kevin Noblet, The Associated Press
2000	Doug Poling, CBS News
2001	Kenneth Freed, *Los Angeles Times*
2002	Bradley Martin, *Asia Financial Intelligence* and *Asia Times Online*
2003	John Brady, *The Artist's Magazine*
2004	Kate Webb, Agence France-Presse
2005	Leonard Pitts Jr., *Miami Herald*
2006	Mark Prendergast, *The New York Times*
2007–11	Mark Tatge, *Forbes*
2011	Andrew Alexander, *The Washington Post*
2012–13	Julia Keller, *Chicago Tribune*
2014–15	Robert Benz, Hanley Wood & Ledge Solutions
2016–17	Julie Agnone, National Geographic Society
2017	Sue Morrow, *The Sacramento Bee*
2018	Julie Agnone reappointed

FOLLOWING IN E.W.'S FOOTSTEPS

By Thomas Suddes

As Franklin Foer wrote in the *New Republic* late in 2014, "These are boom times for provincial autocrats." And that demands robust coverage of the nation's 50 state capitols and its countless courthouses and city halls—that is, avid public affairs reporting.

In 2011, with the financial assistance of the Scripps Howard Foundation, the school launched the E.W. Scripps School of Journalism Statehouse News Bureau fellowships. The paid fellowships partner some of the school's best undergraduates with seasoned statehouse, political, and public affairs reporters in Columbus.

Result: The Scripps School offers tomorrow's journalists an outstanding learning opportunity—and offers additional reporting resources to newspapers and broadcast stations confronting tight reporting budgets. The stories the Statehouse News Bureau fellows report are freely available to other news media nationwide, and fellows' reports that are selected for the Ohio Public Radio-TV Statehouse News Bureau are disseminated particularly by WOUB Public Media, Ohio University's PBS affiliate.

The fellowships had their genesis in discussions I had over several years with Robert Stewart, the school's director. I was an assistant professor with decades of experience covering Ohio's statehouse for *The* (Cleveland) *Plain Dealer,* and I knew of state government reporting programs at Arizona State University, the University of Washington, and the University of Maryland (in collaboration with Virginia Commonwealth University).

An innovative approach

The challenge for Ohio University was to devise a Scripps School program that would be feasible given resource constraints. For example, Arizona State, Maryland, and Washington each maintain what amount to faculty-staffed newsrooms in or near their respective states' capitols. That wouldn't be practical for the Scripps School. So Stewart, with annual scholarship support from the Scripps Howard Foundation, and with the ardent support of news executives at *The Columbus Dispatch,* devised a hybrid.

Rather than create a Columbus newsroom, the Scripps School's students could seek Statehouse News Bureau fellowships. Fellows would report full time, for a semester, at Columbus news organizations covering the statehouse or at the statehouse news bureaus of other Ohio news organizations. I would mentor the fellows in tandem with the fellows' worksite editors.

Journalism students at other universities also would be eligible for the fellowships. (To date, five such students have been awarded fellowships—two students from Ohio State University, two from Kent State University, and one from the University of Cincinnati.)

Among those who have lauded the Statehouse News Bureau fellowship program is Benjamin J. Marrison, former editor of *The Columbus Dispatch,* who was instrumental in the program's success, along with the current editor, Scripps alumnus Alan Miller (BSJ '78). In mid-2014, Marrison wrote, "It's important to train the future journalists on how government—township, county, city, state, federal—actually works by exposing them to it while they're in college. And by putting these [student] journalists next to experienced journalists, we have created a wonderful program that is good for today and tomorrow."

The Statehouse News Bureau fellowships build on Ohio's strong tradition of robust statehouse coverage. According to Osman Castle Hooper, an early historian of Ohio journalism, "There were reporters of the proceedings of the Ohio General Assembly, while the territorial government existed," that is, before 1803.

As a young Ohioan, future novelist William Dean Howells as well as Whitelaw Reid, future publisher of the *New-York Tribune,* were among those covering the Ohio Statehouse and General Assembly before the Civil War. The correspondents association itself was founded in 1893 by a *Cincinnati Enquirer* reporter, James W. Faulkner. He is memorialized each year through a scholarship founded by some of his friends in the Ohio Legislative Correspondents Association and awarded annually by the Scripps School.

Avid coverage of the statehouse, and competition for statehouse news, was spurred by E.W. Scripps, whose Ohio newspapers (first in Cincinnati, Cleveland, Toledo, and Columbus and eventually in Akron and Youngstown) exposed statehouse corruption and contributed to the advance of Progressivism in the state, according to the leading historian of the Progressive movement in Ohio, Hoyt Landon Warner.

Students have been successful

The Scripps School's statehouse program began in fall 2011. As of the 2016–17 school year, 36 journalism students (31 from Ohio University) had been awarded paid, semester-long fellowships. The 36-fellow cohort is diverse, consisting of 18 women and 18 men; of the latter, one is African American, another, Malaysian.

Nineteen fellows have worked with *The Columbus Dispatch;* eight with Ohio Public Radio-TV's Statehouse News Bureau; four with *The Plain Dealer*'s Cleveland.com; one with WBNS-TV, Columbus Channel 10, a CBS affiliate; and four with WCPO-TV, Cincinnati's Channel 9, an ABC affiliate.

As of early 2017, 30 of the 36 Statehouse News Bureau fellows have earned their degrees; the remaining six are completing their degrees as E.W. Scripps School of Journalism students. Of the 30 former fellows who've earned degrees, 26 are working or interning in mass media; one is a law student; two are freelancing; and one is spokeswoman for a labor federation.

Success is measured in countless ways. But it's perhaps notable that one of the first two Statehouse News Bureau fellows was Alex Stuckey, who reported in the fall quarter of 2011 for *The Columbus Dispatch*. Stuckey, a 2012 graduate of the Scripps School, was part of a team that won a 2017 Pulitzer Prize for the *Salt Lake Tribune*. She recently has moved to the *Houston Chronicle*.

Just as notable is this fact: Stuckey's 2012 reporting, while she was on the staff of *The Post,* Ohio University's daily student-run newspaper, sparked a state investigation of the Athens County sheriff. Stuckey's work won an Investigative Reporters and Editors (IRE) award. Three years later, one-time Sheriff Pat Kelly was convicted on 18 criminal counts. He's now serving a seven-year sentence. Then, as now, Stuckey's reporting exemplifies journalism in the public interest—the alpha and omega of the Statehouse News Bureau fellowships.

A PATH TO WASHINGTON

By Kyle Kondik

Contraction in the newspaper industry has been a burden for many but a boon for others. When I was studying at the Scripps School in the early-to-mid 2000s, the idea of bypassing lower-level journalism jobs and moving directly to a national publication almost immediately after college was somewhat ridiculous. At best, many of us hoped we could get a start at a small local paper and work our way up to a place like *The Plain Dealer* or *The Columbus Dispatch*.

But changes in the media world have made it much easier for younger people to get journalism jobs at major publications. And a new collaboration of the Scripps School and the School of Visual Communication is designed to provide the experience that will facilitate that transition. The Semester in Washington program was announced at the National Press Club in February 2017 and was slated to start officially in fall 2017.

Twenty students—10 apiece from journalism and visual communications—will spend several months in the capital, four weeks in a seminar and 10 weeks in a practicum with a participating news publication. The program is designed to give students the chance to learn from industry professionals in Washington, focusing on journalism (print, broadcast, data, and photojournalism), strategic communication, commercial photography, information graphics, data visualization, publication design for print and digital, scripting, and UX design.

The seminars will be facilitated by faculty from both schools. Students will receive credit for the 10-week internships.

That's not to say Bobcats have not been represented in Washington. *The Washington Post* has become *The* (OU) *Post* East—with recent Posties like Matt Zapotosky (BSJ '08), Katie Carrera (BSJ '08), Wesley Lowery (BSJ '17), and others distinguishing themselves there in recent years. Many of my contemporaries at OU have also landed in Washington, including my dear friends Phil Ewing (BSJ '05) and Erica Ryan (BSJ '04), who showed me the ropes at *The Post* when I was in Athens.

These alumni have joined a long list of OU-trained Washington journalists. Among what perhaps are hundreds of former Bobcats (too many to list here), Clarence Page (BSJ '69), Andy Alexander (BSJ '72), Ray Locker (MSJ '84), Greg Korte (BSJ '94), and Sid Davis (BSJ '52) have held and do hold prominent D.C. journalism positions.

In their footsteps, the new Scripps program will further open that path to Washington for Bobcats and allow them to make the connections and get the experience they need to make the most of the opportunities in a media landscape that is increasingly open to younger journalists.

ALWAYS SERVING, ALWAYS LEARNING

By Nerissa Young

R. Smith "Smitty" and Patricia Schuneman. *(E.W. Scripps School of Journalism photo)*

Universities are expected to produce lifelong learners. Two Ohio University alumni are returning that gift and, in turn, leading by example as learners with an annual contribution that supports a spring media symposium.

R. Smith "Smitty" and Patricia Schuneman graduated from OU more than 50 years ago. In retirement, they returned to the school by pledging an annual gift of $33,000 for each of 15 years to sponsor the Schuneman Symposium on Photojournalism and New Media.

The E.W. Scripps School of Journalism is the recipient of their gift, but the campus and the Athens community directly benefit from a program that brings top media practitioners and scholars to Southeast Ohio.

"The Schunemans clearly are lifelong learners, demonstrated not only by their annual attendance at the symposium but also by their enthusiasm for meeting professionals at the cutting edge of communication," said journalism school Director Robert Stewart. "I can't help but think that our students and faculty have taken note of their open-mindedness—indeed, their joy of learning. This may be their main legacy to the students and faculty of this university."

The symposium began as an idea and conversation in 2008, said Thomas Hodson (BSJ '70), who was then the school's director and is now director and general manager of the WOUB Center for Public Media.

Smitty Schuneman (BFA '58, MFA '60) retired from the University of Minnesota after teaching photojournalism. He and Patricia (BSED '59) started their own business in which they produced films and developed media technology. They began a photojournalism symposium at the University of Minnesota.

Broader than photojournalism

"Smitty and I connected originally through Terry Eiler [former director of the School of Visual Communication]," Hodson said. "However, Smitty was interested in sponsoring a symposium that was broader than just photojournalism."

Hodson continued, "We, therefore, talked face-to-face and through email and telephone and hammered out the details of his concept. He and Patricia already had experience with the symposium at the University of Minnesota. He wanted the one at Ohio University to be slightly different, to address 'cutting-edge' trends in journalism and storytelling as well as to address issues facing photojournalists."

The symposium was presented first in 2009 and examined how new media shaped the 2008 presidential race. In 2015, it expanded to two days. Each year, faculty from the journalism and visual communication schools bring together the best in written and visual storytelling.

"The Schuneman Symposium helps us in so many, many ways, but its unique contribution is that we are able to expose our students and faculty to key thought leaders and industry professionals who bring images and words together to tell powerful stories," Stewart said. "Without the gift from the Schunemans, we would be hard-pressed to bring the caliber of speakers to campus that we can with their support."

Hodson echoed Stewart's sentiment: "The symposium gives students and faculty a unique view of media each year. This combination of emerging young journalists with legendary figures with bodies of work spanning decades gives participants the best of the new and the traditional."

A model of cooperation

Stewart said the symposium provides yet one more opportunity for the journalism and visual communication schools to collaborate.

"The fact that we had several symposia prior to moving into neighboring suites in the Schoonover Center really set the stage for us to hit the ground running in the new facility," he said. "The symposium meant that we already had developed very cooperative, friendly dialogue among the students and faculty."

Timothy Goheen, current director of the School of Visual Communication, said the symposium is one of many areas of collaboration between the schools. "I look forward to it being even more influential as we continue the collaboration."

Smitty Schuneman said in the 2015 interview that Ohio University "really still cares about students in a fundamental and absolute way. OU has just never lost its way and it still cares about the students first of all, and it sees to it that they get the best education that they are willing to get."

The Schunemans are doing their part to provide that quality education.

JOURNALISM FOR HIGH SCHOOL STUDENTS

By J. William Click and Virginia "Ginger" Hall Carnes

For more than 70 years, thousands of high school students have gained their first formal taste of journalism as they prepared to lead their newspapers and yearbooks by attending the Ohio University High School Publications Workshop, now called the High School Journalism Workshop.

Growing from its inception in 1946 to become the nation's largest by the mid-1960s, the workshop had its peak attendance of 2,251 participants in 1967, partly because students loved the real-life and memory-inspiring experiences gained through publication of a newspaper or yearbook during the week.

The program grew from a void created on the Athens campus following World War II when very few students attended regular summer sessions. The number was so small that President John C. Baker (1945–1961) and Dr. Rush Elliott, director of the university's summer session, formulated the idea of a two-day conference on student publications to bring students and advisers to campus, both for education and to use university facilities that were lying fallow in the summer.

Journalism Director George Starr Lasher appreciated the idea. He personally handled arrangements, including transporting students from the train station to their residence halls. The workshop began in 1946 as a conference and roundtable discussion with 48 students and two faculty members. Ohio's was the second such workshop, starting about 10 years after similar sessions at Northwestern University. Lasher served as workshop director through 1950.

Beginning in 1951, Ohio originated the idea of writing, editing, and publishing newspapers—mimeographed, letterpress, and offset—and a yearbook signature, which were printed and sent home with the students. The workshop newspapers were special treats. Workshop teachers would feed student-produced stories about the workshop to instructors who coordinated the paper.

Meghan Louttit of *The New York Times* guides students during the 2015 High School Journalism Workshop. *(E.W. Scripps School of Journalism photo)*

Loren Joseph "L.J." Hortin joined the team in 1947, and it was expanded beyond two days in 1949, formally gaining its long-time name, the Ohio University High School Publications Workshop, in 1950. For the next 20 years participants arrived on Sunday afternoon and left the following Saturday after lunch. Enrollment skyrocketed during Hortin's tenure to 1,826 in 1964, when Hortin relinquished his role as director. Workshop instructor John Neff described Hortin as a "very energetic, tremendous guy who had his finger on everything."

Hortin developed the Ohio Plan: students went to class each morning until the 10 a.m. convocation in Memorial Auditorium to hear a major speaker, and then they returned to class. President Baker committed to fund one major convocation speaker each year. Most afternoons featured guest speakers in smaller venues—for example, the AP and UPI Ohio bureau chiefs talking to newspaper students, and photographers or others talking to yearbook students—followed by an extensive recreation program featuring dances, sport tournaments, swimming, tennis, golf, and movies.

The nation's largest workshop

A 1964 *Scholastic Editor* magazine article on summer journalism workshops concluded that the Ohio workshop attracted one in five workshop students nationally. Through the 1960s, students came from 12–13 states, and workshop instructors came from as far away as Massachusetts and Illinois.

Hortin resigned as director of the School of Journalism in 1967 to return to Murray State University and was replaced as workshop director by John William "Bill" Click (MS '59). After earning his master's degree from Ohio, Click taught at other colleges but returned to Ohio to teach in the summer workshop. In 1965 he joined the Ohio faculty at Hortin's request and directed the workshop from 1965–1981.

"I'm certain of Bill Click," Hortin said. "I got him here."

Click spent his career immersed in student publications, as evidenced by his receipt of top awards from scholastic press organizations, particularly the prestigious Gold Key from the Columbia Scholastic Press Association. He chose workshop teachers by watching those who attended and encouraged creativity in students.

Lab sessions taught by veteran high school publications advisers included critiques of the students' newspapers or yearbooks by the instructor—a tremendous amount of work for the teacher but a treasure for the students and advisers. "We offered free evaluation of the publications, but there were no prizes," Hortin said in a 1976 interview. "The idea of this workshop is to help the schools."

The value of the High School Journalism Workshop as a recruiting tool is demonstrated by these students at the 2015 workshop who said they planned to attend Ohio University. *(E.W. Scripps School of Journalism photo)*

Parents and teachers enjoyed the learning environment. “It was the only thing [my daughter] did in high school that was non-competitive,” one parent said in a 1966 survey. “No failures. No grades. It was an excellent learning environment.” It also became a recruiting tool for OU because students had experienced campus life. Many came to study disciplines other than journalism.

The most popular convocations were by prominent cartoonists who did “chalk-talks.” While discussing their careers, the characters in their strips, and how to get ideas, the cartoonists used black chalk to bring their characters to life. These sketches from the creators of such comics as "Steve Canyon," "Popeye," "Funky Winkerbean," and "Little Iodine" were given to students through a random drawing.

The advisers' seminar

The advisers' seminar was one of the most popular innovations. Advisers originally attended classes with their students and shared their problems with others only informally. Some had been thrust into the role of newspaper or yearbook adviser with zero or minimal training. Beginning in 1953 advisers had their own sessions, lived in the same residence halls as workshop instructors, and discussed the staffing and business aspects of yearbook and newspaper advising.

Attendance decreased as similar workshops were started around the country and higher fees were instituted that limited the number of students a school could send, as well as the creation of other summer camps for wrestling, cheerleading, and the like. By 1976, total participation had dropped to 640–567 students, 42 publications advisers, and 31 teachers and workshop staff members. When Click relinquished the directorship in 1981, faculty colleague Tom Hodges took the helm for the 1982 workshop.

One intangible benefit was expressed by a teacher from Brookville (Ohio) High School, who shared one student's comment: "Well, I know one thing now. I am going to college," which pleased his parents and shows that the values derived were not confined entirely to journalism.

—Most data for this story are from Virginia D. Hall's 1976 graduate history project, "From Chaos to Organized Confusion: A History of the Ohio University High School Publications Workshop."

EDUCATION ON THE ROAD

By Jerry L. Sloan

AFTER HAVING SPENT 22 years at Ford Motor Company and another four-plus years as vice president of public relations for American Motors, I had just returned to Ford in 1987 to be executive director of public affairs (what Ford called public relations). In doing a quick review of the many things Ford PA was involved in, I noted cooperative programs with Northwestern University and the University of Missouri. While both were fine universities, and the programs were worthwhile, my question was Why not also Ohio University? Since I was the boss, everyone thought it was an excellent idea. I also was a 1959 graduate of the school.

We started talking with the School of Journalism to see what we might do cooperatively. An excellent program emerged—The Ford Master's Program—to enable middle management Ford PA people to earn a graduate degree from the E.W. Scripps School of Journalism.

As the program developed, we got "sticker shock." Our human resources people thought Scripps saw the name Ford and immediately assumed "deep pockets." It took our best negotiating skills to convince the Ford HR people that this unique program deserved a higher price tag. After some pushing and shoving, the program was a "go."

Note: When the program began I never imagined I would become a professor in the School of Journalism before it was completed. Looking back, I have the satisfying feeling that I threw a pass and somehow was in the end zone to catch it for the winning touchdown.

A program for middle managers

We had 10 middle managers ready to embark on earning an Ohio University master's degree just as we had to make key moves within Ford PA. Men and women were moved around the country, and this resulted in four candidates dropping out of the program before they started. Six students began in fall 1989.

The six Ford PA people were Denise Carmona Bither, Jim Bright, Susan Page Miller, Mike Parris, Jim Trainor, and Joy Wolfe. Instruction was to be provided by six School of Journalism faculty members: Michael Bugeja, Hugh Culbertson, Dru Riley Evarts, Mel Helitzer, Tom Hodson, and Guido Stempel. Administration was provided by Assistant Director Patrick Washburn. Paired with the unique program were interesting experiences, such as Hodson arranging for the Ford group to spend a day at the U.S. Supreme Court when it was in session.

The Ohio University classes in the program were conducted over six quarters in two years. One subject was taught each quarter.

The students met at Ford's World Headquarters in Dearborn, Michigan, at 6 a.m. on a Friday and drove a Ford (of course) van to Athens.They met for a class all afternoon, took a short dinner break, and then continued their class in the evening. On Saturday morning they resumed their class until noon before returning to Michigan.

After a weekend off, the professor teaching that quarter's class would travel to Dearborn, Michigan, to teach a class on a similar schedule at Ford's World Headquarters. Sometimes instead of driving to Dearborn, the professor would conduct the class via videoconference or conference call. Videoconferencing was in its infancy at the time; a conference call was a good alternative.

The classes were Journalism and Communications Seminar; Mass Communication Theory; Public Relations Problems and Programs; Newspaper and Communications Law; Mass Media and Society; and Government and Mass Communication. After completing the six Ohio University courses, the students took additional courses at universities closer to home and then, as was the case with on-campus students, had to do a thesis or professional project.

A result was productive research

Three of the six men and women were able to complete the program and earn master's degrees. All three produced professional projects to complete their degree requirements.

Denise Carmona Bither's project was on employee communication and its effectiveness in the workplace. "I compared Ford to Disney and Hewlett Packard," Bither (MSJ '94) explained. "I visited Disney and HP and was able to interview many of their executives."

She said, "One of the biggest things I learned was prior to Disney embarking on an extensive employee-communication program, it had an extremely high rate of turnover. After it began its program, its turnover rate dropped, and officials thought employee communications played a key role."

For his professional project, Mike Parris (MSJ '94) wrote a 60-page research piece on a story titled "Waiting to Explode" and produced by *Dateline NBC* in which it was reported that certain Chevrolet pickup trucks were exploding on impact. "*Dateline* had hired an outside contractor to do the story," Parris said. "It was later discovered [that] the contractor had set up a Chevrolet truck to explode in a crash test by overfilling the gas tank and shooting a small rocket at the truck to make sure there were flames."

General Motors' investigation of the NBC story discovered the bogus explosion using the rocket. GM went public with its findings and filed a lawsuit against NBC. As a result, NBC's Jane Pauley read a 3½-minute apology on air, an executive resigned, three producers were fired, and the on-air correspondent was transferred from her national assignment to a local station.

For the project, Parris said he was able "to interview the ex-NBC president, key PR personnel from GM, and *Popular Hot Rodding* magazine's editor, Pete Pestere, who broke the story that sank NBC."

Jim Trainor's professional project looked at the impact that distance played on media relations, specifically, how media dealt with a local PR representative versus dealing with someone in a home office located far away. "Remember," Trainor (MSJ '96) said, "this was before the Internet as we were still using pagers and bag phones, so the topic was more pertinent than it would be today."

(In possibly one of the more bizarre defenses of a professional project, Trainor's defense took place in my living room. Ralph Izard and I were on Trainor's committee, and I was confined to my home following two surgeries within the previous two weeks.)

Jim Bright, while not earning a graduate degree, did complete all of his requirements except a professional project. The reason for his inability to earn his master's degree was his success. Ford continually moved him—from Ford Motor Credit PA manager in Dearborn to Southwestern Regional PR manager in Dallas to Ford Division PR manager in Detroit—during the six-year term of the program.

He had several other key assignments before retiring in 2006 as an executive director of Ford Public Affairs. Following his retirement, he was appointed Winslow Professor of Journalism and Public Relations at his alma mater, Indiana University, where he taught until 2010.

Denise Carmona Bither was manager of FCN News (Ford's vast employee TV news operation) when she began the program. She held a number of key assignments before moving to Visteon Corporation, a large Ford spin-off, as executive director of global corporate communications. She later left Visteon to be a stay-at-home mom and raise her family.

When the program started, Mike Parris was assistant manager of Ford Division PA. He moved through a series of assignments before retiring as PA manager for South America and Asia-Pacific. Mike now heads Parris Communications in Birmingham, Michigan.

Jim Trainor was assistant manager of PA at Lincoln-Mercury Division when the program got under way. He also moved through a series of PA positions before leaving Ford as L-M PA manager. He is now senior group manager of Product PR for Hyundai Motor America.

ONLY THE BEST AND BRIGHTEST

By Guido H. Stempel III

The School of Journalism began selective admissions in 1979 at the request of Jim Walters, Ohio University director of admissions. For the school, it was an answer to a problem of growing enrollment with which it had been wrestling for more than a decade. For Walters, it was part of an approach that he felt would bring more and better students to Ohio University.

The school's enrollment doubled in the 1960s, reaching a total of more than 1,000 students. A number of factors contributed to this growth. For one, the university's enrollment expanded, and journalism was a more popular major throughout the country and certainly on the Ohio campus.

The school first sought to control enrollment by establishing a grade-point requirement. But university officials at first said that was contrary to university policy. Later, however, selective admissions became university policy. Walters planned to implement the policy one major at a time, and journalism, with the largest enrollment and applicants with higher class ranks and ACT and SAT scores than other majors, was the logical place to begin. In the early 1970s, university enrollment had declined by one-third, but journalism's enrollment had stayed at about 1,000.

Higher standards stimulated more applications

Walters expressed the opinion that becoming more selective would not only ensure that the school gained the very best students but also cause its number of applications to increase. He was right. Before long we were rejecting more than 100 applicants annually.

In later years, the process was placed in the hands of James B. Piatt Jr. (BSJ '87), who served for five years as assistant director of admissions.

"It was an exciting time to be part of a program which had a national/international reputation for outstanding faculty accomplishment as well as graduate student preparation but was still gaining steam as [a] national attraction for undergraduate students," said Piatt, now vice president of university advancement at Elon University.

The process, in the main, evolved around admissions decisions based on class rank, grade-point average, and performance on the SAT and/or ACT. But, Piatt said, while this helped raise the school's academic profile, it did not consistently guarantee journalistic aptitude among its enrolling students.

"In the spirit of accommodating talented students who fell short of the numbers-oriented admission qualifications for the Scripps School, then-Director Ralph Izard and I reviewed hundreds of appeals each year by students requesting a second look based on demonstrated journalism talent," Piatt said. "Each week, Dr. Izard and I would meet to read through scores of high school newspaper articles and view VHS tapes of broadcast productions, homemade films, and other items submitted by aspiring applicants."

A personal approach

Piatt continued, "This approach provided a uniquely personal touch to a process that we could have allowed to become just the opposite. Instead, we chose to make smart bets on students of all academic calibers. Success in journalism, it could be argued, has always been a result of a certain degree of grit. Those applicants capable of demonstrating that grit were usually greeted with a successful outcome of their appeals."

The numbers varied over the years, but in general, 160–180 freshmen entered each year, and to this number some 40–60 transfer students were added. Stempel noted that many of these transfers demonstrated what Piatt called "grit" by coming to Ohio University anyway even though they had originally been denied journalism admission. They then reapplied at the end of their freshman year.

The process continues. The selective admissions plan set up more than 40 years ago has remained in effect. It has kept enrollment at a size appropriate for the school's facilities and has enabled the school to maintain the quality of the program. And journalism majors are generally recognized as among the university's best and brightest students.

"WHY I WANT TO BE A JOURNALIST"

By Michael Precker

I SET OUT to write a story about my memories of a 1970s era requirement of a 500-word essay for admission to the School of Journalism. But this ace reporter couldn't find any official sources from that era who remembered such a requirement. Nonetheless, it was real to me, which is why a budding 1970s wise guy/too-full-of-himself Postie published his essay as an op-ed in the morning paper. In my mind, I'm pretty sure the requirement was abolished a year or two later. Again, no reliable sources can confirm that or that my column helped kill what may or may not have been a requirement, but neither can they contradict me when I take credit. So, to all subsequent journalism graduates: You're welcome!

Here's what I wrote to comply with what I thought was a requirement:

There's a rule in the OU School of Journalism that requires every student, under penalty of nongraduation, to submit a 500-word statement explaining in precise, lucid detail just why he or she wants to be a journalist.

I am told, and I do not doubt it for one minute, that failure to comply with the requirement, be it useful or not, will result in my being handed a blank sheet of paper in a fancy envelope in that misty-eyed moment in the Convocation Center four quarters hence.

For three years, until this very date in this very column, I resisted the subtle pressure to write such a statement, primarily because my reason for wanting to be a journalist is this: I don't know. I just like to write.

Unfortunately, "I don't know. I just like to write," is only eight words, which leaves me approximately 492 shy of the mandated goal. But the question remains: Why do I want to be a journalist?

Is it because there are now 55,000 journalism majors in college, according to the Association for Education in Journalism, who will compete for good job openings that may number in the hundreds? No, it's not that.

Could it be that most of the jobs that are available pay $105 a week for 60 hours of work, in towns that don't even make a lot of maps? No, that's not the reason.

Is it because, in this Golden Age of journalism, for every *Washington Post* and *New York Times* and (Dayton) *Journal Herald,* there are hundreds if not thousands of *Columbus Dispatch*es and *Athens Messenger*s and (Manchester, N.H.) *Union-Leader*s where they never heard of reporter power or shield laws or responsible journalism or any of the other relevant things we learned in Mass Media and Society?

No, that can't be it either.

Perhaps it's the idea that, unless my uncle happens to be editor or majority stockholder somewhere, my job, if I get one at all, more than likely will be with one of those abominations whose main accomplishment, for the greater glory of journalism, is to waste the precious timberlands of our nation. No, I guess not.

Then why? Why don't I do like my friends and labor long and hard and become an accountant or a doctor or a lawyer and end up in a plush carpeted office with a safe desk job and hefty salary worthy of my middle-class suburban heritage?

Why do I run all day on four hours of sleep trying to be a student, then play with papers and words and glue all night to put out a newspaper so that someday I can be a real live newspaperman?

Why? I don't know. I just like to write.

And that, my friends, is exactly 500 words.

AN INCREDIBLE JOURNEY

By Martha Cordes Towns

THERE'S NO QUESTION about the professional and personal importance of the School of Journalism's providing financial support that enables students to take advantage of off-campus seminars, conferences, and other worthwhile events that involve travel that they otherwise might not be able to afford.

That's what happened to me in 1959.

Long before the Association for Women in Communications, Theta Sigma Phi was the honorary society for women in journalism. As president of the Ohio University chapter, and with the support of funds from the school, I was given the opportunity to attend Theta Sig's 50th anniversary convention in Seattle, Washington. It was unbearably hot in Cleveland that August, and the cool air in Seattle was a blessing. I went west by train and flew home. I had never flown before, and the trip impacted me for the rest of my life.

The one remaining artifact from that weekend was a linotype slug with "1959" engraved on it. I carried it on my keychain for many years until the chain broke and the slug flew so far in the darkening garage of the Terminal Tower that I couldn't find it. Perhaps it was fitting, because it was from that same terminal that I took the first train on my trip to Seattle. Anyway, I would rather have lost a car key; at least that could have been replaced.

Seattle was chosen as the site for the meeting because it was the home of the last remaining founder of Theta Sigma Phi, which was started in 1909 by seven students at the University of Washington. At the 50th anniversary, we were treated royally: lunch at the Seattle Tennis Club, a tour of the Boeing plant, and a beach picnic on Lake Washington, where salmon was roasted on cedar planks. It was the best meal I have ever had.

But the impact of the travel was not lost. It served as a seed that resulted in a terrific career in journalism for me and, in 2004, for establishment of a modest fund within the university by my husband, Ed, and me. We wanted to provide funds for interested students who wanted to go somewhere and do wonderful things.

A lot of salmon have swum upstream in all these years. There have been many more plane trips (including two press trips to Germany) and way too many splendid meals (please don't ask me to describe them).

Journalism has truly been my life, and I mean the newspaper business. The beginning of that life occurred during the summer after my freshman year, when I worked at the *Chagrin Valley* (Ohio) *Herald.* I was paid $25 a week and thought I was rich. I married, had two daughters, and kept on working, always two and a half days a week. After many years at the *Herald,* I wrote for the *Chagrin Valley Times.* In 1985, I was given the opportunity to create and serve as the first editor of *Currents,* a monthly that made covering Cleveland's social life popular again. Every publication in town tried to copy us, but we were the first and the best and are still going strong more than 30 years later.

I believe we will always have newspapers; they are a part of the fabric of our world. There is something solid about them, and you certainly can't hold television news in your hands or clip something out to mail to a friend. And don't ever look askance at weeklies. They are the papers that really care about you and your community. I learned every facet of the newspaper business working for the *Chagrin Valley Herald.*

I bless Ohio University for starting me out on an incredible journey. Good journalism will always be critical to society, and you never can tell where it will take you.

Frank Deaner serves as master of ceremonies at L.J. Hortin's retirement dinner.
(Photo provided by Frank Deaner)

J-BANQUET BEGINNING

By Frank Deaner

"Have you heard?" . . . "Is it true?" . . . "Is he really leaving?!" The news was buzzing through the basement corridor of Copeland Hall, home of our School of Journalism, on that late April day in 1967.

Word was being passed from student to student with an occasional necessary confirmation coming from a faculty member. Indeed, it was true. J-School Director L.J. Hortin suddenly and almost shockingly had informed the faculty in its regular meeting that he would be leaving in a few short weeks.

L.J. Hortin admires his retirement gift from the faculty. *(Photo provided by Frank Deaner)*

The legendary Dr. Hortin, whom nearly everyone thought would retire at OU, announced that he was returning to his old Kentucky home after 20 years on the J-School faculty, including 16 as director, to become chairman of the journalism department at Murray State University.

Within a day or two, Russell Baird, adviser to our chapter of Sigma Delta Chi (forerunner of the Society of Professional Journalists) stopped me in that same corridor to explain that an event had to be planned to honor Hortin, and the logical means to schedule it on short notice was to use our annual SDX chapter dinner. As chapter president, I was given the assignment to convert what would have been a small informal gathering in Baker Center to a much larger event at the Athens Country Club.

The public relations internship I had completed and the '66 Mustang I had gotten that previous summer both served me well as I made many a trip out to the country club to confirm all details with the catering staff.

Besides Baird, others involved in the planning included our chapter officers Chuck Montague (BSJ '68), Tom Douglas (BSJ '68), and Herb Moss (BSJ '68).

With RSVPs pouring in each day, we ended up with about 200 people at the May 19 "Spring Banquet," as it was titled on the cover of the printed program. We crammed tables into virtually every available space and so stretched the limits of the country club that a few tables had paper plates rather than china!

A cooperative event

The banquet was designated as a joint event of SDX; Theta Sigma Phi, the women's journalism society (yes, we were still gender-specific back then); and the Southeastern Ohio Newspaper Association (SEONA), a subgroup of the Ohio Newspaper Association (ONA).

Serving as emcee, I was able to introduce all those who made presentations: Baird and faculty member A.T. Turnbull, who gave L.J. an electric typewriter on behalf of the faculty because Hortin said he planned to "do a lot of fishing and writing" in Kentucky; Sue Bailey (BSJ '67), president of Theta Sigma Phi, who presented a plaque to Mrs. Hortin; and E.D. Southwick, editor of *The Marietta Times,* who presented a plaque to L.J. on behalf of SEONA.

Those adding remarks were Thomas Smith, vice president of Ohio University; Harry Evarts, dean of the College of Business Administration; and Bill Oertel, executive director of ONA.

Besides presenting a portrait of Hortin, our SDX chapter that evening announced the creation of the L.J. Hortin Scholarship for an outstanding freshman entering the School of Journalism.

Evolution into a major student event

That first celebration has grown in recent years into an event that is dedicated to honoring students—the annual school awards banquet. L.J. Hortin, of course, remains a prominent name, along with Frank Deaner and Herb Moss, as the "Spring Banquet" continues today. Hortin is honored annually with the scholarship established at that first banquet and an Outstanding Alumni award given in his name. Both Deaner and Moss join more than 50 other alumni and former faculty who have given back to the Scripps School by establishing scholarships for undergraduate students.

Those scholarships, along with Scripps College of Communication and Scripps Howard Foundation scholarships, now total more than $200,000 annually. In addition to scholarship money, foreign correspondence and Don Perris Internship grants are awarded to support students' professional experience at national and international media. The banquet also features recognition of outstanding seniors and graduate students chosen by the faculty.

The joy of the evening is shared by up to 200 family members, friends, faculty, and donors, said Mary T. Rogus, who has chaired the event in recent years.

"The more than 200 to 500 tweets a year with the hashtag #ScrippsBanquet sum up that shared joy," she added. "It is the one night we showcase the excellence of Scripps Kids, past and present, to an audience of the people who love and support them, as well as help them reach that excellence."

—Mary T. Rogus contributed to this story.

SURVEYS GAIN WORLDWIDE RECOGNITION

By Guido H. Stempel III

A SIMPLE PHONE INQUIRY from Washington resulted in 43 national surveys conducted by the School of Journalism and the Scripps Howard News Service between 1992 and 2012.

The call came in late October 1992 from Dan Thomasson, director of the service and one of the school's best friends over the years. But this call was purely professional. He wanted to do a survey starting in just a few weeks on election evening. Voter turnout in presidential elections had been steadily declining, and it looked as if the 1992 election would be the one in which less than half of eligible voters would participate. Thomasson and his colleagues wanted to anticipate this possibility.

That's why the request was made of me and the Scripps School of Journalism.

I agreed, and on the weekend before the election, Thomas Hargrove, a Scripps Howard reporter who had done a number of surveys, arrived in Athens. By 7 p.m. on election day, we had a questionnaire ready, a sample drawn, and student interviewers lined up. Two days later, by 10 p.m. on Thursday, 600 interviews had been completed. By noon Friday we had a story on the Scripps Howard wire explaining that because of presidential candidate Ross Perot, voter turnout was not less than 50 percent. Instead, it was 56 percent.

Shortly after the first of the year, Hargrove called me again to suggest we do another survey. Soon we were on our way to what turned out to be a whole series of surveys on national issues. We found that unmarried men were more interested in getting married than unmarried women. Next, a survey found that half of Americans believed it was somewhat likely or very likely that flying saucers were real.

Each survey had several topics, and from these results came four or five stories that were distributed to the 400 Scripps Howard News Service subscribers. From clippings and later web searches, the bureau would verify that these stories appeared in newspapers whose circulation totaled 8 to 10 million. These stories displayed the name of Ohio University and its School of Journalism coast to coast and around the world.

The process continued. A 2003 survey found that people under 35 were three times as likely as their parents to have tattoos. A year or so later, the U.S. Army announced a loosening of its standards on tattoos for recruits. The official statement from the army carried only one explanation for the change in policy—the Ohio University–Scripps Howard News Service survey.

A 2006 survey asked respondents if they thought the government had either overlooked or inadvertently aided the 9/11 terrorists. Thirty-six percent said it was either very likely or somewhat likely. That finding went around the world to Great Britain, France, Russia, Japan, and others. More than a year later, *The New York Times* went to the State Department and asked for comment. A front-page *Times* story carried the denial, but to explain why it was asking, the *Times,* in the second paragraph, mentioned the survey from Ohio University.

The surveys ended in 2012 when funding was no longer available. However, my partnership with Hargrove continued. We are coeditors and coauthors of *The 21st Century Voter: An Encyclopedia of Who Votes, How They Vote and Why They Vote,* published by ABC-CLIO in 2015.

GAMES, SURE, BUT CAREERS FOR MANY

By Paul Hagen

It was the late 1970s. Nobody is exactly sure when. Professors Guido Stempel and Ralph Izard decided to offer a course in sports writing. It lasted one quarter. That much everybody agrees on.

"I don't know how we even got it in the catalogue," Stempel recalled with a laugh. "We were both doing a lot of other things. Then it kind of faded. I don't know why. It was something people didn't want to keep teaching. Or, for whatever reason, couldn't. And that's the history of it."

Well, there is another angle to that story. One of the students in the class was Peter King (BSJ '79), who went on to become one of the most respected football writers in the country. He now runs the website *The MMQB*, a takeoff on his long-running *Monday Morning Quarterback* column for *Sports Illustrated.* He still writes occasionally for *SI* and also works for NBC Sports.

Fortunately, taking that class didn't turn out to be a prerequisite for future success. Many who graduated from the Scripps School before or after that long-ago course offering have gone on to have notable careers chronicling the games people play. A sampling follows:

There are columnists. Jay Mariotti (BSJ '81), for example, was a must-read at the *Chicago Sun-Times* for seven years, had a national profile at ESPN, and then became sports director and columnist for the *San Francisco Examiner.*

Paul Hagen. *(E.W. Scripps School of Journalism photo)*

Bob Hunter (BSJ '73) has been a general sports columnist for *The Columbus Dispatch* for more than two decades and has written eight books, seven about sports. Jon Greenberg (BSJ '01) is at *ESPNChicago.com.*

There are those who wrote about college sports. The late Bob Moran (BSJ '74) covered University of Arizona sports for the *Arizona Daily Star* in Tucson and Arizona State for the *East Valley Tribune* in Tempe.

There are pioneers. Susan Reimer (BSJ '73) retired as a news columnist at *The Baltimore Sun* but spent 14 of her 36 years at the paper covering sports. Katie Carrera (BSJ '08) covered the NHL Washington Capitals for four seasons.

There are wire service reporters. George Strode (BSJ '58) was Ohio sports editor for The Associated Press before becoming sports editor of *The*

Allie LaForce interviews former LSU Football Coach Les Miles. LaForce does basketball and football coverage for CBS and TNT. *(E.W. Scripps School of Journalism photo provided by Allie LaForce)*

Columbus Dispatch. Joe Kay (BSJ '77) is in charge of all Cincinnati area sports coverage for the AP.

There are football writers. Tony Grossi (BSJ '79) covered the Browns for years at *The* (Cleveland) *Plain Dealer* and now has the same beat with Good Karma Brands, a website that partners with ESPN Cleveland. Steve Serby (BSJ '71) was Jets beat writer for the *New York Post* and is now a sports columnist who focuses largely on football. Greenberg used to cover the Bears.

There are baseball writers. Anthony Castrovince (BSJ '03) is a columnist for *MLB.com*. Jeff Fletcher (BSJ '92) is the Angels beat writer for the *Orange County Register*. Jeff Lenihan (BSJ '83) covered the Twins for the *Star-Tribune* in Minneapolis. Joe Capozzi (BSJ '87) covered the Marlins for the *Palm Beach Post*. And I, a 1973 graduate, am a reporter and columnist at *MLB.com* after 25 years of covering the Phillies and national baseball for the *Philadelphia Daily News.*

There are broadcasters. Tony Castricone (BSJ '05) is an executive with IMG Sports and current voice of basketball at Clemson University. Allie LaForce (BSJ '11) is a college reporter and Southeastern Conference reporter for CBS and does National Basketball Association coverage on TNT. She serves as cohost of CBS Sports Network's all-female *We Need to Talk.*

Memories of the School of Journalism

Naturally, each alum has a unique memory of how the Ohio University experience affected him or her.

King mentioned a class taught by Dru Riley Evarts: "This was a news-writing class. You've got 10 assignments. Each one is equally weighted. And every one of them, on any paper, if you spell something wrong or have a grammatical error, it's a zero. It's not an F. It's a zero. I remember that as a very valuable lesson. Because you're working fast. You try to work efficiently. But this forces you to work efficiently and work smart."

For Capozzi, it was a writing class with Sandra Haggerty: "This might be obvious to all of us now. But back then I was 19, 20 years old, and she said something in class. 'Always follow the money.' And it was so basic but it stuck in my head and it resonated, and it's so true. Follow the money, that's universal in journalism, I think."

Justice Hill is a faculty member who has a broad background in sports writing and editing, including 7 1/2 years as a senior writer at *MLB.com.* He noted that the scale of the school helps create relationships: "Ohio, in my opinion, is a right-sized school. Ohio U is not a tiny school by any stretch. And it's not huge. So there's an intimacy here you can have that you can't have at some of the bigger schools."

In that atmosphere, networking can lead to opportunities. Fletcher knew early on that he wanted to be a baseball writer. So he arranged to go to

Nicole Bersani (BSJ '12) shows off the trophy received when the Chicago Cubs baseball team won the 2016 World Series. Bersani is the Cubs' digital media coordinator. During her time at OU, Bersani was the CEO of the student-run public relations firm, ImPRessions, and an executive member of the Public Relations Student Society of America (PRSSA). *(E.W. Scripps School of Journalism photo; photo provided by Stephen Green Photography)*

Cleveland when the Twins were in town to hang out with Lenihan. "There are so many OU alums out there that you have the opportunity to connect with. And I've tried to do the same thing. I always try to pay it forward, so to speak," he said.

The importance of *The Post*

While each individual has a unique perspective, in more than a dozen interviews with Scripps grads, two broad themes emerged. Nearly every person who went on to have success worked at *The Post,* many becoming editors. And about half started out interested in writing about something other than sports.

King is an example of both. "I never thought I was going to be a sportswriter," he said. "The whole time I was there I covered Student Senate. I covered all sorts of local news. I covered the statehouse in Columbus a little bit. And my internships were basically news internships. I just always thought I'd end up covering city council or politics or something like that."

He went on to become managing editor of *The Post* in 1978–79. "The weight is all on your shoulders," he said. "Four, five, six, seven people. And it's all your jobs to make sure this paper lands on the doorstep of all the residence halls, all the classroom buildings on campus. And that was really a weighty responsibility, and it was an important responsibility to learn at an early age. It proved to be invaluable for me."

That theme was repeated over and over.

"Just being able to learn on the fly. A paper where you can learn from your mistakes. And we made plenty of them," said Kay, who was managing editor his senior year. "But just doing it every day taught me so much. And the faculty was so supportive of that. They were very much in favor of an independent paper."

Mariotti noted the competitive atmosphere. "I just remember the talent there. Exceptional talent where you really had to hone your skills and work real hard to keep up," he said.

Castrovince summed it up. "It's really cool because it's a very small town, obviously. It's not a small school, but it's not like an Ohio State. You really get to know the other people in your class and school. And from a sportswriter's perspective, you're also surrounded by a Division I program, which is a legit thing. So going on the road with the football team, with the basketball team, with the baseball team. Those experiences were really great preparation for what I'm doing now."

TODAY'S TECHNOLOGY TODAY

By Dwight M. Woodward

In their new home in the Schoonover Center for Communication and the adjoining Radio-TV building, Scripps School of Journalism students have access to 80 computers in four computer labs, the digital broadcast facilities at WOUB Center for Public Media, and an equipment room that provides cameras, lights, audio recorders, and other technologies needed by students to produce multiplatform media.

In Scripps Hall, journalism students in senior capstone courses work in a multimedia loft that supports creative efforts, as well as a social media "smart lab."

And, of course, all have cell phones.

Compare this to the "good old days" when typewriters and pencils were the essential tools of the journalist's craft and trade, before the emergence of computer technology that replaced the ancient California job case for print students and very little else for those in broadcasting.

But leaders at the School of Journalism in Lasher Hall at the time made moves to keep pace with developments in the mass communication industry. The school's response began in 1976 when faculty member Roger Bennett returned from his PhD studies at the University of Texas, presented a discus-

Representing years of technology leadership in the School of Journalism: seated, Tom Hodges and Dick Bean; standing, from the left, Tom Peters, Mary Rogus, Ron Pittman, and Doug Nohl. *(E.W. Scripps School of Journalism photo)*

sion of computer punch cards, and demonstrated an early suitcase computer during the annual Bush Faculty Seminar at the Burr Oak State Park lodge.

"I gave a lecture on computing at Burr Oak and couldn't find a plug for my suitcase computer in the seminar room," Bennett said. "We had to go out into the hall. We talked about bits and bytes and interfaces, terms most professors were not familiar with."

Some faculty members were not happy with the use of the term "dot" for what they saw clearly was a "period" in Internet addresses.

"Don't blame me," Bennett said at the time. "That's what they call them."

FULL-COURT PRESS

SHORTLY AFTER THE School of Journalism moved into Lasher Hall in 1974, the Gannett Company offered the school an offset press.

It seems that Gannett had ordered an offset press for its newspaper on Guam. Trouble was, the order got placed twice and perhaps even paid for twice. Gannett did not need or want two presses on Guam, so its officials offered us one.

On the one hand, it seemed reasonable. Lasher Hall was built originally as the home of *The Athens Messenger*. So the building had once contained a press pit. But the renovation of the building for academic occupancy had resulted in removal of the pit.

Besides, we did not need a press anyway. We had to turn down the offer.

—Guido H. Stempel III

Staffing the computer labs

In 1978, former Scripps Director Guido H. Stempel III led a committee that included Professors Russell N. Baird and A.T. Turnbull. The committee recommended that Richard "Dick" Bean, a supervisor in *The Athens Messenger*'s composing room, be hired to set up the first computer lab in the basement of Lasher Hall.

Bean used private funds donated to the journalism school to purchase eight computers from Newspaper Electronics Corp., headquartered in Kansas City.

"I went out to Kansas City between Christmas and New Year's and came back to Athens and set them up on a Sunday for a class I had on Monday," Bean said. "We had to board up the windows in the basement of Lasher Hall because it was hard to see the little green screens in the daylight."

Bean supervised students taking journalism courses in the lab, where they wrote stories and sent them to a single printer to obtain a hard copy.

Reinforcements arrived in 1981 with the school's hiring of Tom Hodges, who had worked for years as a newspaper photographer, held jobs in public relations, and taught graphics and photojournalism at Eastern Illinois University.

Hodges taught graphics in Lasher Hall and was the journalism school's de facto "IT guy" before such a designation or job description existed. He also worked with Associate Director Tom Peters, who provided a watchful eye and funding for the school's computer needs.

"We had eight remote terminals on a CP/M chassis," said Hodges. "Dick and I flew out to Kansas City and brought back eight computers and expanded the lab to 16 units."

The need for more portable computers

With the advent of the IBM personal computer in 1981, Hodges began looking for portable computers for faculty members. Hodges and Peters agreed to purchase an Osborne I computer, the first mass-produced microprocessor-based portable computer.

By 1982, portable or luggable computers the size of a sewing machine were being manufactured, and a group of faculty and students in the College of Communication purchased Kaypro II computers with their own funds.

"Hodges has an engineering mind, and it didn't take him long to reason things out," Bean said. "He seemed to be able to put together two kinds of equipment and make them work."

Peters provided Hodges with funds to purchase the first personal computers for faculty members. Hodges researched the market and found that off-brand Zorba computers offered a much cheaper alternative to the IBM PC.

"The IBM PC was selling for around $3,700 and the Zorbas were $1,700 originally," said Hodges, who arranged for the purchase of more than a dozen Zorbas. "We got them for $900."

Hodges was in charge of maintaining the Zorbas for faculty members. That IT duty sometimes involved tinkering with the Zorbas.

"At one point, Peters did an inventory and discovered Hodges had cannibalized two of the computers for parts," Stempel said.

EARLY TECHNOLOGY

Q: How could a person crossing the Campus Green of Ohio University in mid-20th-century days identify a journalism major at first glance?

A: Because he or she would be carrying a portable typewriter, of course.

It's true. In those early years, for any course requiring in-class writing, journalism students had to bring their own portable typewriters to class to turn out stories at high speed after hearing the facts from the professor. The school did not yet have desk typewriters on tables in writing labs, and faculty members could not be expected to grade handwritten copy rendered in the haste required to get the news out quickly and accurately.

These typewriters were required in every class meeting of Reporting, very often in Contemporary Issues, and possibly for other journalism courses.

Anyone who had another class immediately before or after his or her typewriter-requiring journalism class had to carry the cussed thing to those classes also. Portable typewriters were heavy. No one wanted to carry one around more than absolutely necessary.

When the school became able to provide desk typewriters (and still later, computers), the requirement to bring one's own portable typewriter died. No one mourned its absence.

—Dru Riley Evarts

The Russell N. Baird Graphics Laboratory

"Apple came along in the late 1980s and 1990s and essentially took over the desktop publishing business," said Scripps Director Robert Stewart. "Within our program, there was some back and forth about how fast to adopt the Apple platform."

That decision was made, and the school purchased 20 Mac IIsi computers in September 1990 from local retailer Vere Smith on Union Street. The first Mac computers—paid for through the equipment endowment account, part of the school's Scripps Howard endowment—were installed in Scripps Hall 006. The computers were connected with a network and a server and featured Aldus PageMaker, Adobe Photoshop, and Adobe FreeHand as software.

Russell N. Baird.
(E.W. Scripps School of Journalism photo)

And that's when Associate Professor Ron Pittman assumed a position of leadership. Pittman had been on the school's faculty teaching graphics since 1988, and his background with Apple computers was just what was needed.

"Ron Pittman was a major contributor on the Mac side," Peters said. "He specified the hardware, the software, set it up, loaded it, and maintained it for years. For no money, as usual. Dick Bean made major contributions to the effort when Macs were adopted for his graphics lab. He did much of the installation and provided support for many years."

Eventually, the facility included four rooms in the Scripps Hall basement and was known as the Russell N. Baird Graphics Laboratory, in honor of a long-time faculty member who, with faculty colleague A.T. Turnbull, wrote a book that, at the time, was the nation's premier text on graphics. The lab was used for graphics, advertising, and various newswriting classes and became the home for *Southeast Ohio* magazine.

Hodges, Bean, Pittman, and others continued to provide instruction to students and technical support to the labs. Bean retooled his skills and, after decades working first with hot type and then teletype at *The Athens Messenger,* began teaching students software programs such as Pagemaker and Word.

"The technology is hard to keep up with," he said. "I'd just go upstairs and talk to Tom [Peters], and he always seemed to find the money we needed."

Based on that beginning, the school in 2015 continued its focus on Macintosh computers, incorporating them into three of its four labs.

The use of PCs in the fourth facility occurred because the school needed to be compatible with WOUB, Stewart said. In 2016, WOUB decided to adopt Adobe Premiere as its nonlinear editing platform, and the school opted to follow suit. At the same time, the school reverted to PCs in that lab because of other newscast software (e.g., AP's ENPS program) used by WOUB.

The move to digital broadcasting

With the development of digital cameras and Internet delivery of video news to users in their homes, similar growth was apparent in the school's broadcast facilities.

"When I was hired in 1987, *ACTV-7 News* had been around a couple years under the direction of faculty member Don Shoultz," said Stewart. "Reporters for the show shared one video camera and one ½-inch editing deck. WOUB News was not part of the journalism curriculum, but many of our broadcast journalism students worked there."

ACTV-7 aired on cable and, with the addition of editing bays and cameras, expanded its broadcast from 15 minutes to a half hour, Stewart said.

"In fact, we were quite late in making the transition to digital editing because we had determined that it was good for our students to know both digital editing, which they were getting at WOUB, and tape-to-tape editing, given that not every entry-level TV market had made the transition. Once the equipment couldn't be repaired, the decision in effect was made for us."

Doug Nohl now oversees the broadcast lab with its 20 PCs that offer video editing for Scripps School students who want a concentration in broadcast journalism. He also oversees the distribution of broadcast equipment available on loan to Scripps students with an OU ID.

"There are 24 shoulder-mount camera kits and tripods available for students wanting to learn how to operate a broadcast camera," Nohl said. "Each kit contains a wireless microphone ensemble, allowing for hand-held or lavaliere microphone use. Each kit contains an LED video light and can be checked out for one day at a time."

The move to Schoonover and the entirely digital format has provided current broadcast "guru" Mary Rogus with state-of-the-art equipment on par with the best technology used at national broadcast outlets. Rogus has developed a series of classes that prepare broadcast students for the variety of jobs available in the ever-changing world of broadcast journalism. She has witnessed the broadcast lab move from a space the size of a storage unit in the basement of Scripps Hall to RTV, where the lab is one of the leading state-of-the-art broadcast labs available to students on college campuses nationwide.

"We put the students together into a cluster of courses designed to provide them with real newsroom experience by producing a daily half-hour

NOT ENOUGH A'S

Students often complain about not getting enough A's.

Here—culled from my recollections as editor of *The Post*—is a different version of that complaint.

I hired a Malaysian student as *The Post*'s wire editor because in interviews, he was most excited about world and national news. So he figured to be a good choice. In my conversations with him, he once pointed out a problem he had in the old hot-type graphics class of the School of Journalism.

The in-class assignment from faculty member Larry Study was to fetch type from the California job case to spell out your first and last name. But my new wire editor was stymied. There simply were not enough A's in his tray to spell out his name—Sankaran Ramanathan (MS '74). It's been something like 40 years, but I've never forgotten that story.

–P.J. Bednarski

broadcast," Rogus said. "We concentrate on local news. Students go to the Athens City Council meetings, and they cover high school sports and events on campus."

The sequence of courses taught by Rogus and others in the broadcast lab results in daily news shows produced entirely by students. The students are responsible for producing a live, half-hour TV news show broadcast weekdays at noon on a Time Warner channel to all Athens County residents.

Students taking the sequence of courses learn how to report and anchor on the air, as well as to direct, edit, provide graphics, and produce an entire package using technology on par with that of large network broadcasters, providing them with marketable skills and hands-on experience to begin working in the broadcast industry.

"NATIVE SPEAKERS" DIRECT SOCIAL MEDIA STRATEGY

By Billy Hartman

When the E.W. Scripps School of Journalism set out to adopt a social media strategy in 2010, it did what any organization should do: listen to social media natives. Fortunately, the school's award-winning student-run public relations firm, ImPRessions, had all the highly motivated social media natives needed to develop that strategy.

When he became director of the school that year, Robert Stewart asked ImPRessions to create a student-run "social media swat team" to help develop a coherent social media strategy for the school.

Prior to the formation of the team, Stewart, as associate director, had run the school's Twitter and Facebook accounts out of his office. Once becoming director, he quickly realized that he needed help, which is when he turned to ImPRessions.

"The fact that it's a student group is beside the point," he said. "A social media swat team gave us a group of people who could help us think strategically about the communication needs of the school."

About the same time that the swat team took shape, the school's faculty was working to retool the curriculum for the transition from quarters to semesters—the perfect opportunity to develop coursework that reflected the importance of social media.

"When we developed our new curriculum for semesters [which went into effect in 2012], we knew we wanted to include courses on social media, the most obvious being a course called Strategic Social Media," Stewart said. "We also wanted to provide several courses that could be part of the Scripps College of Communication's new Social Media Certificate."

Learning by doing

"The fact that our students actually are learning about social media in and out of the classroom, and then applying those lessons on behalf of the school at a very high level, means they are providing a high-quality service to their own program," he added.

Trusting students with protecting the school's brand required courage, but Stewart said he has "never once had a faculty member come in and say 'What the heck is going on with our social media?'" Aside from catching the occasional typo, Stewart has nothing but praise for his swat team.

Social media have changed the way communication inside the school and to alumni is done, and Stewart believes that as a result, the school is more in touch with people who have graduated in the past five to 10 years.

Twitter, in particular, has been used effectively to get the word out quickly about events or school news. He relies on and trusts his students on the swat team to evaluate and relay messages he posts from his own Twitter handle.

Depending on the message the school is trying to get across, Twitter can be even more effective than directly emailing students, he said. It's easy for students to ignore email. "You have to have a great subject line to get students to read [email]. With Twitter and Facebook, students see the messages on media they already are using."

In the school's formal instruction, social media have become integral parts of the way students learn as well as interact with their professors.

"Faculty members incorporate social media as teaching tools on an individual basis," Stewart said. "In J1010 (and J101 before that, under quarters), I've used Twitter to send out *New York Times* articles about media topics, which students have to read for a weekly quiz. Mary Rogus uses Twitter for in-class discussion."

Lecturer Dan Farkas (BSJ '98, MBA '14) creates a hashtag for each of his classes. With the hashtag, he tweets approximately three or four times a week. Whatever Farkas puts on Twitter with the hashtag correlating to the specific class is fair game. Such use of social media keeps students up-to-date on current trends in the ever-evolving digital world.

Engagement and communication

Twitter and Facebook also have changed the way students engage during journalism school events, such as a Scripps Senior Saturday, a Schuneman Symposium, or even the annual awards banquet, when hundreds of congratulatory tweets are generated. "Using a hashtag is an efficient way to get engagement," Stewart said. This allows not only current students but also alumni to interact during events happening in Athens.

Students tweet at their professor to ask questions about class, inquire about a meeting, or even spark a discussion.

"It's cool to go on Twitter and see what your professors are saying on there," senior Chris Saulnier (BSJ '15) said. "You can read the 'about me' section in their syllabus, but you can learn so much more about your professor by looking at the Twitter page, or Instagram. It closes the gap between teacher and student. You get to know them on a personal level."

But the bottom line for the school is to make sure that its students are thinking carefully about how to use social media as communication professionals, according to Stewart. After all, Facebook, Twitter, Instagram, Snapchat, and the many other social media platforms are no longer just applications on a smart phone but have become means of communicating, getting messages out, and developing a brand.

"Professor Farkas says if you want to know how customers think of your brand . . . ask them. Social media provide a great opportunity for that to happen," Saulnier said.

In the future, Stewart's strategy is to work with his social media swat team to "keep tweaking the tweets, [and] be smart and professional about it." He's relied on the swat team to make recommendations about how and when to best use newer social media platforms as they've come along, including Instagram, Yik Yak, and Flickr.

A mirror of the society we serve

The E.W. Scripps School of Journalism's mission statement makes reference to helping students work in "a multicultural and fast changing world." Such a statement highlights the importance in all forms of mass communication and in education of ensuring inclusion of the total society. Students and, indeed, all citizens have a right to expect a celebration of difference involving attention, for example, to race, sex, sexual preference, religion, cultural background, and abilities. Effective education and effective mass communication require such dedication.

Facing page: RTVC Building, home of the school, 1969–74. *(Photo courtesy of the Peter Goss Photograph Collection, Mahn Center for Archives and Special Collections)*

A TIME OF TRANSITION

By Clarence Page

LOOKING BACK, I feel very fortunate to have gone to journalism school when I did. The half decade of 1965 to 1969 was a period of seismic change for journalism, for our generation, and for the world.

A video about the Class of '69 unspooling in fast-forward would show us morphing fashionably from preppie to hippie, perhaps ending with hints of yuppie, a look that would not take hold for another decade or two.

Clarence Page. *(© Ken Steinhoff, all rights reserved, reproduced with permission)*

Unlike most of my freshman classmates, who still seemed to be making up their minds, I arrived in Athens with my love for journalism fully loaded. I chose Ohio University because of its reputation for excellent journalism education and for the valuable experience offered by its independently published five-day-a-week student newspaper, *The Post.*

From those platforms, my fellow J-majors and I received one of the most valuable gifts that our profession offers: a front-row seat on changing times.

When I think about what it was like to be a black student in those days, I think about how it was a time of transition from an old racial order to a new one. "Roommate preference" forms disappeared after my freshman year. Then almost reappeared by my senior year as a new black militancy demanded separate dorms and other facilities.

I think about humorous moments like the look on the face of my white freshman roommate when I removed my sunglasses and he discovered to his visible astonishment that *black people tan.*

I also recall such not-humorous moments as the night when some white friends and I had to fight our way out of a roadside coffee shop near Nelsonville. Some of the local blue-collar men made it quite clear that they didn't like black people. They didn't like white people who liked black people, either. I have not stopped at a strange roadside coffee shop since.

Keys to a better future

Episodes like this were constant reminders that we black students were in a place that was not necessarily intended for us. But we would make the best of it. This university offered us the keys to a better future. We were "Keepers of the Dream" about which the Rev. Martin Luther King Jr. preached.

Yet for the few of us who pursued journalism, race was the elephant in the room that seldom received much discussion. That was a tragic oversight at a time when President Lyndon B. Johnson's historic 1967 Kerner Commission report on civil disorders singled out news media as having "failed to analyze and report adequately on racial problems in the United States and, as a related matter, to meet the Negro's legitimate expectations in journalism."

"By and large," the commission said, "news organizations have failed to communicate to both their black and white audiences a sense of the problems America faces and the sources of potential solutions." Yet the only discussions of this topic that I recall in the J-School were when I brought it up —and even then the discussion didn't last long.

I felt a very different sense at *The Post.* Although I was the only black staffer of my generation who stayed at the paper for more than a few months (a diversity challenge that, by the way, still persists at campus newspapers across America), I think all of us who had writing and editing positions were acutely aware of the racial and political issues that were part of our college communities and of the larger society in which we were about to make our careers.

The Post and the rest of journalism attracted me because I wanted to be judged not by the color of my skin but by the content of my copy. "Just prepare yourself," my family elders had encouraged me, "so that when the doors of opportunity open up, you will be ready to step inside." Fortuitously my faith in media opportunities was rewarded by the time I was looking for internships and jobs after my junior year. By then editors were looking for reporters and photographers who could be sent to "the ghetto" without looking too conspicuous.

Fortunately, I was ready. I knew from J-School how to find stories, gather information, and write the narratives. Most important, I knew how to think like a journalist.

I would be prepared well by our journalism school, directed in my freshman year by the long-tenured and grandfatherly L.J. Hortin, whom I fondly remember mostly for his "Hortinisms." That was the title given by my *Post* colleagues to his hilariously folksy observations, which we posted as the "Hortinism of the Day" in the daily's front-page masthead. My favorite: "Getting out of a Volkswagen Beetle is like being born again."

Looking back, it is ironic to see how humbly the School of Journalism was tucked away in the basement of the College of Business Administration in Copeland Hall. Hortin retired in my junior year after preparing the way for Bobcat journalism to hit the big time in a new College of Communication in 1968. Its first dean, John R. Wilhelm, a distinguished former war correspondent and director of McGraw-Hill World News, oversaw a grand expansion of print and broadcast journalism education that coincided with new changes in the industry.

Top professionals came to campus

Instead of having to look elsewhere for top-notch news professionals, we experienced such notables as CBS News' Walter Cronkite, *The New York Times*' Turner Catledge, and AP's Wes Gallagher—as well as pioneers in media theory like Marshall McLuhan—who were coming to visit us.

The times were a'changing, and we were part of it. Journalism itself was changing, along with its social impact, even as we were learning it. New technology brought televised presidential debates, Vietnam combat news footage, live coverage of demonstrators outside the 1968 political conventions, and ad campaigns that sold candidates as elegantly as they sold Cadillacs.

And traditional news skills were changing with the times, too. Reporters with strong literary voices like Tom Wolfe, Gay Talese, Joan Dideon, and Jimmy Breslin—plus essayists with a strong news sense like Norman Mailer and James Baldwin—excited those of us who still believed in the power of the printed word.

It is comical now to think back on how much some teachers and faculty resisted change. We had a program director at WOUB Radio—where I volunteered as a freshman to learn how to write news for broadcast—who went through the station's record library, censoring tracks of music with nail polish if they had a beat. He wasn't just anti–rock-'n'-roll and anti-R&B. He even banned upbeat Broadway show tunes.

I remember a magazine-journalism instructor who offered an automatic A to any of us who sold an article during the semester. He tried to renege when I sold a short political piece to *Evergreen Review,* the famously artsy and controversial New York–based political and literary magazine, which my teacher didn't like. Yet it was the sort of groundbreaking publication for which I wanted to write, a magazine that was shaking up the national conversation on race, war, poverty, and other issues. As a matter of principle, I appealed his decision to a sympathetic superior, and eventually I received my A—a small victory, in my view, for the New Journalism.

Our era would be followed by the era of Watergate and other scandals that would bring a new stardom to investigative reporters. More surprises would unfold. That's why we call it "news." But I will always look back on our era as a great watershed. It was a time that put some old issues to rest while raising new ones, many of which Americans are still trying to resolve, even as they make more news for new generations of journalists to report.

IT'S ABILITY THAT COUNTS

By Laralyn Sasaki Dearing

Laralyn Sasaki Dearing. *(Photo provided by Laralyn Sasaki Dearing)*

During my freshman year, faculty member Ralph Izard suggested that I apply for the clerkship at *The Cincinnati Enquirer.* The program was offering *minority* internships, and I was hesitant to be labeled or singled out because of my Asian heritage. After all, I wanted to "earn" an internship "on my own merit."

Riz looked me in the eye and gave me advice I have used for 30 years: "Being a minority only means you can apply. You will get the job based on your ability."

Something worked, and I managed to have five major internships during my OU career: *Cincinnati Enquirer* clerk, *Cincinnati Enquirer* reporter, *Wall Street Journal* (Cleveland Bureau) reporter, *Los Angeles Times* (Washington Bureau) reporter, and UPI Paris reporter.

Even if that's not a record, they were wonderful experiences that taught me a lot about being a journalist.

THE POWER OF ASKING QUESTIONS

By Beverly Jones

From the moment of my arrival as a freshman in 1964, Ohio University felt like home to me. But while I loved being in Athens, I was impatient with my first-semester coursework. I had come to OU to become a reporter and was eager to start taking journalism courses.

After a few weeks on campus, I wanted to at least see the journalism school. So late one afternoon I walked down the steps to the basement of Copeland Hall, home of the Business College, where the J-School was then housed. I found my way into an empty classroom decorated with an old Linotype drawer filled with a jumble of tiny metal letters of various fonts. As I stared at the relic, I felt excited to be so close to the world of newspapers.

I was startled by the arrival of a small, energetic, white-haired man who asked, "How can I help you?" I said I wanted to be a journalist. After introducing himself as L.J. Hortin, school director, he started with the five W's: Who was I? What did I want to do with my life? When had I enrolled at Ohio University? Where was I from? Why was I in the journalism school? After a few minutes of being intensely quizzed about my hopes and dreams, I felt like I'd had my first lesson as a professional. The J-School director had taken me apart, seemed to suggest I'd passed his tests, and taught me an important lesson: Questions can be powerful.

At the time, women students at Ohio University endured suffocating restrictions. Among the most annoying were the "women's hours" curfews that required us to be back in the dorms by 10 or 10:30 on weeknights. Dress regulations also were strictly enforced, and it seemed particularly silly that we had to wear hose and high heels for Sunday dinner in the dorms. While smoking was commonplace, it was a punishable violation for a "lady" to be seen puffing on a cigarette while standing.

A time of change

But attitudes were starting to change. The civil rights movement in the early 1960s foreshadowed widespread social upheaval in opposition to deepening U.S. military involvement in Vietnam. And women at Ohio University, like those at schools around the country, were chafing at the *in loco parentis* regulations that made them second-class citizens.

Through the mid-1960s, some women held prominent editorial positions in campus media outlets like *The Post.* They were accomplished young journalists who were every bit as talented and devoted as their male counterparts. They had little trouble finding work at newspapers when they graduated; journalists were in high demand then. But then more than a few were pigeonholed in the "Women's Section."

Nationally, groundbreaking women journalists were just starting to be recognized. Famous broadcast journalist Barbara Walters was hired by NBC's *Today* show in 1961 as a researcher and writer, and several years later she became the "Today Girl," handling mostly fluff assignments. But male hosts took the lead in all joint interviews, and not until 1974 was she recognized as coanchor of the morning program (and then only after the male host died). Legendary wire service reporter Helen Thomas broke ground for UPI in 1960 when she followed the presidential campaign of John F. Kennedy and was rewarded with an assignment to the White House.

At Ohio University, a steady stream of the nation's best-known print and broadcast journalists visited campus during the 1960s and '70s. But only a few women—like *The Washington Post* publisher Katharine Graham and *Newsweek* columnist Shana Alexander—were among them.

Still, in that era, women were welcomed at Ohio University's journalism school. From the start, one thing I liked about the J-School was that women and men were treated in much the same way. During high school I'd been one of the few girls in an intensive four-year math/science program. There we were reminded that colleges and employers weren't interested in female scientists and engineers. But from the time I met Dr. Hortin, I regarded the J-School as a place where women were taken seriously.

Beverly Jones. *(Photo provided by Beverly Jones)*

That view was not universal at Ohio University. I was shocked in my senior year, when I took a fresh look at the treatment of women around the university. It all started as I was writing an honors thesis in literature, and my topic title was "Woman as Existential Being." My idea was that the female characters in early novels were more self-aware than the males because being social outsiders gave them perspective.

I didn't complete my thesis, however, because my English Department adviser rejected the topic. He argued that the Existentialist writers said women "cannot be fully actualized beings" but instead must be defined by their relationship to male lives. He said they believed women aren't capable of an existential experience. And he seemed to share the view that women simply should serve and support men, since they don't themselves have what it takes to become fully developed adults, either in novels or in life.

A standoff ensued. I declined to back away from writing that female characters were the first in fiction to be capable of self-awareness. My adviser said he would give me a failing grade. I said "OK" because I didn't need the credits to graduate. But under the university's grading system for honors projects, a student could be given the grade of "Incomplete" but not an F. So I had "Incomplete" on my record and was declared ineligible for graduation.

While the stalemate lingered, I started noticing more about the limitations and assumptions that shaped not only a woman student's campus life but also her career opportunities after graduation. As we approached May 1968, which should have been my graduation date, I put an ad in *The Post,* proposing a discussion group for women who wanted to challenge the status quo. Two showed up that first night. We established ourselves as the Women's Information Group and began asking questions and giving speeches in classes or any gathering that would have us.

In the following year, while I was still on campus doing clerical work in Cutler Hall, I was visited by Harry Evarts, the innovative young dean of the College of Business. He had noticed my efforts to raise awareness of gender inequality. And he invited me to become the first woman to enter Ohio University's MBA program. I accepted and agreed to be his graduate assistant. As my first day of school approached, my undergraduate college degree finally arrived in the mail.

A shift to WOUB

Still fascinated by journalism, I shifted my studies to part time and took a job writing for WOUB. It gave me the platform to ask questions even more loudly, including through a radio program interviewing "women of achievement." My goal was simply to draw attention to some of the many women in the community who were engaged in creative and important activities. By then, in the early 1970s, the percentage of women enrolled in the J-School was increasing. Many of those who graduated got hired as "hard news" print and broadcast reporters and were at the forefront of the push to elevate the status of women in journalism. I had access to a microphone, so I remained prominent.

After I had spent about a year at WOUB, President Claude Sowle summoned me to his office. He invited me to write a detailed report substantiating my claims that Ohio University was systematically discriminating against women. Sowle gave me an office adjoining his, as well as the title of "assistant to the president for women's affairs." Most important, he spread the word that the questions I would be asking should be treated seriously.

I was gripped by self-doubt. I wasn't confident of my mandate and wasn't sure how to go about such an ambitious project. But as a journalism grad, I knew how to do research and ask questions. I began interviewing women, methodically working through every unit and level at Ohio University. I spoke with about 90 students, faculty members, and administrators, from housekeepers to the dean of women.

Drawing on my J-School training, I considered myself a reporter, not a leader. As my journalism instructors had taught me, credibility came from simply laying out the facts—accurately, fairly—and letting them demonstrate that the university was engaged in pervasive, systematic discrimination against women. I was particularly grateful to Professor Ralph Izard, who had managed to hammer into my head that every little detail—including spelling—matters.

My 1972 report included 21 recommendations for change. They ranged from adjusting faculty salaries and bringing women into the administration to allowing women to join the ranks of the "110 Marching Men," the highly acclaimed all-male OU band. President Sowle endorsed the report and asked me to lead its implementation. By the time I headed off to Georgetown law school in 1975, Ohio University was established as a leader in the movement to ensure equality for academic women.

The report had made a difference. I'd had no training in organizational change, but I'd developed critical tools in J-School. My education began with that encounter with the energetic white-haired man I had met as a freshman in the basement of Copeland Hall. In one brief conversation, L.J. Hortin had taught me an enduring lesson. I had learned the power of asking questions.

WOMEN IN THE J-SCHOOL

By Susan Crites Price

When I arrived in Athens in fall 1968, it was common practice for newspapers to have separate classified ad columns for "Help Wanted—Male" and "Help Wanted—Female." That included their own ads, where they routinely advertised editorial jobs under the male column. Women were largely found in secretarial positions or selling classifieds.

The few women reporters were mostly relegated to covering soft news and features, usually for the Women's Section. Broadcast journalism was even harder for women to break into, especially for those not deemed attractive enough for TV. And women commonly received less pay than men for the same jobs.

Why, then, did any females want to pursue a journalism career?

Here's why, in my case: Circleville High School in 1967 sent me to the journalism school's summer publications workshop, run by faculty member J.W. Click, and I was hooked. I was impressed by the faculty and learned a lot that I could take back to my high school newspaper and yearbook. When it was time to choose a college, I chose OU because of the journalism program's excellent reputation.

Apparently, it didn't occur to me and my female classmates that we might not succeed in our chosen career field, probably because we didn't fully understand the barriers women faced. By the time I graduated, however, the news profession was on the cusp of major change. The experience of OU women in the journalism school was changing, too.

I should say at the outset that I never felt discrimination in the journalism school, although I can't speak for the rest of the women students in my classes. I received a solid education that helps me to this day—I still make my living as a writer. But the school reflected the times. For one thing, we lacked role models. I don't recall any women on the journalism faculty. This was partly because of the employment pipeline. Many of my professors had come from careers as working journalists, a nearly exclusive men's club. But this lack of women on the faculty was also typical of the university as a whole. In my four years as an undergraduate, I recall only one woman instructor—for a philosophy class in logic.

Susan Crites Price. *(Photo provided by Susan Crites Price)*

The Post was a critical part of my journalism education. I started writing for *The Post* as a freshman and worked my way up the ranks to associate editor—second in command—in my junior year. *The Post* had a good mix of women and men in key editor positions; it was only later that I that realized the top job hadn't been held by a woman since Elsie Uncapher (BSJ '62) in 1961. There wouldn't be another one until Susan DeFord, a 1976 graduate, took the position in 1975.

The perspectives of recruiters

The journalism school encouraged all of us to pursue work experience and, to that end, hosted recruiters seeking summer interns. I applied at the end of my sophomore year and interviewed with a veteran newsman from the *Cleveland Press* who questioned whether I'd be able to cover events at night or how I'd find a safe place to live. That interview went nowhere.

Luckily, the recruiter from *The* (Dayton) *Journal Herald* had no such qualms, and he hired me. Pat Ordovensky was a 1954 OU journalism grad who had edited *The Post* in 1953. He hired two of us Posties that summer. Steve Shaunessy was put on the general-assignment desk, while I landed on the all-female staff in Modern Living (formerly the Women's Page). And, yes, I wrote stories about fashion—a subject I knew nothing about—but also wrote about education, health, personal finance, and even women's rights, a topic that had largely been ignored by the media but was starting to heat up in 1970.

I could see why my professors felt real-life experience was such an important part of a journalism education. And it truly was eye-opening. While I had many opportunities to write stories of importance to both men and women, I also could see how certain sexist practices still prevailed in newsrooms. Here are two examples: The Modern Living staff was the only group in Editorial that had a dress code; our editor would not allow us to wear pants suits, only skirts or dresses. Also, the employee cafeteria was open only to women. It was a throwback to the days when the publisher, former Ohio Governor James M. Cox, worried that his female employees might be harassed—or worse—if they went outside in search of a restaurant. (Sometime after my internship, male reporters finally protested that this was discriminatory, and the result was not what they'd hoped: the paper closed the cafeteria and installed vending machines.)

It took a long time for the news media to take the women's movement seriously and give it the coverage it deserved. When *Newsweek* decided in 1970 to run a big cover story on it, only one of the magazine's 52 staff writers was a woman: Lynn Povich, who had climbed from the all-female ranks of researchers to the all-male writing staff by agreeing to cover fashion.

Realizing the story had to be written by a woman, the editors assigned the story to a freelancer. The women staffers, outraged about being passed over for this important story and tired of the complete lack of opportunities to advance, filed a sex discrimination suit on the same day the special issue hit the newsstands. They inspired women working at other media companies to sue their employers, including *The New York Times,* as Gail Collins said in her 2009 book, *When Everything Changed: The Amazing Journey of American Women from 1969 to the Present,* published by Little Brown.

The women's movement

The women's movement was taking hold on the OU campus, too, and it became part of my beat at *The Post.* There was so much to cover. Birth control information was scant, and abortions were illegal except in New York (as of 1970). There were few women faculty members and no women's studies courses. New organizations such as the Women's Information Group formed to raise awareness and push for campus reforms.

Seizing on the idea of attaining power through control of the news media, we women at *The Post* decided to publish a special tabloid about the women's movement, both on campus and beyond. It appeared on November 19, 1970, and the only male byline was that of the editor, Rudy Maxa (BSJ '71), who penned a "guest" column. Unfortunately, we didn't get the reaction for which we'd hoped. In a story for the 1971 "Athena" yearbook about the progress of the women's movement on campus, I wrote that the special issue had received little reaction from the university community "except some sordid comments from men and one letter to the editor." But change was starting to happen. I wrote that "a women's literature course was allowed to slip into the curriculum for spring, and women's hours were finally abolished."

I didn't apply for the editor job at *The Post* at the end of my junior year, because I was offered a full-time job as a general-assignment reporter at *The Athens Messenger.* The journalism school supported my efforts to finish my degree part-time while working as a reporter full-time. I patched together some independent study and some evening classes.

I've always valued the education I received from the journalism school and have fond memories of many of my professors—even though none of them was a woman.

TRAINING MINORITY JOURNALISTS

By Ted Pease

The idea for the Midwest Newspaper Workshop for Minorities—which now seems a quaint and somewhat paternalistic name—was born in the mid-1980s as a simple way to help address the long-standing disconnect between the news business and a diverse nation.

Talk about creating the Ohio workshop, and its sister program at the University of South Carolina, started during meetings of the American Society of Newspaper Editors' Task Force on Minorities. The task force was a coalition of ASNE editors and representatives of the four minority journalists groups (the National Association of Black Journalists, the Native American Journalists Association, the National Association of Hispanic Journalists, and the Asian American Journalists Association), plus a handful of interested journalism educators.

The group convened regularly through the mid- and late 1980s, a manifestation of newspaper editors' and publishers' concern that their publications were falling short both in covering their increasingly diverse communities and in populating their newsrooms with journalists who were not white.

The way I remember it is that newspaper people in these conversations regularly voiced a frustration that sounded like an echo of the 1960s, when editors lamented criticism by the Kerner Commission after the 1967 race riots, saying, "We can't find qualified Negroes" to provide better coverage of black communities. In the 1980s, newspapers' consciousness about their shortcomings in covering diversity was much greater than it had been in the '60s, but the difficulties in recruiting a more diverse workforce were exactly the same.

"We can do this"

This, thought the journalism educators involved in these conversations, should be easy to fix: training new journalists is what we do. The University of South Carolina's program got off the ground first, in about 1986, and the OU-based Midwest program followed in 1988. The idea locally came during a conference of the Association for Education in Journalism and Mass Communication when I, then a doctoral student, Director Ralph Izard, and faculty member Sandra Haggerty attended a panel discussion about the South Carolina program.

Before we left the room, we had decided: "We can do this."

Izard and I spent much of 1987 planning the Ohio workshop and forging partnerships with foundations and regional newspapers to help pay for the program. The concept was to find people of color who had already graduated from college, in any discipline, who could commit to a full-time 10-week training program that, if successful, would launch them onto new career paths with our newspaper partners. Besides getting the full news-editorial undergraduate curriculum in 10 weeks—newswriting, reporting, feature writing, copy editing, media law, ethics, and more—for 10–12 hours a day through the Athens summer, students would publish two or three tabloid newspapers and serve a two-week internship with participating newspapers.

Because the participants had already graduated from college and in many cases were a couple of years into other careers, they brought to the table maturity as well as expertise in a variety of subject areas from religion to sociology to juvenile justice that made them de facto specialists. Our job was simply to overlay their knowledge base with the tools to report and write for newspapers that needed their perspectives.

Participants received free room and board in OU residence halls, plus stipends of $50 per week. It was basic training, "journalism boot camp," except that after 10 weeks the survivors would emerge with press passes instead of military dog tags.

REFLECTING A CORE VALUE

BEFORE THE NATION welcomed its first black president, before the Internet changed newspaper journalism forever, before the world changed, the nation continued to struggle with race relations—and the journalistic response. The E.W. Scripps School of Journalism had an answer: the Midwest Newspaper Workshop for Minorities.

Picture this: the late 1980s. The school offered an opportunity for aspiring journalists of diverse backgrounds with little or no newspaper experience. The goal: place them in newsrooms around the Midwest. Not only did the program succeed, but participants exceeded anyone's expectations. Many became reporters at metropolitan newspapers such as the *Akron Beacon Journal,* and Colette Jenkins Parker earned a Pulitzer Prize as part of a series on race.

The workshop raised the school's profile nationally as one that cared about diversity and took the lead in that regard, said Ralph Izard, school director at the time and workshop cofounder.

"I think it was a successful program," he said. "From the standpoint of the students, many found jobs. From the standpoint of the Scripps School, it was an opportunity fulfilled that reinforced a tone of interest in diversity, equality, and helping develop a kind of journalism that was broad-based and multicultural. These were core values in the school."

More than that, he added, the regular student body and faculty members learned important lessons about racial relationships, and the program had some impact "on deepening our curriculum and the color of our student body."

Support from foundations and newspapers

Major financial support for the OU workshop came with $10,000 each from the Gannett Foundation, Thomson Newspapers, and the school's long-time partner, the Cincinnati-based Scripps Howard Foundation. Many newspapers in Indiana, Ohio, Michigan, and Pennsylvania also sent newsroom staff to serve as short-term instructors.

The first Midwest Newspaper Workshop for Minorities opened in the summer of 1988 with eight students from Ohio, Indiana, Pennsylvania, and Tennessee. There was one full-time staff person—me—supported by courses taught by journalism faculty. In subsequent years, the workshop

The conviction was that anyone could learn journalism basics in 10 weeks, said faculty member J. Frazier Smith, director of the program in its last two years and later metro editor at the *Dayton Daily News*. It was difficult, but a determined student could get through. "Ten weeks is enough," Smith said. "If you take a willing soul, you can teach him or her to do anything. But the soul has to be willing."

Diversity came not only from race. Even though the original intent was to focus on the Midwest, it became quickly clear that organizers should yield to a much broader demand. That's why participants came from coast to coast. Among African American participants, for example, Quwan Spears came from Los Angeles, Demetrius Patterson and Kevin Sanders arrived from Chicago, Colette Jenkins Parker came from South Bend, Indiana, and George Thomas came from Cleveland. Others were Asian Americans and Hispanics. Many came from big cities, but the need was elsewhere.

"We wanted to especially diversify the smaller and medium-size newsrooms where the editors played the game of not being able to find anybody [of color]," Smith said. "So we found people for them."

Applicant numbers were increased by recruiting those of varied backgrounds. The workshop's founding director, Ted Pease, said the selection committee favored those without journalism experience because "people with undergraduate degrees in journalism should be able to find ways into the industry. We wanted to expand the pool."

The formula worked for six years, but when funding became much more difficult, the school was forced to discontinue the program.

"We closed the workshop with great reluctance," Izard said. "But we believed we had a good run and made real contributions to newspaper journalism."

—Steve Woo

added full-time staff, in particular J. Frazier Smith (MSJ '91), who succeeded me as director in 1991, and Justice Hill, a current faculty member in the school.

The three of us taught classes, as did Scripps faculty Izard, Dru Riley Evarts, James Alsbrook, Don Lambert, Sandra Haggerty, Dick Bean, Pat Washburn, and others. Reporters and editors from partner newspapers—the *Pittsburgh Post-Gazette, The* (Cleveland) *Plain Dealer,* the *Dayton Daily News, The Columbus Dispatch,* the Richmond (Indiana) *Paladium-Item,* the *Detroit Free Press,* and others—came for short courses, day-long reporting crisis simulations, and one-on-one time with the prospective interns/employees, as well as to watch, kibitz, and evaluate the program.

From Day 1, everyone was running at full speed. In just weeks, students had to go from learning the basic WhoWhatWhereWhenWhyHow to applying interview skills and writing complex, multisource stories for publication in the real world.

It was intense. It was tiring. It was a blast.

Despite the proven success of training workshops like the ones at Ohio and South Carolina at identifying, training, and placing journalists of color in U.S. newspaper newsrooms, by the mid-1990s foundation support had dried up, and neither the newspaper industry nor the individual newspapers that benefited from growing more-diverse newsrooms were willing to underwrite the costs.

Over my three years with the program, the workshop recruited, trained, and placed some extraordinary journalists. We were proud of a 70 percent placement and retention rate for program graduates five years out. And although I've lost track of most of the alumni, I do know that some continue in the newspaper business, bringing readers in the communities they cover diverse perspectives that are essential to a changing nation.

"I CAN DO THIS," SHE SAID. AND SHE DID

By Colette Jenkins Parker

I STEPPED ONTO the Ohio University campus in the summer of 1990 to participate as a fellow in the Midwest Newspaper Workshop for Minorities with a promise that elicited some reasonable doubt.

The director, Edward "Ted" Pease, and codirector, J. Frazier Smith, had assured me that after completing this 10-week intensive journalism-training program I would be prepared to work as a reporter in a newsroom. They also said the newspaper industry was supporting the fellowship program because of the industry's commitment to diversity.

Believing the latter was easier than accepting the notion that after 10 weeks, I would be a trained journalist. It was difficult to conclude that a young woman with a psychology degree who had never written for her high school or college newspaper could become a competent journalist in 10 weeks.

But because of who I am—a person who tries to be optimistic—I decided to be open to the possibility that Ted and Frazier could make good on their promise. My belief that the skills I had learned as a psych major at Indiana University and those I had acquired in the workforce were transferrable also gave me an "I-can-do-this!" spirit.

During the 10 weeks, I (along with about a dozen other fellows) endured Dru Riley Evarts—"Dru the grammarian"—who made it very clear that none of us would survive the program without passing her grammar test. I was thankful to all of my English teachers from the past that I was able to pass the test on my first try.

Good journalism is common sense

Then, there were what I considered the commonsense lessons Ted and Frazier imparted—"Stay in tune with what is going on in the world." . . . "Listen to the news and read more than one newspaper each day." . . . "Be a good listener.—Do you really hear what the person you're interviewing is saying, or are your biases creeping in?" . . . "Don't be afraid to ask questions.—No question is a stupid question, especially if it gives you a better understanding or more clarity." . . . "Be fair and accurate.—Get it right the first time because nobody reads corrections."

Ted and Frazier also stressed the importance of choosing words carefully when writing and not falling into a habit of using gender-specific terms (e.g., firefighters, not firemen). They shared their writing lab instruction with a guy named Justice B. Hill, who wasn't shy about embarrassing anyone who had what he considered weak writing skills. Justice had no problem glancing over the shoulder of a fellow to see what was written on the computer screen and yelling at the top of his lungs, "What is that!!??"

The first time I observed Justice expressing his displeasure in what he read, I was horrified and amused simultaneously. I remember walking up to him after writing lab that day and saying, "Don't you ever do that to me!" He laughed, and I said, "I'm serious. I won't respond well to that!" Surprisingly, Justice seemed to be impressed that I had the audacity to challenge him, and we began to develop a rapport that has led to a growing friendship over the years.

I didn't hang out much with Tom Hodges—who spoke in layout language, using terms like "agates," "column inches," "grafs," "legs," "sigs," "teasers," and "wraparounds." While Tom was a very likable and pleasant person, I wasn't interested in learning his language, because visually oriented instruction and work has never been my strong suit.

I met some wonderful people during my time in the Scripps School as a fellow, and to my surprise, the training I received there led to an impactful 26-year journalism career. I started with the (Warren, Ohio) *Tribune Chronicle* and in 1992 began what turned out to be nearly 25 years with the *Akron Beacon Journal,* which included being a bylined reporter on a 1994 Pulitzer Prize–winning series called "A Question of Color."

Questioning the industry's commitment

During my career, I discovered that instead of doubting the workshop's effectiveness in preparing me as a journalist, I should have questioned the newspaper industry's commitment to diversity, because what I found on the inside were newsrooms devoted to what I call "window dressing."

I observed a number of newsroom management teams who were engaged in the decorative exhibition of diversity—counting the number of nonwhite male faces on their products' pages and hiring newsroom staffers of different complexions who shared the same mindset of those making the hires.

I left the industry feeling like I had done what I could to tell the stories of people who have been historically underrepresented on the pages of news papers, particularly women, minorities, and the marginalized. I wish I could have done more to change the biased mindset that is still alive and well in the industry.

What troubles me most is that the newspaper industry does not seem to recognize that its inability to diversify by including a variety of voices in its coverage has directly led to its decline.

Colette Jenkins Parker. *(Photo provided by Colette Jenkins Parker)*

Tales of accomplishment

Thousands of journalism graduates from Ohio University have achieved distinction in their chosen professions. Unfortunately, they cannot all be included in this volume, and those who are omitted surely have earned our respect and our apology. What is provided here, therefore, is little more than a representative sample of successes based on a solid background gained during years in the School of Journalism. Certainly, they have earned our pride in their achievements.

Facing page: Pamela Shoemaker (BSJ '72, MSJ '72) is honored as the inaugural recipient of the Guido H. Stempel III Award for Journalism and Mass Communication Research in 2014. Shoemaker is the John Ben Snow Professor at the S.I. Newhouse School of Public Communications, Syracuse University. *(E.W. Scripps School of Journalism photo)*

RISING INTO JOURNALISM'S ELITE

By Lindsay Friedman

Up the stairs, camera in hand, a young journalist races to the roof of Athens' East Washington Street parking garage in 1971 to get a better view of a raging fire at the Athens National Bank (now Chase) on Court Street.

Despite the intense heat, Ohio University student Skip Peterson (BSJ '74), a *Post* reporter and photographer, won't stop until he gets his shot.

Peterson breaks into a run the second he realizes cops from the Athens Police Department have spotted his perch. He is caught on the stairs after taking his photos, and police threaten to take his camera.

Later he recalled that it was a good thing an editor from *The Athens Messenger* was there to confirm his legitimacy.

He was only one of a cadre of talented young staffers from *The Post* who dedicated themselves to journalistic pursuits around Athens. The group included then–young photographer John Kaplan (BSJ '82, MS '98), who remembers the motivation among his colleagues, who would often sleep in the newsroom.

"They were beyond incredible student journalists," Kaplan said later. "They had dedication that I've never seen surpassed in my 30-plus years in the field."

Years later, both Peterson and Kaplan were involved with Pulitzer Prize–winning journalism. That's an accomplishment earned by only a few, from reporters and writers of news and columns to editors, designers, and photographers. Not all were formally named as winners, because of how the Pulitzer organization awards prizes: some by name, some for team accomplishments, and others collectively for a publication's staff.

Excellence requires many contributors

But it is the case that many individuals contribute to the work that is cited for Pulitzer excellence. At Ohio University, some began their career on Athens' brick streets and embarked on the path to journalism greatness later, and some earned the prize before their OU association. Some were students, and a few others were faculty. They covered the top local, national, and international news stories: the 9/11 terrorist attacks, the impact of race, the spread of Ebola, airplane crashes, the health system, the Boston Marathon bombings, and presidential campaigns and other elections.

And the School of Journalism does not stand alone at Ohio University. Colleagues from the School of Visual Communication and the College of Fine Arts may boast of their own lists, including one VisCom faculty member, Professor Marcy Nighswander.

The success of Ohio University alumni is not a surprise for Leonard Pitts Jr., former Scripps Howard Visiting Professional (2005–06) and himself winner of the 2004 Pulitzer Prize for Commentary. Pitts has taught at a number of top-ranked universities, including Princeton, but said some of his most talented students were those from Scripps Hall.

"Let's just say some of the sharper students were at Ohio University," he said.

No matter the name, year, award, or contribution to Scripps, each journalist helped provide an insightful annotation of the world being witnessed. Their circumstances vary, but they are joined together by their examples of journalistic excellence.

For example, three-time Pulitzer winner Michel du Cille was deeply involved with visual communication during his time at Ohio University, where he received his master's degree in journalism in 1994. Du Cille won three Pulitzer Prizes for photography (in 2008, 1998, and 1986) in public service, feature, and spot news photography. The visual journalist continued to produce extraordinary news photography until his death in 2014 while in Africa depicting the Ebola outbreak for *The Washington Post.*

Michel du Cille, three-time winner of the Pulitzer Prize.
(E.W. Scripps School of Journalism photo)

A second repeat winner, long-time *Chicago Tribune* columnist Clarence Page, received the 1989 Pulitzer Prize for Commentary recognizing his consistently provocative columns on local and national affairs. Years earlier, in 1973, Page was a member of a *Tribune* team that worked undercover to reveal flagrant violations of voting procedures in the 1972 primary election. He worked undercover as a poll watcher on Chicago's South Side as part of the project that won the Pulitzer Prize for Local General or Spot News Reporting.

Another *Chicago Tribune* columnist, Paul Gapp (BSJ '50), won the 1979 Pulitzer Prize for Architectural Criticism. Likewise, Donal Henahan (BS '43) of *The New York Times* won the Pulitzer in 1986 for criticism, in this case music criticism.

A prize-winning idea

In an article heralding its receipt of the 2016 Pulitzer Prize for National Reporting, *The Washington Post* credited Ohio University alumnus Wesley Lowery (BSJ '17) with the idea that stimulated one of the most ambitious projects in the newspaper's history.

"After covering several high-profile incidents (including the Michael Brown shooting in Ferguson, Missouri) . . . Lowery was surprised to discover that there were no official statistics about such fatalities," *The Post* said. "So Lowery pitched an idea to his editors: The newspaper, he suggested, should collect the information itself and analyze it for patterns in law enforcement."

His editors accepted the idea, and Lowery became a member of the team that eventually developed a database containing the details of 990 fatal shootings by police across the nation in 2015 and provided a series of articles describing trends in the data.

Lowery also was involved when *The Boston Globe* staff won the 2014 Pulitzer Prize for Breaking News Reporting for its coverage of the Boston Marathon bombings. *The Globe* was cited for "using photography and a range of digital tools to capture the full impact of the tragedy." Lowery was among those staff members who contributed tweets to that coverage.

The staff of *The Wall Street Journal* won the Pulitzer Prize for Breaking News Reporting in 2002 for "its comprehensive and insightful coverage, executed under the most difficult circumstances, of the terrorist attack on New York City," and June Kronholz (BSJ '69) was among the principal contributors. *The Journal* carried three bylined stories on the front page of its September 12, 2001, edition. Kronholz, working out of Washington, supervised the reporting and wrote one of these stories.

When TWA Flight 800 crashed off the coast of Long Island on July 17, 1996, Joanne Utley-Baksh was at her desk as an art director in *Newsday*'s Editorial Art Department, primarily charged with doing front page and news page design. The crash occurred after deadline and prompted a flurry of activity as the staff launched into coverage that eventually won the 1997 Pulitzer Prize in Spot News Reporting.

The *Newsday* staff was cited for its enterprising coverage, and Utley-Baksh and her desk colleagues contributed by making and remaking the pages as new information and photos poured in. The rapidly developing stories were made complex by the deaths of 230 people, the third-deadliest aviation accident on U.S. territory, and by speculation—eventually discounted—of terrorist activity.

"First, we went with a page with only words announcing that the plane was lost," Utley-Baksh said. "Eventually we got a photo of some burning debris in the ocean and added that to the tabloid page. Several inside pages were also revamped on the fly. I worked with the other front page designer that night and over the next couple of days to present the photos and stories that came pouring in."

Colette Jenkins Parker of the *Akron Beacon Journal* did not attend Ohio University as a regular student; instead, she came to Athens for one summer in 1990 to attend the School of Journalism's Midwest Newspaper Workshop for Minorities. She was among bylined reporters who wrote about education as part of a team examination of the impact of race on education, housing, employment, and the criminal justice system. The team was awarded the 1994 Pulitzer Prize for Public Service.

In the late 1980s, three Ohio University graduates working at *The Courier-Journal* in Louisville, Kentucky—Durell Hall (BFA '78), James Henahan (BSJ '73), and Marc Norton (MSJ '67) were among staff members who won the 1989 Pulitzer Prize for General News Reporting for sustained coverage of a bus crash that claimed 27 lives.

Joe Mahr (BSJ '94) of *The Blade* in Toledo was one of three who wrote a series on atrocities by the U.S. Army during the Vietnam War. Their 2004 prize was for investigative reporting. The next year, Steve Hymon (BSC '88) of the *Los Angeles Times* was among bylined writers for a series that won the 2005 award for public service. It was cited as a "courageous, exhaustively researched series exposing deadly medical problems and racial injustice at a major public hospital."

In 2017, reporter Alex Stuckey (BSJ '12) was an important member of a team that won for *The Salt Lake Tribune* the Pulitzer Prize for Local Report-

Pulitzer Prize winner Wesley Lowery. *(E.W. Scripps School of Journalism photo)*

ing for its groundbreaking investigation of rape at Utah colleges. Judges said the paper's staff earned the prize "for a string of vivid reports revealing the perverse, punitive and cruel treatment given to sexual-assault victims at Brigham Young University, one of Utah's most powerful institutions."

In addition to Leonard Pitts Jr., one other former Scripps Howard Visiting Professional, Julia Keller (2012–13), earned Pulitzer credentials. She was awarded the 2005 Pulitzer Prize for Feature Writing while at the *Chicago Tribune* for her work characterizing the intersecting perspectives of multiple strangers who were trapped together in a deadly tornado.

Kaplan and Peterson led visual investigations of their own. Interested in the dissection of sociological structures, Kaplan conducted a critical analysis of the age 21, providing a visual narrative of different paths of life by young adults. Inspired after covering a 21-year-old murderer, he followed celebrities, the poor, the average, and the rich. As a result, working for Block Newspapers in Toledo, he received the 1992 Pulitzer Prize for Feature Photography.

At the *Dayton Daily News,* Peterson was identified by the paper as the lead photographer for a series disclosing flaws and mismanagement in the military health care system that won the 1998 Pulitzer Prize for National Reporting.

Given that each of these journalists was effectively armed with a curious mind and the skills needed to pursue these stories, it is not surprising that some cite their time at Ohio University as a factor leading to their success.

"Ohio University is where I learned that excellence matters," Kaplan said. "Ohio University is where I learned that this field is truly important. It's beyond important; it's foundational in a democracy."

TAKING DISSERTATIONS TO THE NEXT LEVEL

By Patrick S. Washburn

Douglass Daniel (PhD '95) experienced what few doctoral students have shared when he was in the journalism program at Ohio University.

In the summer of 1994, I showed Daniel a flyer from Syracuse University Press, which noted that it had a new book series about popular television shows. This fit perfectly with the work he was doing for his dissertation. A former reporter with a long-time interest in journalism and film, he was conducting research on the *Lou Grant* show, which ran on CBS from 1977 to 1982. He was interested in what the award-winning weekly series told its audience of up to 25 million about journalism and how much the show mirrored reality.

Douglass Daniel. *(Photo provided by Douglass Daniel)*

Daniel met with Syracuse's acquisitions editor, submitted a proposal and several chapters by mail, and was given a book contract before he finished his dissertation. He sent Syracuse his dissertation before defending it in the spring of 1995 and was asked to start putting it into book form immediately.

Realizing that this would be a mistake before having his defense and seeing what his committee suggested to improve the manuscript, he had to hold off Syracuse until gaining that approval. The book was published in the following year, with the star of the show, Ed Asner, writing a foreword, and it received a favorable review in *Entertainment Weekly.*

Most have examined historical subjects

While no list has been kept by the journalism school of dissertations that graduate students converted into books, at least 16 have been published. Most have examined historical topics, ranging widely and including President Dwight Eisenhower's use of prime-time TV in the 1950s; sex columns in college newspapers and magazines; Asian Americans and the mass media; the influence of the *National Police Gazette* in creating the modern American man from 1879 to 1906; the government's Office of Censorship and the effect it had on the press and radio in World War II; and the Scripps newspapers in World War I.

I chaired 12 of the dissertations that were published, and the other four were chaired by faculty colleagues Joe Bernt, Anne Cooper-Chen, Marilyn Greenwald, and Mike Sweeney.

The 16 students, all of whom have had university teaching and professional positions since graduating, had varying experiences in getting their dissertations published.

For example, Steve Hallock (PhD '05) found the process "really easy." He contacted three or four publishers, and Praeger Publishers immediately accepted his proposal and gave him a $2,000 advance contract. He found that editing his dissertation was "quite simple," and with no significant changes, his book on the dwindling marketplace of ideas in today's news was published in 2007. Since then, he has published two more books, which he attributes to the self-confidence he gained in publishing his dissertation.

Reed Smith (PhD '93) had much the same experience with his dissertation about Samuel Medary, publisher of a copperhead newspaper in Columbus, Ohio, during the Civil War. Because Medary's papers were at the Ohio Historical Society in Columbus, and his newspaper was published there, Smith approached only the Ohio State University Press, which published the book a year and a half later, in 1995. While he had to add some material to the manuscript, he said changes to it by an editor were "minimal."

In contrast, Dale Zacher (PhD '99) finished his dissertation on the Scripps newspapers in World War I in 1999, but it was not published by the University of Illinois Press until 2008. His progress was slowed in those nine years because he taught at four universities as well as working full-time as the communications director for a gubernatorial candidate in North Dakota in 2000. In 2001, he contacted Illinois, which asked him to cut 150 pages (about a third of the manuscript) to make it more economical to publish. It was finally accepted about four years later and then took several years to appear in book form.

The effort of writing a book

"I have been surprised how few administrators understand the effort it takes to write a book," Zacher said. "Too many vanity publishers make it easy to be a 'book author,' and some administrators don't know how to distinguish between the two. . . . Moreover, some seem to just count how many publications you have—and thus a book is just one such publication!"

Sweeney, who received his doctorate in 1996 and joined the OU faculty in 2009, had a somewhat similar experience. After Oxford University Press turned down his manuscript, he went to the University of North Carolina Press, which said it could not consider the manuscript unless he trimmed it from 714 pages to fewer than 400. After going through the same arduous process as Zacher, including various reviews and editing, his book about the Office of Censorship in World War II was published in 2001 and won the first book-of-the-year award from the American Journalism Historians Association. That was followed by more than a dozen books, many of them for National Geographic, and several more awards.

"I don't owe much to the book that came out of my dissertation—just my financial security, my tenure and promotion, and my reputation as a scholar," Sweeney said wryly.

All of these students say their book-publishing success stemmed to some degree from the OU doctoral program. For example, all 16 took the historical research course, which affected what they did. Many also learned to write better, which was stressed by the faculty. And in some cases, the faculty provided the seed for what became a dissertation.

Steve Siff (PhD '08), for example, recalls Bernt's eyebrows "rising" when he showed him a 1960 *Time* magazine article that compared the effects of LSD with the passions of some Catholic saints. He is still thankful to Bernt for "encouraging me to pursue what might have seemed an oddball idea [for a dissertation]." And Ed Simpson (PhD '12), who turned his dissertation into a book in only 14 months, still recalls what two of us told him. Bernt advised him to "go look" at what had been done before choosing a topic, or it might be a waste of time, and I told him that I wrote articles and books "one sentence at a time." And when I was satisfied with that sentence, I moved to the next one, thus avoiding sloppy drafts. He says those pieces of advice are still his "constant companions."

Jim Foust (PhD '94), whose book on the history of the Clear Channel Broadcasting service was published six years after he finished his dissertation in 1994, sums up what it is like to publish a book.

"I . . . probably made about $400 on the book, after investing thousands in grant money and at least hundreds in my own money," he said. "But it is definitely a cool experience to get a box full of your freshly published books from UPS. . . . I think there are a lot of people in academia, and even really good researchers, who maybe don't have the attention span or the desire to commit to something long term like a book project. And so I think that if you are somebody who has done that and has been able to take it through to fruition that you get quite a bit of respect from your colleagues."

Perhaps the most recent book to emerge from a Scripps School dissertation was written by Tom Hrach (PhD '08). His book—*The Riot Report and the News: How the Kerner Commission Changed Media Coverage of Black America*—was published in 2016.

One thing is for certain: there will be more. Scripps School students seem to have this kind of talent.

YOU CAN COME HOME AGAIN

By Andrew Alexander

Martin Savidge was comfortable delivering the news to a worldwide TV audience. But for the veteran CNN journalist, delivering Ohio University's 2003 undergraduate commencement address was another matter.

"To speak to a packed house on a campus I knew and loved took my public speaking angst up to a whole new level," recalled Savidge (BSJ '81). He worried that he wouldn't "live up to the significance of the day."

Over the years, a handful of Scripps journalism alums have returned to Athens as undergraduate commencement speakers. Aside from the honor of being chosen, most recall feeling special pressure to do well at their alma mater. They also have vivid memories of the commencement pageantry and being touched by nostalgia.

"I looked out over that crowd, [and] my mind flashed back to when I was sitting in the back of that hall," said Pulitzer Prize–winning *Chicago Tribune* columnist Clarence Page (BSJ '69), who delivered the keynote address in 2001.

Page was right. For me, the lasting memory was the size of the audience. While accompanying university leaders to the stage before giving the 2013 commencement address, I scanned the cavernous Convocation Center. The place was literally packed to the rafters.

Van Gordon Sauter. *(Photo courtesy of the Ohio University Archives, Mahn Center for Archives and Special Collections)*

Thousands of high-spirited seniors in their caps and gowns occupied chairs on the floor. Thousands more, family and friends, surrounded them. All told, roughly 13,000 attended. And that was just the morning ceremony. In the modern era, undergraduate commencements have become so large that speakers must do double duty; there's an afternoon ceremony of the same size.

It's daunting. You're humbled to be the featured speaker and receive an honorary doctorate. You've spent weeks polishing gems of wisdom for the young graduates. And you're apprehensive. This is an important moment in their lives—and yours. You want to do well.

Then, as you're about to speak, several things hit you.

No one is unhappy at a commencement

First, no one is unhappy at a commencement. You quickly realize it's an easy crowd. The students are festive. The parents are proud (and in many cases, relieved).

Second, few will later recall much of what their commencement speaker said. Within several years, many can't even remember who spoke. That's oddly comforting as you ascend the podium.

"Graduates typically remember little or nothing that their commencement speaker said. I certainly don't," Page noted in recalling his 2001 keynote.

In some cases, even the speakers themselves can't recall precisely what they said. "What did I say? No idea," confessed legendary broadcast executive Van Gordon Sauter (BSJ '57), who delivered the commencement address in 1983 when he was president of CBS News.

Savidge, a native of Canada who grew up in the Cleveland suburb of Rocky River, agreed. "I remember everything about what it was like to be there and little, very little, about what I said," he recalled.

In his commencement speech, acclaimed sports journalist Peter King (BSJ '79) revealed that the thought of addressing fellow Bobcats had been more unsettling than writing for *Sports Illustrated* or delivering commentary for NBC's *Football Night in America* on Sundays. "Preparing a commence-

Clarence Page. *(Photo courtesy of Ohio University Archives, Mahn Center for Archives and Special Collections)*

ment speech is far more harrowing than talking to millions of people or writing for millions of people whom I can't see," he told graduates in 2008. King, who met his wife at Ohio University, spoke on the 28th anniversary of their marriage in Galbreath Chapel on the College Green.

Sauter, a burly and bearded raconteur who grew up in Middletown, Ohio, recalled that his audience in 1983 "was in high spirits—and in some cases, I do mean high—and was quite generous."

Page, from the same hometown, remembers a scene after the ceremony. "I completed my speech, feeling quite proud of myself for how far I had come since Middletown, Athens, and the class of '69," he said. But afterwards, as he strolled virtually unnoticed through the crowd of fresh graduates and their families, he recalled, "I was humbled again to be reminded of what every commencement speaker should remember: All of these nice people did not come just to hear me."

Several used their speech to pay tribute to Scripps faculty who were instrumental in their careers.

King talked about Professor Dru Riley Evarts—nicknamed "Conan the Grammarian" by students—whose precision-language class was among the most demanding in the journalism school.

"She was a big influence on my life," King told the graduating seniors. "And the reason was that any paper you wrote for her class would get an automatic F if there were any misspellings or grammar mistakes." He added, "Her theory was a good one. There's never an excuse for giving less than your absolute best."

In my case, I confessed to being an inattentive student who left Ohio University in 1970 without a diploma because I didn't have enough credit hours to graduate.

"I owe my college degree [in 1972] to one journalism instructor, Dr. Ralph Izard, who nudged me to do an independent study project to get the necessary credit hours," I told the students. Izard, then assistant director of the journalism school, went on to become its director.

Like me, the absence of academic excellence did not preclude Sauter from being a commencement speaker.

"With a barely concealed mix of joy and relief, the Ohio University business school escorted me to the door after I managed abysmal grades—F's—in the required courses of accounting and statistics," he recalled years after his commencement address. "I was adrift, perilously devoid of career direction. Where to turn? Why, to the journalism school, of course."

There, he flourished under the school's director, L.J. Hortin, "a generous and harried man [who] found potential in every aimless student, whatever his or her outlandish dreams."

Advice for the graduates

Regardless of whether their audiences remember, the journalism school commencement speakers were full of advice to the new graduates.

Sauter urged students not to be discouraged by previous decades that had seen the assassination of political leaders, years of struggle for racial equality, and upheaval over the unpopular war in Vietnam. "Mankind is moving toward a 'golden age,'" he told them, adding that Ohio University had provided them with "a value system, formed by the history and traditions of the institution," that would enable them to create a better world.

In his speech, Page shared advice he had received from his grandmother, a retired public school teacher, when he graduated from high school in 1965. "Today is not the end of your education, but the beginning," he told them.

Savidge, who had recently returned from covering the onset of the U.S. war in Iraq, relayed advice that had been given to Marines about to enter combat. "Rely on your training. Trust in those that have experience. Never forget that above all you are a human being," he told them.

In my 2013 address, I implored them to give back to Ohio University. "Not years from now, when you've been promoted to that big job with the large corner office," I said. "Rather, as soon as you can after you leave Athens" by volunteering to mentor students, talking to classes, or prepping graduating seniors for job interviews.

King relayed advice he had gathered by asking famous sports figures what he should tell the graduating seniors.

From Dick Ebersol, longtime head of NBC Sports: "Always ask why."

From NFL quarterback Peyton Manning: "Never forget where you came from. Make your family a part of your everyday life."

From sports broadcaster Bob Costas: "Things are rarely black and white. Don't demonize."

And King ended with one of his own. Noting that the United States accounts for only a fraction of the world's population, he implored the new graduates, "Live in the universe, [but] don't go thinking you're the center of it."

Note: Since the completion of this article, two additional journalism graduates have served as speakers at the Ohio University commencement. Wesley Lowery (BSJ '17), national correspondent for *The Washington Post,* spoke in 2017, and Allie LaForce (BSJ '11), reporter and anchor for CBS Sports and Turner Sports, was featured in 2018.

EDITING AN ACADEMIC JOURNAL IS LIKE BEING A PARENT

By Michael S. Sweeney

Professor Patrick S. Washburn received a warning in 2000 when he was formally offered the post of editor of *Journalism History,* the nation's oldest academic journal of mass media history.

"When I took over from Barbara Cloud [at the University of Nevada at Las Vegas], she told me, 'This is like handing over my child,'" Washburn recalled 15 years later. "She said, in so many words, that I had better not screw this up."

He said he came to understand what she was talking about when he retired from the E.W. Scripps School of Journalism in 2012 and handed the editorship to me, one of his advisees during work on my 1996 PhD degree. Being editor of an academic journal is like being a parent: It demands one's attention; encourages creative thinking and problem solving; and shapes something the world regularly judges as a reflection of its producers. And when the final result appears, more often than not it's a source of great pride.

The E.W. Scripps School of Journalism has had more than its share of national journal editors among faculty and alumni. The publication list includes *Journalism and Mass Communication Quarterly,* the flagship journal of the Association for Education in Journalism and Mass Communication (AEJMC), as well as *Newspaper Research Journal* and other specialized journals in subfields of communication research.

For the editors, the work is its own reward.

It took Guido H. Stempel III, longtime editor of *Journalism Quarterly* (it became *Journalism and Mass Communication Quarterly* after he stepped down in 1989), a few years to realize how much he enjoyed his stewardship.

"When I was a grad student at the University of Wisconsin, I didn't say to myself, 'That's what I want to do,'" Stempel said. "But after I had been editor for a few years, I got a call from a grad student at Penn who was doing her master's thesis on journal editors. She had a list of questions, and one was, 'What did you really want to do?' I said, 'This is it.'"

"I had people tell me how much they had appreciated what I had done," he said. "Some people want an article to be published the way they wrote it. I wanted it to be clear. I would make some changes that I thought would clarify things, but I would not rewrite the style of the article, for heaven's sakes."

Reviewers must be experts

Stempel also had the commonsense idea of selecting reviewers for a manuscript based on their expertise in the subject matter, rather than having a secretary make assignments based on who was due in the rotation. Anyway, for most of his career, he didn't have a secretary.

"I think picking the right reviewer was the single most important thing an editor could do," Stempel said. "Get an expert review!"

He said he was proud of the number of manuscripts he supervised each year (about 250), the quick responses from his reviewers, and the average number of articles printed—about 120 each year, including research-in-brief.

Former OU faculty member Daniel Riffe (MSJ '76) first encountered *Journalism Quarterly* in the 1970s, when he was a master's student at Ohio University. "Taking courses in law and methods from Guido Stempel, along with theory from Hugh Culbertson, I began to read the journal, first for seminar assignments, but then each issue that arrived in the reading room at Lasher, cover to cover!" he said.

Riffe reconnected with the journal when he began his PhD program years later at the University of Tennessee. That led to three and a half decades of association with *JQ/JMCQ* as a contributor, a reviewer, an editorial board member, an associate editor, and, most recently, for 14 years as editor.

Riffe saw his job as helping scholars get good work into print, rather than looking for ways to reject work that was less than complete or satisfactory. "The real rewards of editing came when I was making a publication decision, and I felt that we had genuinely helped a scholar make her or his work better and that it was 'ready,'" he said.

Under Riffe's leadership, *JMCQ* moved from "snail-mail" submissions and reviews to digital submissions and other communications. He stepped down from the position in 2014.

Unlike Riffe's taking over a healthy journal from Stempel, Washburn inherited a nearly moribund publication in *Journalism History*. He said he had decided in the mid-1990s that he would like to be a journal editor and settled on *Journalism History* because of his interest in mass media history and his belief that the journal's quality of scholarship, production values, large format, and use of photographs made it the premier publication in its discipline at the time.

He approached Cloud and said he would be interested in being editor if she ever decided to retire. She made that call in 2000, and he met her in Las Vegas after attending an AEJMC conference in Phoenix. In their discussions, Cloud agreed to complete her last issue as editor in January 2001 and let Washburn get out the next issue in April. When Washburn asked for the journal's files to be transferred to Athens, Ohio, he learned that Cloud had left him without any accepted manuscripts scheduled for publication. The April issue was empty, and he had three and a half months to fill it.

He said, "Gradually we worked it out so that within two to three years, we had stuff accepted nine months to a year before it appeared. And later, we expanded to five articles instead of four, simply because we had the money and we could do it."

Washburn said that of all the things he did in his career, being editor of *Journalism History* gave him the most satisfaction.

The school's impressive record

Journal editors associated with the E.W. Scripps School include the following:

- *Business Case Journal.* Professor Craig Davis, coeditor (2014–).
- *Journalism History.* Patrick S. Washburn, editor (2000–2012); Professor Joseph Bernt, associate editor (2000–2012); PhD recipient James J. Foust of Bowling Green State University, associate editor (2012–); PhD recipient and Professor Michael S. Sweeney, associate editor (2009–12) and editor (2012–); Professor Aimee Edmondson, associate editor (2012–); and master's degree recipient Katherine Bradshaw of Bowling Green State University, book review editor (2010–).
- *Journal of Media Economics.* Professor Hugh Martin, coeditor (2011).
- *Journalism Quarterly/JMCQ.* Guido H. Stempel III, associate editor (1970–72) and editor (1972–89); Daniel Riffe, professor from 1995 to 2008, editor (2001–14); Professor Randall Murray, managing editor; Professor Russell Baird, managing editor (1977–78); Professor J. William Click, managing editor (1978–89); PhD recipient Ted Pease of Utah State University, book review editor (2008–13); 2005 PhD recipient Ronald R. Rodgers of the University of Florida, book review editor (2013–16).
- *Journalism and Mass Communication Educator.* PhD recipient Maria Marron, now dean of the College of Journalism and Mass Communication, University of Nebraska–Lincoln, editor (2012–17).
- *Newspaper Research Journal.* Former visiting faculty member Gerald C. Stone, founding editor (1979–88); former Director Ralph Izard, editor (1988–2000); PhD recipient Ted Pease of Utah State University, associate editor (1988–91); Professor Guido H. Stempel III, associate editor (1990–2000) and senior research editor (2000–2016); Professor Marilyn Greenwald, managing editor (1994); Professor Ron Pittman, production editor (1994–2000); and PhD recipients Sandra Utt and Elinor Grusin of the University of Memphis, coeditors (2001–17).
- *Web Journal of Mass Communication Research.* Guido H. Stempel III, cofounder and coeditor (1997–2016); Professor Hans Meyer, coeditor (2010–); Director Robert Stewart, coeditor (1997–).
- *International Communication Research Journal* (*ICRJ*). Professor Yusuf Kalyango, editor (2014–).

FIRST PHD RECIPIENT

By Ralph Izard

BIRTHNEY "BERT" ARDOIN (PhD '71) came to Athens from Monroe, Louisiana, and when he left he carried with him the first PhD from Ohio University's School of Journalism.

Based on that academic background and his earlier professional career, he spent 14 years as professor and chairman of the Department of Journalism, University of Southern Mississippi, and 19 years in California as professor and graduate director in the Division of Communication at Pepperdine University. He retired in 2004 and now resides in Corinth, Mississippi.

Ardoin's primary teaching areas were in advertising and public relations. His dissertation, completed under the guidance of Guido H. Stempel III, was titled *A Comparative Content Analysis of Newspapers under Joint Printing Agreements*."

Birthney "Bert" Ardoin. *(Photo provided by Bert Ardoin)*

A SHORT CAREER AS THE "GO-TO" MAN

Dan Reimold (PhD '08) wrote his Ohio University dissertation on sex columns in college newspapers, then went on to establish himself as one of the nation's leading scholars of college media. Reimold died in 2015 at the age of 34.

"He was undisputedly the foremost scholar on college media today," said College Media Association President Rachele Kanigel. "I can't think of another person who came close to his stature in the field. His independent news site College Media Matters was the go-to spot for all news about college media, and his writings were widely cited by journalism educators and researchers."

Reimold was an assistant professor of journalism at St. Joseph's University in Philadelphia, where he was the adviser for *The Hawk* student newspaper and taught basic and advanced journalism classes.

"Losing Dan is a huge blow to College Media Association and Associated Collegiate Press but also to college media in general," said Kelley Callaway, vice president of member services for CMA, of which Reimold was an active member. "He was energetic, funny, innovative, and engaging. His loss is a personal and professional one."

Reimold was known for successfully bridging the gap between collegiate journalism and academics, publishing scholarly articles in *College Media Review* and *Newspaper Research Journal* and journalistic pieces for *USA Today* and *The Huffington Post.* Reimold was the campus beat columnist for *USA Today* College and maintained a monthly column on the student press for the Poynter Institute.

His textbook, *Journalism of Ideas: Brainstorming, Developing and Selling Stories in the Digital Age*, was published in 2013 by Routledge. A book based on his dissertation, *Sex and the University: Celebrity, Controversy, and a Student Journalism Revolution,* was published in 2010 by Rutgers University Press. He also had recently begun holding weekly Twitter chats about college media.

—Adapted with permission from College Media Association release posted August 2015

COVERING THE JFK ASSASSINATION

By Dru Riley Evarts

Covering the Kennedy assassination, being one of only three reporters to witness the swearing-in of Lyndon B. Johnson on Air Force One, and being the first reporter/eyewitness to announce to the world that Vice President Johnson had become the 36th president of the United States.

These tragic moments were among the highlights of Sid Davis' long career in broadcast journalism.

Again and again, Davis (BSJ '52) relived and retold everything about the assassination of President John F. Kennedy and Johnson's installation, most recently at the 50th anniversary in November 2013. Many publications, broadcast programs, and groups consulted him for details, beginning with the first shot he heard through the experience at Parkland Memorial Hospital and all that had happened during the subsequent days and weeks as the nation mourned.

In describing the tragic scene at the assassination announcement by Assistant White House Press Secretary Malcolm "Mac" Kilduff, Davis said, "Red-eyed and choked by grief, Kilduff struggled to speak. 'President John F. Kennedy died at approximately 1 p.m. Central Standard Time here in Dallas,' he said. 'He died of a gunshot wound to the brain.'

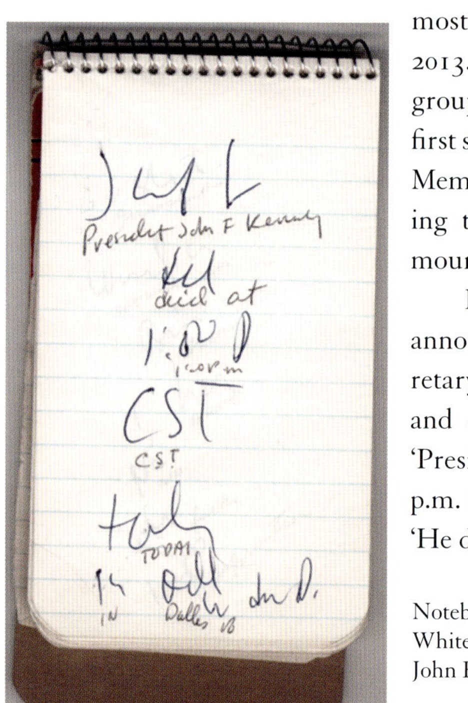

Notebook used by Sid Davis when he was informed by the White House press secretary of the assassination of President John F. Kennedy. *(Photo provided by Sid Davis)*

"We ran for the phones. It was bedlam. While we were filing, [UPI reporter Merriman] Smith, [*Newsweek* reporter Charles] Roberts, and I were nabbed by a White House official, Edwin Fauver, who told us we were to be the pool reporters who would witness the inauguration on Air Force One. . . . We were herded to an unmarked police car, then driven through Dallas' streets at speeds of up to 80 miles an hour, running red lights, heading for Love Field, where the swearing-in was to take place. Police-car radio silence was being maintained in case there were conspirators about, but we heard a headquarters transmission that a suspect had been apprehended.

Sid Davis. *(Photo courtesy of the Ohio University Archives, Mahn Center for Archives and Special Collections)*

"Arriving at Air Force One, Roberts and I were told there were only two seats left on the plane for press. Smith would board because he was a wire-service man; Roberts and I would have to flip a coin for the remaining seat." Davis volunteered to leave the plane and brief the other press in Dallas and then would broadcast his eyewitness account from Love Field.

"Staying on Air Force One would have meant being airborne, out of pocket, during the three-hour return to Washington, and I needed to be on the air and available in Dallas, " Davis said. Over the 50-plus years since that day, two visions remain embedded in Davis' mind: the courage of Jacqueline Kennedy, her clothing blood-splattered from her husband's wounds, attending the swearing in of her husband's successor; and the compassion and calm resolve of President Johnson in taking charge. The Associated Press said of him that day, "It was as though a giant hand had reached down and soothed the heart of a grieving nation."

Davis covered nine presidents

Davis covered President Johnson from the moment he assumed the presidency until he retired, coming to know Johnson on a personal level as well, observing his pain during the Vietnam War as well as his historic triumphs on civil rights legislation. In all, Davis covered nine presidents, but he ranks as one of his most exciting presidential trips the opportunity to fly to Athens, Ohio, in the press group to cover President Johnson when he made the first of his "Great Society" speeches on May 7, 1964.

Beyond his role as one of the central figures in coverage of the Kennedy assassination, Davis' life included many other highlights—becoming vice president of NBC News and chief of its Washington Bureau, becoming program director of the Voice of America after his retirement from NBC, and remaining a successful researcher/writer and lecturer, both for the Brookings Institute and as a freelancer.

In addition to being a distinguished broadcaster and broadcast administrator, Davis has written for *The Washington Post, American Heritage* magazine, *TV Quarterly, The Washington Times,* and *Broadcasting Magazine.* He also has done media commentary for National Public Radio.

Sidney A. Davis is his formal name, but everybody (including himself) calls him "Sid." And the byline "By Sid Davis" has come to mean well-reported and documented news and follow-ups from the time he was a student in the School of Journalism and a reporter on WOUI (the predecessor of WOUB) until his reporting from the highest places.

Davis had enrolled at Ohio University in 1948 to utilize the GI Bill to earn a college degree. Much as he admired George Starr Lasher and other faculty members, it was broadcast journalism for Davis from his earliest days in the school.

As Davis became more of a fixture on WOUI, he used the summer between his junior and senior years to do one of the School of Journalism's earliest internships—at the newly opened WJEH in Gallipolis. Upon graduation, he landed a reporting job at the Westinghouse station in his hometown, Youngstown. His work there came to Westinghouse's corporate attention, and his achievements led to his being selected as the White House reporter for all of Westinghouse's stations.

An active supporter of Ohio University

Davis has always been an active supporter of Ohio University and its students. He has made generous donations of both written and recorded materials related to the Kennedy assassination and its 50-year anniversary. He has gone far beyond any expectations in welcoming students to Washington and arranging interviews and other experiences for them.

He has said of his experience in the School of Journalism, "I recall how much I enjoyed OU. Journalism was right for me, and OU was the place to be. It became a decompression chamber for me after the U.S. Navy. The atmosphere was totally friendly, and its size (about 6,000 at the time) contributed to the attention we received. I can't think of a single professor I didn't like or admire. Yes, I could have hit the books harder, but the personal treatment and attention was always there."

Davis has been recognized by the School of Journalism (with the L.J. Hortin Distinguished Alumnus Award in 1995), by the Scripps College of Communication with induction into the Ohio Communication Hall of Fame in 2004, and by Ohio University with the Medal of Merit Award in 2012.

TALENT RUNS IN THE FAMILY

By Dru Riley Evarts

IT IS ALMOST poetic that the 2-year-old girl who moved to Athens, Ohio, with her parents because her father had been asked by Ohio University to establish a journalism program should die just as the book chronicling that program was entering its final editing.

Four 1942 BSJ recipients—Edwin Darby, Dorothy Patterson, Mary Elizabeth Lasher, and Sol Kalichman—work to produce *The Post* in this 1941 photo from the "Athena" yearbook. *(Photo courtesy of the Ohio University Archives, Mahn Center for Archives and Special Collections)*

Mary Elizabeth Lasher, born on March 14, 1923, died on March 9, 2016, five days before her 94th birthday. She had grown up in Athens, where her father, George Starr Lasher, was respected, even revered, for the success of his department, then school, of journalism. She stayed in Athens after high school to study journalism and received her BSJ in 1942.

Known both in and out of the school as "Mary Lib," she became the first woman editor of *The Post.* She met her future husband, Kenneth A. Barnette, while she was doing a Reporting Practice course at *The Athens Messenger,* where he was a reporter. After college and a competitive stint on a New York fashion magazine, she landed a job as the first woman to be hired in a professional editorial position at *Editor & Publisher* magazine, followed by being

I Love My Prof---He's My Dad

By Mary Elizabeth Lasher

People ASK, and they ASK all the time: "How does it feel to have your father for a professor?" It isn't a feeling—it's a fact. I have him for a professor and I like it.

(Ed. Note: Prof. George Starr Lasher is director of OU's School of Journalism.)

Of course, when he calls the roll and says, "Miss Lasher," it seems unnatural, and yet all my other professors do the same. Why shouldn't he?

It's one class I'll probably never cut. It's one class for which my assignments will be in on time. However, the same is true for most of my other classes.

Like some 40 other persons I'm getting the benefit of the service my father has to sell, and it's the same service to me as it is to them. From 10 till 11 Tuesdays and Thursdays, I'm just the third girl in the second row who has to be taught the same thing as the second girl in the third row.

I like the class. It's fun. And best of all, I haven't heard his stories at home. In fact, I never realized till now how little journalism I hear at home compared to the amount he gives us in class.

Although the boy next to me in class thinks it impossible to love a professor, it is not only possible, but natural to love a professor—if he's your father.

This column, written by Mary Elizabeth Lasher about her father, appeared in *The Post. (Reproduced with permission from* The Post*)*

the first woman to become public relations director of the American Newspaper Association.

After World War II, she married Barnette, and they settled in the Buffalo, New York, area. She was involved in journalistic and public interest areas as she raised their three daughters. Upon her husband's middle-age death, she took over editorship of his paper*, The Amherst Bee.*

Her other journalistic experience included reporting for the *Tonawanda News,* copy editing for the *Buffalo Courier Express,* and two more public relations directorships—first for the Buffalo Philharmonic Orchestra, then for SUNY Buffalo.

Upon her return to Athens and Ohio University, university people and townspeople alike knew her for her public service, such as chair of Athens High School's largest scholarship committee, vice president of the Athens Foundation, member of the Ohio Valley Summer Theater Board, alumnae adviser to Pi Beta Phi sorority, and donor of the School of Journalism's Lasher Living Legacy Award (with her sister Dorothy) and the Lasher-Evarts Quality of Writing Award.

Paul Gapp. *(Photo courtesy of the Ohio University Archives, Mahn Center for Archives and Special Collections)*

HIS WORDS MADE CHICAGO MORE BEAUTIFUL

By Ralph Izard

It is high praise when the editor of a major metropolitan newspaper says one of his staff members was "an architecture critic so excellent that he actually made Chicago more beautiful by his words."

The comment was made in the 1992 obituary of Paul Gapp (BSJ '50) by *Chicago Tribune* editor Jack Fuller, who added on a personal note that Gapp was "one of the true gentlemen of our trade."

Gapp was among those who distinguished the Ohio University School of Journalism by winning a Pulitzer Prize in 1979. During a 42-year career, he worked at two other newspapers, but it was as architecture critic for the *Tribune* that he attracted the greatest attention.

"By studious and elegant effort, he made architectural criticism an important factor in Chicago newspaper journalism," Franz Schulze, professor of art at Lake Forest College and a widely published critic of art and architecture, said in the *Tribune.*

Gapp was noted in Chicago as being a tell-it-like-it-is journalist. This made him a force in the city he characterized both as "a sprawling, muscular, free-wheeling, big-spending, bragging, bustling, exciting, go-to-hell town" and as "the last of the great American cities, a city of great elegance and great charm," the *Tribune* said.

The praise of Gapp's work had not diminished 20 years after his death when the Urban Communication Foundation honored him during the 2012 convention of the Education in Journalism and Mass Communication in Chicago.

Gapp posthumously was awarded the Lifetime Achievement Award from the foundation for architectural criticism. During the program, Gary Gumpert, foundation president, praised Gapp as part of a unique group that provides a remarkable path of both journalistic and literary excellence.

"Who speaks for the city?" Gumpert asked. "It takes a special vision—a unique human who understands the interface of motives, structure, and community."

Gapp's acceptance of that challenge provided the basis for his Pulitzer for a series of 1978 columns that took readers on a newspaper tour of the city's 46 official landmarks and historic sites. The *Tribune* praised Gapp's work for its demonstration of "an abiding concern for the city's environmental destiny" and "even handed, reasoned judgments with a style that's selectively scalding, often witty, always incisive, and never excessively technical."

Born in Cleveland, he worked following graduation for *The Columbus Dispatch* for six years and for the *Chicago Daily News,* where he was a reporter, feature editor, and editorial writer for 10 years. He also worked as an account executive for a Chicago public relations firm and directed the Urban Journalism Fellowship Program at the University of Chicago. He served terms as executive director of the Chicago chapter and the Illinois Council of the American Institute of Architects.

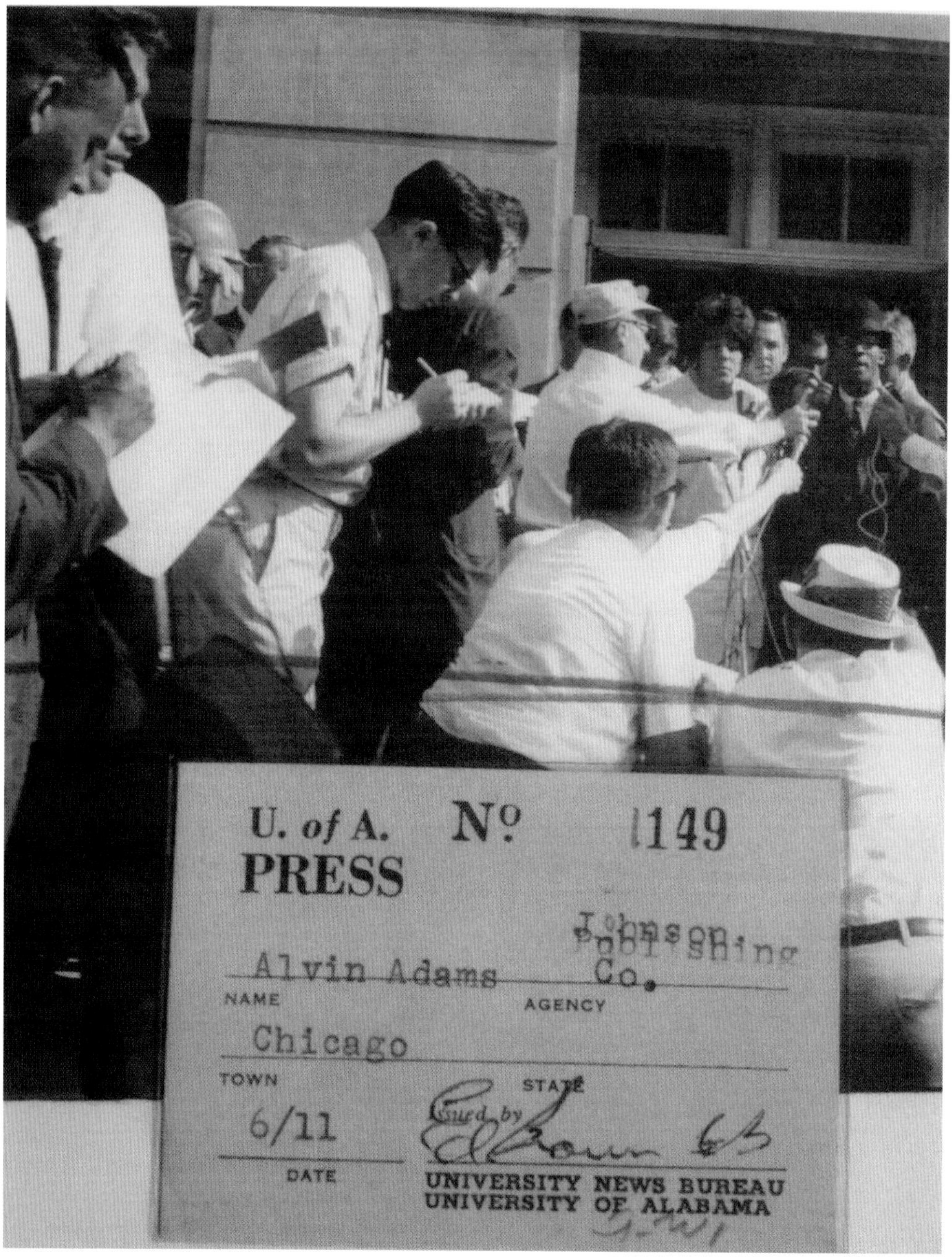

The press pass used by Alvin Adams when he covered the historic June 11, 1963, standoff at the University of Alabama between the U.S. government and Alabama Governor George Wallace. In the photo, Adams is on the far left taking notes. On the right are Vivian Malone Jones and James Hood, the first African American students to register at the university. *(Photo provided by Ada Woodson Adams)*

Alvin Adams. *(Photo provided by Ada Woodson Adams)*

AN AFRICAN AMERICAN JOURNALIST DURING THE CIVIL RIGHTS ERA

By Robert Stewart

Alvin Adams, one of the first African American recipients of the BSJ, graduated from Ohio University in 1959. He had a distinguished career during the civil rights era in print journalism and public relations with the UAW and the Illinois Power Company. The comments in this story are excerpts of an interview with his wife, Ada Woodson Adams, conducted by Robert Stewart. The comments have been edited slightly. The full interview is available at http://bit.ly/1TxyF6Y.

How did college come about?

"Al always wanted to go to college. His father died when he was a baby. And his mother was working very hard not only to raise her two kids but also her siblings because, being the oldest in the family, Al's mother took on the responsibility of raising her younger brothers and sisters. So Al was just planning on graduating from high school and getting a job, and maybe later on figure out some way to go to college.

"But he had a teacher in his high school, sophomore to junior year, who took an interest in him and saw that he had an ability that needed to be nurtured. Her name was Bonnie Kindle, and Bonnie Kindle told Al that she was going to take him to OU and introduce him to Professor [L.J.] Hortin and see about getting him enrolled at Ohio University. She did that. She took him to a meeting at OU and she walked up to Professor Hortin and said, 'Professor Hortin, see this young man right here? He's coming to OU. I want you to take care of him.' And so, that's how he got to OU."

What was it like to be an African American student at Ohio University from your perspective and what you know about Al's perspective?

"Al was told that he was going to be graded harder than anyone else because life out there in the world was going to treat him differently. So, in a way, the professor was preparing him for the outside world but also giving him a harder time to achieve greatness while on campus. But it made him more attuned to what he would have to do once he left the university. Al's biggest challenge was to meet the criteria of the professors and to get good grades. Mostly, his grades were probably B's and C's but he was more of an A–B student in my judgment."

What was it like for you two after graduation?

"Al graduated in '59 and applied for [journalism] work around this area—Athens County, Columbus, anywhere in Ohio. But they weren't hiring blacks at the time. Finally, *The Chicago Defender* sent him a note to come for an interview. He started working for *The Chicago Defender* in 1960, and he worked there until 1961. In 1961, he was hired by Johnson Publishing Company, and he started working for *Jet* magazine. I graduated in 1961 and began working in Chicago as a teacher. Our life was steady, non-eventful. Just struggling to make ends meet as a young married couple with new jobs.

"Then Al started covering the civil rights movement, and that's when our life really started to change because then is when we really became more aware of what the southern life was like. He was able to see firsthand what was happening, get to know the people at that time. Eventually he got so moved by what was happening he thought he wanted to be more of a part of the movement other than just reporting what was happening. And I kept saying to him that I want to be there too. So we decided to take a leave of absence from our jobs. We went to Tennessee and eventually to Georgia and Mississippi.

"The year was 1964. Al took part in the Freedom Summer, but I did not. I left the movement in April of '64. Al took a year and three months off from his work. But they kept him on the payroll and, after about six months, they gave him a part-time job of sending stories and pictures back to *Jet*. He was like a consultant. He actually couldn't get involved in the civil rights movement as a reporter, but by taking a leave of absence, he could become actively involved and picket and help people register to vote.

"Many times the police officers would ask, 'What are you? Are you black or are you white?' At one point we were in a car, and we were stopped. There was a white woman in the backseat of the car, and the officers asked her to get out of the car. Fortunately for us, they let us go. I don't know why they did because, as you know, black and whites often get killed for being together."

What do you recall about Al and what he remembered about interviewing Martin Luther King Jr. or Malcolm X or any of the other civil rights leaders?

"He interviewed Dr. Martin Luther King Jr. several times, including after Dr. King got the Nobel Peace Prize. One time the King organization asked Al to work for them, but he chose not to. Malcolm X and Al had pretty good rapport. They communicated back and forth. Malcolm X mentioned Al in one of his books, and Al also had a letter signed by Malcolm X complimenting him on a story. Dr. King and Malcolm X were sort of like 'good cop, bad cop.' Martin Luther King was the good guy, and Malcolm X was sort of seen as the bad. But they both had one objective: change.

"Today, things have changed. They haven't changed enough, and there is still room for change. I think racism is still here in America, and I still think we have a ways to go."

What role do you think the media play in bringing about change?

"The change would not have happened had it not been for print media. Change would not have happened had it not been for television. Because it took the word getting out to the people about what was happening in the South long before the civil rights movement. There were other Rosa Parks before Rosa Parks who sat on the bus and wouldn't get up. There were other people who were involved in bringing about change. But because in the media, journalists got the news out to the world, and it brought about change. And I think we still need this.

"We are in the digitized age right now, and so much of our news is going to be lost because it's not in hard copy. You write an email to somebody, and they put it in the trash. All of the letters that Al got from other people are an important part of our history, an important part of the fabric that makes up who we are. They aren't going to be lost if people save them. People can throw letters away too, but it's so much easier to throw emails away. We need to have our books and our papers."

Why did Al decide to stop being a traditional journalist and switch gears?

"For him, I believe it was money, because he always liked to write. When he started out, he was making $20 a week, back in the '50s and '60s when we got married, probably bringing home less than $5,000 a year. Even working at *Jet* magazine, the pay was good but it wasn't good enough to raise a family. So that's when he decided to move into PR. Even in PR he still was writing, but it was a different type of writing. I think I discovered maybe two or three books that he had started. One was going to be a novel, and one was going to be a sort of biography. He did write one book. Well, actually, he put together two that he had more or less finished. One is in print, and one is not in print."

Why did his high school classmates like him so much?

"You know how some people have a way of making you feel important? Well, Al had that way of listening and making you feel important. He would write about people. Even if a kid was a bully, Al would write about it in such a way that it would come across being positive. Al wrote about people who touched him, and his classmates were one such group. I think he wrote a poem for everyone in his class. And he would, out of the clear blue sky, one day hand somebody a poem that he had written about them. I think that kind of endeared him to them."

THE MAN WHO MADE MAYBERRY

By Jack G. Ellis

One of Ohio University's most devoted graduates stands tall among the most successful talent managers in the entertainment industry, directing and managing the careers of such notables as Andy Griffith, Jim Nabors, Jerry Van Dyke, and Frankie Avalon.

Richard O. Linke (BSJ '41) has always stated that his matriculation to Ohio University and Athens, Ohio, from his hometown of Summit, New Jersey, in fall 1937, was an early defining point in his life and one of the best decisions he ever made. Linke's journalism education, his friendship with students, faculty, and staff, and his Sigma Chi fraternity were the basis for many lifelong relationships.

Together, they were the foundation for his remarkable career in the entertainment business, including successful and top-rated television series and record sales for many noted vocalists, and for his success in career direction and management of entertainment personalities. He has been called

"The Man Who Made Mayberry," a reference to the setting of CBS's very popular *The Andy Griffith Show.*

How did it all begin?

When Linke was in high school, he already knew he wanted to be involved in the entertainment business. Following his graduation from Ohio University with his degree in journalism (emphasis in public relations), he returned to New York City, where he began his career with The Associated Press, starting as a file clerk. After two years with the AP and learning how to make contacts, a Linke trademark throughout his career, he joined the respected public relations firm Earle Ferris & Co., where he handled publicity for 40 radio stations.

He soon moved up the ladder to a major advertising agency, Newell-Emmett Co., where one of his accounts was a new show called *The Chesterfield Supper Club,* starring a young singer named Perry Como. That also began a friendship that lasted until Como's death in 2001. Linke's mentor, PR legend Michael Nidorf, told him in 1947 that he should be in the record business, which led Linke to a newly formed company, Capitol Records, working with recording artists such as Nat King Cole, Mel Torme, Peggy Lee, and bandleader Stan Kenton.

Mentor for entertainment greats

A business decline in 1949 led to his dismissal from Capitol, but as one door closes, another opens, the next with fellow Ohio University alumnus and prominent bandleader Sammy Kaye. After a successful stint with Kaye, Linke formed his own company, Richard O. Linke Publicity, and his first two clients were young singers Doris Day and Gordon MacRae. This success led to a call again from Capitol Records, which rehired him, this time as national promotion manager.

In 1953, while at Capitol, Linke remembered hearing about a young high school music teacher in North Carolina who was entertaining on weekends and recently had cut a record titled "What It Was, Was Football" for a regional record producer. Linke met Andy Griffith, bought the record rights for $10,000, and signed Griffith with Capitol Records. The record became a national hit for Griffith and Capitol. Linke began personally managing Griffith, getting him exposure in New York with shows such as *The Ed Sullivan Show* and doing club appearances, all the while refining and developing Griffith's skills and nightclub act.

Linke accepted a new position with Columbia Records as national singles sales manager, and there he became friends with songsters such as Rosemary Clooney, Jerry Vale, and Tony Bennett, who remained good friends throughout their lives. Bennett, also known as an artist, visited Dick at his home in Hawaii, presenting him with a gift of one of his esteemed paintings, in acknowledgment of their long friendship.

When, in 1957, Linke left Columbia to focus on his company, Richard O. Linke and Associates, he devoted full time to managing Griffith. Two years later, TV producer Sheldon Leonard called Linke with an idea for a new TV series starring Andy as a small-town sheriff. Linke and Griffith, along with their families, moved to the West Coast and Hollywood and, in 1960, began filming this new series called *The Andy Griffith Show.*

The man who made Mayberry

With the decade-long run and success of the series, Linke began building his enterprise of clients, which included Griffith, Jim Nabors, Bill Bixby, Jerry Van Dyke, Ken Berry, Forrest Tucker, Larry Hovis, Maggie Peterson, Frankie Avalon, Bobby Vinton, Ronnie Schell, and others. Linke's technique was to get each of these new faces in substantial roles within his established series, then launch them into their own starring roles elsewhere. Throughout the 1960s and early '70s, he was arguably the "hottest" manager in Hollywood as well as part owner of four of the top television shows of that era: *The Andy Griffith Show, Gomer Pyle, U.S.M.C., Mayberry R.F.D.,* and *The Jim Nabors Hour.*

After semiretiring from the business, Dick and his wife, Bettina, moved to Athens, where he became an adjunct professor with the Ohio University School of Journalism, teaching an upper-level course, Entertainment Public Relations. While in Athens, in 1995 Bettina also earned her BSJ, joining Linke's daughter, Nanci, who received her BFA from Ohio University in 1971, as alumnae.

Linke became a trustee of The Ohio University Foundation and established the Richard O. Linke Scholarship at the J-School. The Linke award provides the largest monetary scholarship given annually to an exceptional rising senior student majoring in journalism.

I know firsthand the influence of Richard O. Linke, as it was Linke who recommended that then-President Vernon R. Alden "take a look at a young man" in Los Angeles as a candidate for the vacant position of executive director of The Ohio University Alumni Association. Through Linke's introduction, my family and I moved to Athens in 1967, and I began a career with Ohio University that spanned 30 full-time employment years, 12 years in a consulting capacity, and a continuing interest in university events while in total retirement.

Until he passed away in 2016 at the age of 98, Linke lived with Bettina on the Big Island of Hawaii and continued to keep in touch with his many entertainment friends and his connections at Ohio University.

LINKE SCHOLARSHIP LED TO 40-YEAR CAREER

On a recent visit to Ohio University, a must stop for Jean Gianfagna (BSJ '76) was at the Richard O. Linke Office in Scripps Hall, a facility designed to pay tribute to Linke that includes photos of some of his more prominent clients and the furniture he used during his career as a television manager.

She wanted to add her personal tribute and her thanks to the highly successful OU graduate.

"I am eternally grateful to Dick Linke for helping me pay my college tuition," she said. "He helped start me on a very successful 40-year career in advertising."

In 1975, Gianfagna (then Jean Merritt) received the Linke Scholarship, one of the largest in the school. That helped propel her to selection as the school's 1976 Outstanding Journalism Graduate.

Gianfagna founded Gianfagna Strategic Marketing Inc., a marketing strategy and consulting firm in Cleveland, in 1992 after holding high-level advertising and marketing management positions in Washington, D.C.

Among her awards for marketing achievement and entrepreneurial success are a lifetime achievement award from the Direct Marketing Association of Washington and an Enterprising Woman of the Year Award from *Enterprising Women* magazine. On campus, she also had been awarded a Sears Congressional Internship and was selected to attend the Direct Marketing Association's Senior Collegiate Institute. She served as managing editor of the OU yearbook (then called "Spectrum Green").

–Ralph Izard

Jean (Merritt) Gianfagna offers thanks to Richard O. Linke. *(Photo by John Kiesewetter)*

THE SAGA OF SONNY LINKE

The following are excerpts from an interview with Richard O. Linke (BSJ '41) by Director Robert Stewart for the School of Journalism website. The interview was uploaded on April 25, 2011, and may be accessed at www.youtube.com/watch?v=BYNo9WVECeM &sns=em.

THE SUMMER BEFORE I graduated, two buddies of mine from Summit [High School in New Jersey] came over to see me. They had gone to Ohio University for one year, and they were going back. They brought a brochure. I was interested in journalism so I looked at it. This school was supposed to have, even then, a good school of journalism. I didn't even tell my folks. It sort of whetted my appetite. And I didn't think I could get in because I didn't have the credentials.

So there was a formal application. I filled it out and sent it in. Lo and behold, I got a letter back from the admissions office from Athens, Ohio, Ohio U, that they would accept me conditionally. I had never heard of that before.

I got to Athens at about 5:30 in the morning. I didn't know anything. Nothing. Luckily there were some Delts with an automobile at the station. At least, I was smart enough to say, "Can you give me a ride uptown?"

Then I start walking around looking. And the next day we met at Memorial Auditorium. I had a test they give for IQ. Then the signing-in process, registering, was in the men's gym. A lot of chaos. And what the hell do I know? What the hell would I be taking?—English, algebra. Zoology was my science. I registered, and I started in, and there's no way that I could pass the course in zoology. Absolutely lost. The first year was tough. I thought I'd never see a C or a B.

We went home the first Christmas, and I remember my mother was in bed resting, and I went in and actually cried and I said, "Look, I can't make this, Mom. I can't make it. I'm going to drop out, and I'm gonna go over to the stock market, and I know I would get a job there." She said, "Don't do that, Dick"—well, she called me Sonny. I was called Sonny in high school. I should have kept it; I would have made a fortune after the Godfather pictures, Sonny Linke.

She said, "I'll make a deal with you. You stay the rest of this year, until June. Then if you feel this way, call us at home and everything, move in with us." So, reluctantly, I said OK. I went back the next semester. I started zoology. I took geology, studied rock formations. I took algebra and passed it. I thought I was going to go right down the drain with geometry. Well, I don't know how I lasted, trust me.

After my sophomore year, don't ask me what happened. Something happened. A transformation. I don't know if it was maturity, or what. I paid more attention. I caught on. I started doing well in class. I was big in the fraternity. So I guess I have to thank Ohio University and the faculty a lot for hanging in with me.

And to end up this sad saga, on June 9, 1941, I received my bachelor of science in journalism.

[After graduation] we're all getting in the car, and the awful feeling [hit me]. You don't want to go. I wanted to stay. Get a job in Athens, I don't know what I would do. Columbus, it was an empty, empty, empty road up there. Well, you can only take it so much, and I broke down and cried. But when we got on the road toward Columbus, I had simmered down. I got control of myself and off to the races.

[If I were graduation speaker . . .] I would stand up there and say, "You know what? You finished four years. You should be proud. You're graduating from one of the greatest educational institutions in America: Ohio University, Athens, Ohio. Now you've had four great years, we call them four years of heaven, and you're going out, and please don't forget Ohio University. Sign up as alum right away. Don't wait. Come back. See your professors. They'd like to see you."

That's what I did. Did you know that I made 55 homecomings? And I got better and better and better. I don't know what you would call me academically, but I did make it.

–Richard O. Linke, interviewed by Robert Stewart

Mayberry's Richard O. Linke and Andy Griffith. *(E.W. Scripps School of Journalism photo provided by Richard O. Linke)*

THE GRAMMY MAN

By Isaac Noland

Ken Ehrlich has experienced some of the music industry's finest moments, and he knows most of the biggest stars, but it was a special time when he returned to Athens on March 14, 2016, for his induction into Scripps College's Ohio Communication Hall of Fame.

It had been more than 40 years since he and his wife, Harriet, last set foot in Athens and more than 50 years since he received the BSJ in 1964. "A lot of memories come rushing back," Ehrlich said over lunch with a group of students. "I won't remember what we had for lunch, but I remember everything from that year."

His time at OU was a memorable era for the nation, as well. During his last years there, President John F. Kennedy was assassinated, and the Beatles gave their first U.S. performance on *The Ed Sullivan Show.* His freshman year roommates in Gamertsfelder Hall were an American ROTC cadet and a Vietnamese student whose father was part of South Vietnam President Diem's government.

Little did he know that his career—highlighted by more than three decades of producing Grammy and Emmy Award ceremonies—eventually would harken back to those historic days at OU.

Originally interested in being a sports writer, Ehrlich was warned by his mother that he wouldn't make a living focusing on that path unless he became "one of the greats." He remembers it now as a surprisingly prescient estimation of the turmoil print journalism would eventually go through.

After graduation Ehrlich moved to Chicago and worked in public relations for years, although in retrospect he doesn't think he was particularly good at it. In 1974 Ken and Harriet were about to move back to Athens, where he had accepted a job in what was then the Office of Development,

Ken Ehrlich with Bruce Springsteen and Aretha Franklin. *(Photo provided by Ken Ehrlich)*

when a last-minute going-away lunch turned into a surprise job offer. He was whisked back to the Chicago PBS station, where he became a producer, creating *Made in Chicago,* which later would become *Soundstage.*

Ehrlich had found his calling. "It was more about keeping an eye open," he said. "When opportunity comes along, recognize it."

A few years later Ken and Harriet moved to Los Angeles, and by 1980 he was producing the Grammy Awards telecasts for CBS. He is now most often described as the man who created "Grammy moments," those surprising, energizing, and captivating spectacles. Often-cited examples include the duets between Elton John and Eminem, Tina Turner and Beyoncé, or a bald Melissa Etheridge performing a Janis Joplin tribute following her chemotherapy for breast cancer.

After decades with the Grammys—including the Recording Academy's President's Award in 2010—it became apparent that some of Ehrlich's most memorable professional experiences were inspired during his time at Ohio University.

Ken Ehrlich with Paul McCartney.
(Photo courtesy Kevin Mazur, WireImage)

"The Beatles were my idols, one of the reasons I wanted to do what I did," he said. So it was fitting that he produced the 50th anniversary special "The Night that Changed America: A Grammy Salute to the Beatles."

But until the final planning stages, the surviving Beatles were not fully on-board. "All I wanted was for them to perform," Ehrlich said. "They were teasing me, not committing."

Then he got a call from Paul Mc-Cartney, who said the group would play and asked him what their set should be.

"Now a Beatle is calling me and asking me what he should play on my TV show," Ehrlich said, thinking back to when he watched that fateful *Ed Sullivan Show* on TV in his landlady's parlor in Athens.

Ehrlich's professional life is punctuated with famous names and legendary performers. Some productions are celebratory, others somber, such as the July 4, 1987, "Welcome Home" show for Vietnam veterans in Washington, D.C. He invited renowned guitarist and singer John Fogerty, who was happy to perform. After rehearsing his solo work, Fogerty realized how important his Creedence Clearwater Revival songs were for many of the veterans present. He ended up launching into "Born on the Bayou" and performed CCR favorites to an exuberant, emotional crowd of veterans.

The Vietnam Veterans Memorial stood nearby, erected five years earlier and designed by young artist Maya Lin from Athens, Ohio. Ken's old ROTC roommate from OU, Gary Shy, was one of the names on that wall.

"Our pop culture is music, literature, film, art," Ehrlich said. "This is what peppers our lives."

In a congratulatory video for the hall of fame induction ceremony, CBS executive Jack Sussman described one of Ehrlich's quirks: When something goes right, when one of those "Grammy moments" goes off, he rolls up his script, smashes it down, and yells, "Go Bobcats!"

Most of Ehrlich's favorite places at OU are now long gone. He was introduced to his wife while he played piano at The Lantern (currently the site of a clothing store next door to what was then the Varsity Theater, now a Chipotle restaurant). He remembers Club 33 and pizza places such as Angelo's, Campus Pizza, and The Spot. An empty patch of grass stands where his fraternity house used to be.

Despite the past, Ehrlich made it clear that his acceptance speech at the induction ceremony was for the present students of OU. "What I have to say is really about them," he said during the speech. "Life started for me when I got here in September 1960."

His final remarks addressed questions that eager students ask him, such as "How to get started?" or "What advice do you have?"

"I tell them, I don't know," he said. "There are no rules. Life happens. All we have to do is wait for the right train. Even if we take the wrong one, all we have to do is wait for the next station and get on another one."

ACCIDENTAL JOURNALIST

By Burton Speakman

When recounting the history of the Scripps School, it's impossible to leave out the contributions of the accidental journalist who ended up changing broadcast news.

Van Gordon Sauter (BSJ '57) came to Ohio University in 1953 with no plans to major in journalism, but after some academic struggles in math, he decided on journalism as a major. Once he made that move, Sauter showed a level of creativity that eventually led *The New York Times* to question, "Is Van Gordon Sauter a TV visionary? Or is he a destructive provocateur?"

After Sauter became president of CBS News in 1981, *The Times* reported, he made drastic changes. News budgets were cut, and a number of longtime reporters were either laid off or forced into retirement.

But perhaps his most controversial move was a change in content. Sauter was the first national TV executive to bring feature stories to a regular status on national news broadcasting. Although such emphasis is typical today, the early shift away from straight news reporting anchored mostly in New York and Washington, D.C., to more soft features angered many in the business.

"To many CBS News staffers, the changes were appalling, epitomizing the triumph of style over substance," *The Times* said. The newspaper referred to Sauter's era of running CBS News as "controversial and tumultuous."

Sauter's rise within CBS was dramatic as he moved from correspondent in Chicago to news director, then to New York to run special events for the radio division of the company, according to *People* magazine. He returned to Chicago in 1972 to be news director for the television station. He was the network's censor in 1976 and, in 1977, moved to KNXT in Los Angeles to manage the station and sent ratings skyrocketing. This was his last stop prior to taking over CBS News.

Sauter even had a role within Fox News, being appointed to lead the Fox news division in 1992. This was prior to the creation of the Fox News cable channel in 1996. While Sauter did not ever run the conservatively focused cable channel, he did lament the liberal bias at his former employer, CBS News.

In a January 13, 2005, op-ed for the *Los Angeles Times,* Sauter wrote about CBS News: "I stopped watching it some time ago. The unremitting liberal orientation finally became too much for me. I still check in, but less and less frequently. I increasingly drift to NBC News and Fox and MSNBC."

Van Gordon Sauter chats with Director Cortland Anderson during a visit to the Ohio University campus. *(Photo courtesy of the Ohio University Archives, Mahn Center for Archives and Special Collections)*

Fox tasked Sauter with the creation of a nightly broadcast news schedule, something that eventually was given up as the company shifted focus to its national cable news network.

Criticism of public broadcasting

Sauter created further controversy in his professional career by criticizing public broadcasting. He stated that stations that received government funding were doomed in the long term and that they should move away from taking funds from the Corporation for Public Broadcasting.

These comments were made when Sauter worked as general manager of KVIE, the PBS station in Sacramento, California. He further suggested that PBS could become more commercial, a statement that many still consider heresy.

Despite the opinions of others, Sauter said he never thought about his ideas for CBS or public broadcasting as being risky or controversial. He just believed they were what needed to be done. They were changes he felt were necessary for the changing media landscape.

These days, he remains an avid consumer of news, reading two to three newspapers a day and watching Fox News, CNN, and MSNBC. With the Internet and 24-hour news networks, he said, it's easy to get the news without having to follow the network schedule.

"I don't watch the broadcast news unless they have something special that I can't get anywhere else," he said.

Sauter's time in Athens foretold his willingness to go against the grain.

At Ohio University, he showed a gift for pushing buttons and going against the traditional. He did work at *The Post,* but he and some other student friends revived a college humor publication called *The Green Goat* that sometimes put him on the wrong side of the university's leaders.

He and his fellow publishers kept *The Green Goat* off campus to avoid being removed from the university.

"We had our office above a local bar," he said. The staff would run up a tab each month on food and beer and then give advertising to the bar owner to pay off the debt.

"It was a good life, but I can't remember what happened [to *The Green Goat*] after I graduated," he said.

After graduation, it was some time before Sauter moved into television. He even spent a year in advertising working in the days of the Mad Men at McCann Erickson Worldwide.

"I took on the projects that no one else wanted to do," he said. This meant he spent a lot of time working with television advertising, which was his first exposure to broadcast.

First in print, then to broadcasting

Sauter earned a master's degree from the University of Missouri in 1959 before starting a print career with *South Coast Today,* the newspaper in New Bedford, Massachusetts. He followed with a stint at the *Detroit Free Press,* and finally went to the *Chicago Daily News,* which has since closed, before leaving print. "I did enjoy print, but I was not a good reporter," he said, explaining that his writing was greatly influenced by television even before he got into the broadcast industry.

"I was always fascinated with TV," Sauter said. "I always tried to bring visual elements to my print stories." The power of images was cemented in his mind on a trip to Mississippi, where he had been sent to cover the kidnapping and murder of civil rights workers.

"There was this old black man who was in a boat slowly dragging a river to look for the bodies of those kids," Sauter said. "I looked down and thought that would be a great story. Then I looked at the bank and saw a TV crew down there filming."

Television has the ability, by its nature, to capture stories visually and tell them in a way that is hard for print to match, he said. Television news has a cinematic quality.

Sauter's broadcast career started in 1968 when he was hired by CBS-owned WBBM radio in Chicago, one of the nation's first all-news stations. He started as a correspondent and eventually was promoted to news director. From there he was promoted by CBS Radio to run special events for the network's news operation in New York.

His first job in television was in 1972 when he was named news director at WBBM-TV. After that job, he spent time as the CBS censor and at KNXT in Los Angeles, where he gained a reputation as a problem solver for the network and was known for being eccentric.

"While running KNXT, he wore the rags of a beach bum to the office, lived on a 45-foot cabin cruiser, commuted to work in a much-dented Jeep, and referred to himself as Maximum Leader," a *People* magazine profile noted.

Throughout his career, Sauter's attitude toward journalism may be summed up through the idea of telling stories well. No matter what the form of the story, the audience needs to be able to "feel like they are in that spot," he said.

PEER PRESSURE

In my days there, the School of Journalism was filled with characters and amiable cliques. Mine was dominated by kids from Cleveland and New York City. Brash. Opinionated. Aspiring wits, arguing over books and movies, newspapers, and magazines. We constituted a floating, and at times fatuous, city room. And our place of convening was the OU *Post*.

Though still new to journalism and its ethos, I even wrote a regular, presumably jaunty, column for *The Post*. Great fun, but hard and time-consuming work. And one time on deadline I took a shortcut. I lifted what I recall to be an idea or riff from a vaguely popular syndicated columnist.

It was, if memory serves me correctly, low-grade plagiarism. Somewhat defensible. Harmless. But insufferable and very bad form. Far too close to a firing event.

My little clique from the school swung into action. They—guys with names like Tavcar and Bowers and Bennett—conducted what I think the 12-step programs call an intervention.

You can't do this, they warned me. You will stunt your career. Blight the newspaper. Embarrass the school. Pay attention. Or find new friends. And a new career. The message was clear and compelling.

The experience was so emblematic of the journalism school. It forcefully advocated good journalism. And the students embraced it. And for me, a bumbling newcomer, they enforced it. Thank goodness I failed statistics and accounting and had to leave the Business School. My move to journalism was among the best things that ever happened to me.

–Van Gordon Sauter

References made are to Larry Tavcar (BSJ '58), Frank Bowers (BSJ '57), and Saul Bennett (BSJ '57).

CHAMPION OF THE MIDDLE CLASS

By John Kiesewetter

DOZENS OF OHIO UNIVERSITY journalism majors spent parts of their careers in the nation's capitol, but only one was sent there by voters.

Don J. Pease, a 1953 graduate and former editor of *The Post,* was elected to serve in the U.S. House of Representatives from Ohio's 13th District in 1976. The Democrat served eight terms through 1992. The former editor and copublisher of the weekly *The Oberlin News-Tribune* previously had served on the Oberlin City Council, in the Ohio House of Representatives (1969–75), and in the Ohio Senate (1965–67; 1975–77).

"Congressman Don Pease represented the very best Ohio has to offer—hard work, dedication and a focus on helping the American worker," said U.S. Senator Sherrod Brown (D-Ohio).

Pease, a Toledo native, started his journalism career in Oberlin after earning a master's degree in government from Ohio University; completing graduate work as a Fulbright Scholar at King's College at Durham University in northern England; and serving two years in the U.S. Army (1955–57).

With his experience as *Post* editor in 1951–52, Pease "could have gone almost anywhere," said classmate and long-time friend Dru Riley Evarts. He "specifically chose to go to the weekly paper in Oberlin in order to groom himself for Congress. How about that! Is that forward-thinking or not? And it worked!"

Human rights activist

In his first term, as a member of the Foreign Affairs Committee, Pease earned a reputation as a strong human rights activist by sponsoring and rallying support for legislation banning U.S. coffee imports from Uganda in protest against Idi Amin's genocidal regime.

Pease was appointed in 1981 to the powerful House Ways and Means Committee, where he distinguished himself as an opponent of President Ronald Reagan's "Reaganomics" by seeking lower tax rates for the poor and middle class and fewer tax breaks for the wealthy. In the federal budget debate of 1990, he authored a compromise limiting tax deductions for individuals making more than $100,000, which became known as the "Pease Plan." *The New York Times* praised Pease as one of the lawmakers who "broke the budget deadlock."

His journalism background was evident in the day-to-day business of the U.S. House of Representatives. He warmly supported open "sunshine" government rules and consistently opposed closed mark-up sessions, according to his Oberlin College Archives biography. His integrity was acknowledged by *U.S. News and World Report,* which called him one of the "straightest arrows" in Congress in 1989.

"Don's friendliness and his humor, his keen mind and ability with words, and the integrity with which he approached each given task were distinguishing characteristics wherever he was and whatever he did," said a 2002 tribute in the *Congressional Record* written by Edward F. Weber, his classmate at Jesup W. Scott High School in Toledo and former House colleague. Weber also noted that Pease forfeited his term as Scott High School senior class president in favor of being editor of the high school paper because of a rule that prohibited one person from holding two major titles.

Advocate for the Cleveland area

"He was a strong advocate for the Cleveland area and a champion of the middle class," said Brown, who succeeded Pease as the 13th District representative (1993–2007) before being elected to the U.S. Senate. "His long career in public service was well spent in pursuit of policies to protect American workers from unfair trade and to reform our tax code."

After retiring from Congress in 1992, he returned home to teach politics at Oberlin College. But he wasn't finished with government service. President Bill Clinton in 1993 appointed Pease to the Amtrak board of directors. He served five years.

Pease died in Oberlin on July 28, 2002, two months before his 71st birthday. In October that year, the Federal Building in Medina was renamed the Donald J. Pease Federal Building. The Oberlin City Council honored him in 2009 by naming a 3.1-mile paved bike and walking path cutting diagonally across the city as the Don J. Pease Memorial Bike Path.

"THE BEST DECISION I EVER MADE"

By Burton Speakman

The first female African American justice on the Ohio Supreme Court came to Ohio University in 1978 not sure what she was going to do when she graduated.

"I changed my major four times. I had worked for my high school newspaper and yearbook and thought that was fun," said Yvette McGee Brown (BSJ '82). "Then I moved to broadcast, was in advertising for a short time, and then decided to focus on public relations."

Her plan to become the spokesperson for a politician in Washington, D.C., changed in a moment of serendipity in a conversation with Sandra Haggerty, now professor emerita.

During an advising session, Haggerty asked McGee Brown what she wanted to do with her degree in public relations.

"I told her I loved political science and had a passion for politics," McGee Brown said. Haggerty stated that if she wanted to work in politics in D.C., then McGee Brown should go to law school.

"She told me that everyone in D.C. has a law degree," McGee Brown said. "Sandra Haggerty changed the trajectory of my life."

Important advice from her grandmother

The decision was sealed after McGee Brown had a conversation with her grandmother about Haggerty's advice. Her grandmother had grown up in the Jim Crow–era South, and while she wasn't educated, she was wise.

"She was sitting on her chair and crocheting. She listened to me and then without looking up said, 'You're going to live to be 25 years old. You might as well be 25 years old with a law degree,'" McGee Brown said.

Professionally, McGee Brown has varied experience as both a lawyer and an activist. She was a judge in the Franklin County Common Pleas Court in the Division of Domestic Relations and Juvenile Court from 1993 to 2002 and founded the Center for Child and Family Advocacy at Nationwide Children's Hospital. The center serves as a resource for victims of child abuse and family violence. She was appointed to the state's supreme court by then-Governor Ted Strickland, taking office in 2011 and serving until the end of 2012. She is now a partner in the Columbus office of the Jones Day law firm.

McGee Brown credits much of that development as a leader to the confidence she gained during her time as a student at Ohio University.

Yvette McGee Brown.
(Photo provided by Yvette McGee Brown)

Opportunities at Ohio University

"Attending Ohio University was the best decision I ever made. I grew up there. I don't think I'd be the person I am today without it," she said. In Athens, she was able to take advantage of the opportunities at the school—serve on committees, work at *The Post,* and even host her own show, *Black Talk,* which aired on WOUB every Sunday at 10 p.m.

In addition, the education she received in the Scripps School helped to prepare her for her time both as a lawyer and as a judge, she said. It helped teach her how to dig for more information.

"I tell my clients all the time, it's not what you know happened, it's what you can prove," McGee Brown said.

Furthermore, learning about the who, what, how, when, where, and why of journalism helped with putting together legal briefs. Writing a legal brief isn't all that different from journalistic writing, she said.

The time in the Scripps School also taught her how to recognize an organized argument and, conversely, a poor argument, which has been useful to her as both a judge and an attorney.

Her goals as a politician were formed as a student in Athens as well. One political science professor stated that it would be great in politics for someone to run who didn't really care if they won, who would be able to say whatever she or he truly believed.

That advice influenced McGee Brown, she said, and she tried to live up to it any time she ran for public office.

Janet Jackson, a former Franklin County Common Pleas Court judge and Columbus city attorney, who had worked with McGee Brown in the 1980s, stated in an article with *Capital Style* magazine that she had never seen another with the potential of McGee Brown.

"I knew she was going to make such a difference in the world," Jackson said in the article. "And she has done more than I ever even imagined."

Obviously, the Scripps School was equally impressed when it awarded McGee Brown its 2017 L.J. Hortin Distinguished Alumna Award.

Ludel Sauvageot. *(Photo courtesy of the Ohio University Archives, Mahn Center for Archives and Special Collections)*

A LEADER AMONG WOMEN PROFESSIONALS

By Laura McMullen

Before she became Ludel Sauvageot, identified by the Ohio Women's Hall of Fame as "an outstanding role model for both aspiring and practicing public relations professionals everywhere," she was Ludel Boden, an Athens girl bound for Ohio University.

"I always wanted to write," she told *The Ohio Journalist* in 1988, more than 60 years after she became the first woman to graduate from the OU School of Journalism. And that's what she did, first for *The Athens Messenger.*

As a reporter, Sauvageot covered the pulse of the town—which looked a little different at the time. "Athens is a peculiar town in many respects," she wrote for the *Messenger* in 1926. "It has few alleys and but a few short dirt streets."

Among other articles, she published a series about the popularity of canning among Athens women. And she wrote about it with flourish. "A rare conserve or an unusual jelly often transposes a commonplace dessert or simple meal into an interesting and delectable feast," she wrote in 1926. She "transposed" that zeal into her series about Athens gardens in the same year: "The intoxication of beauty leaves nothing to be desired."

Intellectual curiosity

Sauvageot had a "tremendous intellectual curiosity about the world—the desire to learn and to teach," says the older of her two sons, Andre, who now lives in Reston, Virginia.

Her curiosity wasn't confined to Athens. After graduating in 1927 and leaving the *Messenger* in 1928, she bounced among newspapers in Ohio and Illinois. In the '30s, she moved to Philadelphia—and to what she's best remembered for, public relations. Her role with a Methodist mission group took the Athens native to "the slums of Cuba, as well as the hills of Appalachia," according to *Profiles of Ohio Women, 1803–2003,* by Jacqueline Jones Royster.

In Philadelphia, Ludel Boden met and married cardiologist Paul Sauvageot, and in Akron, Ohio, they began raising two boys, Andre and Jules. It was Akron, Andre says, where the young family lived when Japan bombed Pearl Harbor.

Sauvageot continued her public relations work: for the U.S. Army Air Corps during the war and for Akron General Hospital (now Akron General Medical Center) afterward, upon moving back to Ohio.

The "women's role" in hospital PR

She helped establish the first public relations department in any Akron hospital, according to Royster's book. The Ohio Women's Hall of Fame, to which she was inducted in 1990, goes a step further: "Ludel Sauvageot was a pioneer in the field of hospital public relations and forever changed the women's role in the field."

It wasn't just the idea of a woman working up the ranks in PR that was remarkable at the time. It was the fact that Sauvageot, who was a teenager before American women could vote, worked at all. When discussing her professional identity in a 1980 interview with *The Ohio Journalist,* she put it like this: "It was a struggle, because doctors' wives didn't work."

But not only did she work; she seemingly never stopped. "In the context of the time, she was a feminist in the sense that she was always leaning forward and doing things," Andre says.

After leaving the hospital in the 1950s for the International Council of Industrial Editors, Sauvageot returned to Akron General in 1967 and worked there for 10 more years, until she retired at age 70.

The retirement didn't last long. She returned to the hospital as a consultant a month later, according to Royster, and taught journalism at Kent State University.

Sauvageot taught in more ways than in a classroom throughout her more than 60-year career. She wrote four books, mentored countless young professionals, and returned to Athens several times to speak to Scripps students.

She died at age 90 in 1996, but her impact on students and journalism still live through namesake scholarships, one given in the School of Journalism and Mass Communication at Kent State University, another given by the Akron Press Club.

HE COULD BE A JERK, BUT "BOB MADE US ALL BETTER"

By Burton Speakman

Bob Tkacz, in his student days, wasn't the shining star of the Ohio University journalism program.

He was successful as a student, yes, rising to the position of managing editor at *The Post*. But Tkacz (BSJ '76) didn't leave the school with a job lined up at a major paper or with the goal of winning Pulitzer Prizes. Instead, after a couple of years at small newspapers, Tkacz left Ohio to work in Alaska covering politics and the environment. He spent most of his career as a freelance writer.

In Alaska, he truly made his mark.

He became one of the better-known and respected political writers in Alaska and was a prime example of how hard work, intelligence, and determination can result in great journalism. Tkacz died on May 27, 2014, at his office in Juneau, leaving a hole in the Alaskan press corps after covering the capital for more than three decades. He was 61.

During his time as a student, Tkacz provided hints that he might end up writing about politics and the environment, although much more of his work at the time seemed to focus on nontraditional religions such as Satanism and Wicca or even a church being put up for sale.

Only one of his *Post* stories—an article on professors protesting strip mining—focused on an environmental issue. The environment later would become a defining issue for him. As a general-assignment reporter for *The Post,* Tkacz also covered student government, court cases, and downtown events and wrote a lot of features stories.

For sale: One bullshit meter. Used multiple times daily over a span of decades. Very sensitive to even the first bit of BS. Never failed. Can purchase with a spin sensor at a discount. Price to be determined only after hours of argument. No spineless media members need to bother with an inquiry. See Bob Tkacz's ghost of reporters past for details.
(Lisa Demer, *Alaska Dispatch News*)

A passion for journalism

However, the records and notes he kept even as a student showed a talent for organization and a passion for journalism. A profile of Tkacz, published in *The Post* during his time as managing editor, showed the personality that would make him so respected in Alaska journalism circles.

The profile, while picking on Tkacz, contained some truths. It mentioned his unwillingness to take no for an answer, a trait that became legendary as part of his interviewing style.

His willingness to afflict the comfortable and comfort the afflicted appeared in articles focused on campus communists and socialists, taking on bookstores when there was a shortage of books for students, or criticizing the local rental market for students.

"Comparing the problems Athens renters face to venereal disease is not as ridiculous as it sounds," Tkacz wrote in a January 30, 1973, *Post* article.

He even managed to show the biting wit that would make him famous, notorious perhaps, among members of the Alaska press corps when writing about chess.

The opening paragraph of his January 9, 1973, article on a chess team triumph said, "At a time when financial allotments for new sports are practically non-existent, the University's newest squad, the chess team, received all the cash it asked for and skillfully used its funding to establish itself as a rising collegiate chess power in the Western Hemisphere."

A critic of government and the media

His Alaskan colleagues said Tkacz was tough and relentless and could be a jerk. "Crusty" was one of the nicer descriptions. However, they respected his tenacity in reporting and willingness to push to get answers to his questions.

"Bob Tkacz wouldn't let anyone duck the hard questions, and Alaska is a better place for it," said former House Democratic Press Secretary Mark Gnadt in an article in the *Alaska Journal of Commerce.* "Many times I would warn legislators with 'Bob won't let you get away with that answer.' Bob Tkacz was the one reporter you wanted to show up at the other guys' press conferences."

Tkacz was often a critic of the other media in Alaska and was quoted saying, "I have always had a hard time understanding the relative spinelessness of the major media in this state, and particularly the TV stations, but that's just me."

In addition to being critical, his journalistic colleagues said, he could be giving and kind and was often willing to offer his insights and knowledge from years of covering politics in the state.

One of the more infamous incidents of Tkacz's career came in 2006 when he stormed out of a press conference being held by Governor Frank Murkowski after Tkacz became upset that Murkowski twice cut off his ques-

Bob Tkacz, among the most notable of Alaska's governmental journalists, interviews state Senate President Charlie Huggins at the Capitol during the final week of the 2015 legislative session. *(Photo by Michael Penn/Juneau Empire)*

tions. The governor's office responded by refusing to send any correspondence to Tkacz for a couple of days until convinced otherwise by the rest of the capital pressroom.

After Tkacz's death, Frank Ameduri, publisher of the *Alaska Budget Report,* wrote about the legacy Tkacz left as a reporter: "The real tribute to Bob would be for each of us to step up our game a little, and try to be a little more like him," Ameduri wrote.

The greatest compliment Tkacz may have received after his passing came from Rhonda McBride, reporter for KTUU, who wrote simply that while Tkacz was hard on other reporters, "In truth, Bob made us all better."

Tkacz didn't seem to care what others thought about him or worry about his own level of fame even when he was a student. His goal was simply to write the truth, inform people, and make sure the difficult questions were not just asked, but answered.

TRIBUTES TO BOB TKACZ

Bob Tkacz was known for his reporting on maritime and fisheries issues, publishing his own newsletter, Laws for the Sea, *which he established in 1994. When Tkacz died, colleague Jennifer Canfield, now with public radio station KTOO, compiled a personal and professional tribute in what was defined as the newsletter's final issue. Here are a few excerpts from that publication.*

Christopher Clark, former reporter for KTOO, KTUU, KINY, KJNO, and the *Alaska Budget Report:* Bob's barbs were not limited to politicians. He often would mix it up with fellow reporters. We were too soft. We asked easy, no-shit-Sherlock questions. We were clueless and weak. We were superficial. . . . Hanging near his desk was a message that read, *"Writing well is the best revenge."* And the most poignant note of all, written in his own handwriting: *"Be a good person today."*

Robert Sewell, a friend in Juneau: Bob was the real deal. He was someone who lived life on his own terms. I've watched people my whole life; yet I have known very few whom I would call "self-actualized." Bob was one of those. He explored, he thought, he constructed, and in the end, he found and lived by his own gyroscope. He knew who he was, he knew what he was and what he stood for, and he accomplished that by age 61.

Mike Doogan, writer and former state representative: It was amazing—at least for me—that he covered the legislature year after year without letting anybody blow smoke up his skirt. And he didn't take any guff. I have fond memories of watching Bob sink his teeth in a governor and not let go. I believe I saw one or two actually bolt for the safety of their offices.

Gregg Erickson, Erickson and Associates and the Alaska Budget Report: Bob Tkacz believed in, and spent his professional life striving for, objectivity. More important, he knew that neutrality was not the same thing. Bob was objective, not neutral. He didn't think much of neutrality. I asked him once if he thought neutrality was a sin. He said he didn't know, but would not advise reporters who believed in heaven to expect that neutrality would help them get there.

Jesse Kiehl, city and Borough of Juneau assemblyman and legislative aide: FWIW, Bob Tkacz probably wouldn't WANT to rest in peace. I bet he's giving G-d the third degree right now.

Tim Bradner, copublisher of the Alaska Legislative Digest: Bob worked with us for years on *Legislative Digest* and he would frequently get under the skin of influential legislators. Periodically they would call us and try to get us to fire Bob, and even threatened us. My brother Mike (copublisher of the *Digest*) loved getting these calls. He would usually reply using language not appropriate here, and he would call me suggesting we give Bob a raise!

–Compiled by Jennifer Canfield

A JOURNALIST OF MANY TALENTS

By Chip Gamertsfelder

My uncle, the late John R. Whiting (BSJ '36), was born in 1914 in New York City. He spent his early years living in a small village north of the city near the Hudson River and in the vicinity of the Appalachian Trail. Large rock formations dominated the area, and he envisaged those rocks as sailing ships. He was the helmsman in his young make-believe world. His early imagination helped fuel what was to be part of the content of a career in journalism.

Later, other interests, including his enthusiasm for writing, editing, and photography, were strengthened because his grandfather had a printing business. As my uncle explained in his notes about his life, "almost everything in the shop would have been a familiar sight to Gutenberg: a metal holder called a stick in which hand-set type was composed, wooden cases to hold the type, printers ink, rollers, presses." The Red Diamond Press had a typewriter, and this typewriter formed the foundation for my uncle's interest in journalism.

He found a deep satisfaction in interviewing his grandfather about his life with the Second Maine Cavalry during the Civil War. Whiting had also been taking photographs at this time and bought a Corona portable typewriter. His first publication was a series of feature articles for the ship newspaper of the Clyde Line's SS *Seminole,* going down the East Coast. The series was called "Round the Boat with Randolph" because Randolph was my uncle's middle name. "I was in the world of reporters, city editors, writers of books, printing presses," my uncle proclaimed, "and eventually in the world of newsreels, news magazines, press photographers, picture magazines, great photographers, and television."

When he reached college age, his tendencies toward meticulous research led him to the decision to enroll in the respected journalism program at Ohio

University. The Depression was in full swing in the early 1930s when my uncle boarded a train that, after a stop in Washington, D.C., brought him to the small town of Athens, Ohio.

Whiting's years of college study were fulfilling in many ways. He not only learned the profession of journalism from professors such as his teacher and friend George Starr Lasher; he also met Helen Gamertsfelder, whom he dated and later married in the backyard of her home on Morris Avenue in Athens. My grandfather, Dean Walter S. Gamertsfelder, later to become the 13th president of Ohio University, performed the service.

Among his favorite activities at OU was the English Club, which was an honor to him because Dean Edwin Watts Chubb conducted the meetings every fourth Tuesday in the living room of his home.

Worked for campus and local media

As many students have done in Athens, Whiting took advantage of opportunities to use his interviewing and writing skills. He worked for both *The Athens Messenger* and the Ohio University campus newspaper, then called *The Green & White.* Among his most memorable assignments was an interview of the well-known poet and newspaperman Carl Sandburg, who had come to the university to speak at Memorial Auditorium as part of the Lecture and Music Program. Whiting interviewed Sandburg at the Berry Hotel on Court Street.

"He mostly interviewed himself," my uncle said. After the interview for the college paper, Whiting had a front-row seat to watch Sandburg play the guitar, read poems, sing songs, and talk about *The American Songbag.* Years later, Whiting met Sandburg again in Chicago when he was assigned to do photographs of him, through the picture agency Pix, for the *New York Herald Tribune* Sunday book section.

From his early days, Whiting loved the sea and sailing and all the technical aspects of the subject. As a result, he produced books on boating, two of which were *You Can Sail* (1981) and *On Deck* (1985), the latter of which I worked with him on in the summer of 1984 after my graduation from Ohio University's Institute of Visual Communication.

John R. Whiting. *(Photo provided by Chip Gamertsfelder)*

He served as publisher of *Motor Boating and Sailing,* a Hearst magazine, and later was editor and publisher of Hearst Marine Books.

As an accomplished photographer himself, part of which was rooted in his days at Ohio University as a journalism student, Whiting was convinced that words and pictures must work together as a means of strong communication. His photojournalism book, *Photography is a Language,* was published in 1946 by Ziff Davis Publishing Company.

The one photographer my uncle spoke of most often was W. Eugene Smith, who is thought of by many as a legend in the history of photography and especially in photojournalism. As editor of *Popular Photography,* Whiting had given Smith his first assignment in the Pacific during World War II. Smith later continued to document World War II in the Pacific for *Life* magazine. My uncle remained friends with Smith for many years.

As a precursor to Ohio University's tradition of bringing top professionals to campus, Whiting teamed up with Smith again when the pair—joined by *Life* magazine picture editor Wilson Hicks—visited Ohio University by train to give a workshop to students.

He knew the celebrities

Whiting knew many of the celebrities of his time—photographers, artists, entertainers, and other known individuals, including famed actors Gary Cooper and Marlene Dietrich and producer Samuel Goldwyn. While working for *Click* magazine, he once planned a photo session with the artist Salvador Dalí. His staff went all over New York City in search of props. And as my uncle described it, the items used for the legendary artist were "a large doll with blond hair, a large wig with blond hair just like the doll's, a human skeleton, a store-window mannequin, half a dozen glass eyes, two dozen live ants, a phonograph record, ostrich feathers, two ballet dancers from the Metropolitan, and a nude model." The photo shoot was a success.

An example of the respect that Whiting earned as an editor is found in his relationship with Henri Cartier-Bresson, the French photographer well known for his worldwide documentary work in photojournalism and one of the founders of Magnum, a photographic cooperative owned by its photographers and founded in 1947. Cartier-Bresson was known for not allowing his pictures to be cropped. But as my uncle wrote on a yellow piece of note paper referring to the iconic French photographer, "He stamped all his prints 'No cropping,' but when he did a story for me [in *Science Illustrated*], he said, 'You can crop any of these.'"

Among other celebrities with whom Whiting worked or knew are artist Andy Warhol; television newsman Walter Cronkite, who used to drop by Hearst Marine Books to talk about boats; cowboy star Gene Autry; *Life* photographer Alfred Eisenstaedt; editor and writer Richard A. Wolters; photographers Andre Kertesz, Peter Barlow, Ansel Adams, and Philippe Halsman; scientist/engineer Charles Kettering; and Beaumont Newhall, once curator of photography at the Museum of Modern Art and Eastman House in Rochester.

Throughout the 1980s and '90s, I would correspond with my uncle, and for several summers spent time with him at his summer home on Block Island, Rhode Island, taking a break from my job as a photographer and photo editor of the *Kettering-Oakwood Times* in the suburbs of Dayton. I was always captivated by my uncle's long memory of his life as a journalist, photographer, and editor. Even as he grew older in retirement, he was always learning new things, working on his computer, and planning projects and books.

His achievements in journalism were extensive. He was managing editor of *Popular Photography;* had numerous articles and photographs published in *The New York Times Magazine, Harper's Magazine,* and *The Philadelphia Inquirer;* and was editor of McGraw-Hill's *Science Illustrated.* Whiting was a writer of the back page of *Life* magazine—"What's in a picture?" He was editor of *Flower Grower* magazine and *A Treasury of American Gardening,* executive vice president of Popular Science Publishing Company, publisher of *Motor Boating* and *Sailing* magazines (both published by Hearst), and editor and publisher of Hearst Marine Books. He knew a lot of people and met a lot of people, but above all he enjoyed being a journalist.

John R. Whiting died on December 16, 1998, in Chester, Connecticut.

JOURNALISM IS PERSONAL

By Michael Clay Carey

Keith Rathbun (BSJ '74) had a way of connecting with anyone he met. Which is good, because he met lots of different kinds of people.

During a news career that spanned more than three decades, he forged friendships with famous rock-and-roll musicians, Amish bishops, international journalists, and small-town newspaper editors.

Rathbun was 63 when he died on January 26, 2016, following a heart attack. In his journalistic work, as in his life, he treasured personal bonds, building relationships with the people he wrote about, with his coworkers, and with others who shared his passion for newspapers.

He was also an alumnus of and strong advocate for Ohio University and the E.W. Scripps School of Journalism, supporting the school financially, visiting journalism classes, and organizing activities for visiting international scholars.

After graduating from Ohio University in 1974 with a degree in journalism, Rathbun returned to his hometown of Cleveland, eventually becoming publisher and part owner of *Scene,* an alternative newsweekly. In Cleveland, he worked to help establish the Rock and Roll Hall of Fame, and he was an outspoken supporter of keeping the hall in the city.

In 2000, Rathbun left *Scene* to become publisher of *The Budget,* a weekly newspaper in Sugarcreek, Ohio. In Sugarcreek, a small town in the heart of Amish country, he was far more likely to cover village councils and bake sales than AC/DC or Billy Joel. But during a 2012 interview, Rathbun told me his philosophy behind producing *The Budget* was not really that different from the approach he took at *Scene.* "We published a great music newspaper and a great alternative weekly [in Cleveland]," he said. "I wasn't a huge music fan. I just find people who are passionate and let them do their jobs."

At the same time, he recognized the importance of building intimate relationships with his readers. When community journalists are engrained in the towns they cover, he told me, "your neighbors know you, and they know you care about the community." He frequently attended business association meetings and was a member of the Sugarcreek Rotary Club and the Tuscarawas County Literacy Coalition. He was instrumental in keeping Sugarcreek's annual Swiss Festival in operation during the 2010s.

"He was looked to as a pillar in the community," said Bev Keller, an editor at *The Budget.* "This community absolutely treasured him."

Rathbun became a national expert on the relationship between community newspapers and the U.S. Postal Service, advocating for publishers and editors on policy matters such as proposed reductions in mail delivery days, centralized post offices, and increased postage.

He also was an important partner in Athens of the Study of the U.S. Institute on Journalism and Media (SUSI), an annual summer program that brings media scholars to the United States. The program is funded by the

Keith Rathbun discusses his newspaper, *The Budget,* with a group of Study of the U.S. Institute–sponsored journalism scholars from around the world. *(E.W. Scripps School of Journalism photo)*

U.S. Department of State and administered by the Institute for International Journalism and the Scripps School. The program included a regular stop at *The Budget*.

When SUSI scholars would come to the newspaper, Rathbun would line up experts on Amish culture, show them around the newspaper, and arrange community dinners for them with members of the Sugarcreek Rotary Club. SUSI scholars typically left Sugarcreek on the day the newspaper was published. Rathbun always made sure the group's visit was covered on the front page of the newspaper so that the visiting scholars could take a copy with them when they left town.

"Keith's generosity went far beyond what was expected or even asked for," said Bill Reader, a Scripps professor who worked with the SUSI program. "It's that personal touch Keith brought to everything he did."

Ray Locker. *(Photo provided by Ray Locker)*

COVERING THE WHITE HOUSE

By Ray Locker

If you had asked me in 1984, when I was working on my master's degree in journalism, if I thought I would be leading the White House coverage for the nation's largest-circulation newspaper with another Ohio University grad, I would have been happy at that thought but probably wouldn't have believed you. At the time, it seemed very far away.

But as I reflect on all the 33 years since then, I realize how much my time in Athens and at OU helped mold me into the journalist I am today and how much the training still helps me do my job. I benefited from working with some of the best minds in journalism education and also spent countless hours soaking up the wisdom of Cortland Anderson, then the director of the Scripps School. As much as anything I learned in the classroom, which was a lot, it was the intangibles of being forced to be focused and organized that have stayed with me the most.

Cortland was a master of management. As his graduate assistant, I would sit in his office every day and listen to him work the phones or talk to various faculty members as they came in to see him. He could motivate, cajole, and direct people to get things done, and he seemed to know everyone. One of the best things I ever did at OU was drive guests to the school back to the airport, which gave me 90 minutes of uninterrupted time to talk to various people in journalism about their jobs, views on the business, and overall philosophies.

Beyond that, however, I use the skills I developed at OU virtually every day in my current job. I took a full load of courses each quarter, worked on Saturdays at *The Athens Messenger,* and taught a beginning reporting class. All of that happened while I was working on my thesis. That forced me to manage my time as never before, and that skill is needed more than anything while covering the White House, a demanding job that can take up all of your waking hours if you let it.

My thesis research forced me to prioritize. I wrote about the demise of the *Cleveland Press* and the failure of afternoon papers. I had to limit my writing to certain papers and places, and that's something that's essential in managing the White House or any beat. To break consequential stories that our competitors don't have, we have to pick certain aspects of the presidency and focus on them. In my work with Gregory Korte (BSJ '94, BA in Political Science '94), we specifically look at the exercises of presidential power.

By focusing on this thread of White House policy, we have been able to tap into existing flows of information that are apart from whatever the White House press office distributes. We use regularly scheduled releases of information to analyze patterns of behavior and decision-making. We can then take those analyses back to White House policy makers to get them to explain what they're doing. It puts us in control instead of making us reliant on whatever daily spin they want to dish out.

That allows us to set the agenda more than many of our competitors, who are often caught in the daily flow of the news cycle. It also allows us to generate exclusive enterprise stories that force the administration to deal with us. As a result, our access to key decision makers has increased, and our stories get better play in *USA Today* and more pickup elsewhere.

Now, with newly elected President Trump in office, those skills are in even greater demand. We need to cope with the torrential flow of information and misinformation from the White House by being smart and organized. Our experience covering previous administrations means we know where to look and then how to act quickly. We're doing that while we cope with the numerous executive orders and leaks coming from all over the administration.

The intervening 33 years since my departure from Athens has helped me get to this point, but the foundation built at OU made that possible. I learned the critical thinking needed to separate the reality from the propaganda and to better understand data to put together stories that can make a difference. Those skills are needed more than ever.

PRESIDENTIAL PRESS CONFERENCE

When President Gerald Ford gave an unusual press conference at the 1974 Society of Professional Journalists convention in Phoenix, among the questioners was Scripps School Professor Norman Dohn.

Q. Norman Dohn, Ohio University. That is where Bill Hess is a football coach, not Woody Hayes.

My question is in regard to foreign policy. Senator-elect John Glenn of Ohio and others have suggested that despite Dr. Kissinger's very fine track record, perhaps foreign policy is such a complex and delicate matter that the machinery of foreign policy ought to be spread out over a broader base. Do you have any plans to do this under your administration?

THE PRESIDENT. I have no such plans. I can't imagine someone who really is not an expert in the field of foreign policy giving advice to a man who has conducted foreign policy with great skill and great success. If you have got someone who is doing a good job, I don't understand why anyone in seriousness would advocate that he be taken off part of the job and turn it over to someone who might not do as good a job.

I respect the right of the Senator-elect to make the suggestion, but I don't think it makes very much sense.

–Contributed by Gregory Korte

SHARING JOURNALISTIC COMMITMENT

If any question dominated the 2017 White House Correspondents' Dinner, it was about what to expect in 2017. President Donald Trump's absence only made him more present, but it also provided unexpected clarity. At the end of the day, we all knew what mattered.

"The stage may look different, but the purpose is the same," said Jeff Mason, president of the White House Correspondents' Association.

The weekend was not without its glitz and glam, though. Many celebrities were not invited or chose to attend a different event. Editors from infamous publications surrounded us in black tie, feet away from striking up a conversation.

It was an honor for us to be invited to attend the dinner because the Scripps School had selected us as its inaugural recipients of White House Correspondents' Association scholarships.

The night was symbolic of the journalism industry as a whole: adversity only increases our determination. Objectivity cannot be a philosophy to only some. The WHCD casts a spotlight once a year on journalists who work every day for hours on end because the news must and will be reported.

That continued diligence applies not only to our coverage but also to our professional network. At the dinner, it didn't matter who your employer was. Journalists from dozens of publications stood together as peers and colleagues, united by a common purpose and regard for the First Amendment.

We witnessed that commitment in action, not only at the dinner but also in the White House press briefing room. E.W. Scripps school alum Gregory Korte (now of *USA Today*) arranged for a brief tour of the press room, as well as the adjoining offices. We saw reporters from the AP, *The New York Times, The Wall Street Journal,* and so many more crammed shoulder to shoulder, frantically typing up the news of the day; however, none was too busy to stop to chat with three aspiring journalists.

The three of us also had the opportunity to learn from journalists who cover the White House during a luncheon titled "The Press and the Presidency." A panel discussion held during the luncheon included journalists from publications such as *The New York Times, The Washington Post,* and Bloomberg News. The panelists discussed different topics in journalism ranging from the challenges associated with covering the White House to how to build source relations.

Ohio University recipients of the prestigious White House Correspondents' Association Scholarship earned a special treat in 2017 when they were invited to the annual White House Correspondents' Dinner in Washington. Here, the school's first recipients—from the left, Cat Hofacker, Megan Henry, and Marisa Fernandez—pose with Gregory Korte, White House correspondent for *USA Today. (Photo provided by Marisa Fernandez)*

That was the true experience—the opportunity to get a glimpse of the ranks we will join after graduation, a community that is not only tenacious and hardworking beyond belief but also incredibly supportive. From offering career advice to suggesting potential mentors, the journalists of the WHCA and the White House press pool showed us how professional competition is one of their greatest assets.

While we may write for different publications and reserve the right to protect our individual scoops, we respect each other as dedicated and talented journalists.

—Cat Hofacker, Marisa Fernandez, and Megan Henry

Lasher
Hall

Student organizations

Student organizations in the School of Journalism since the beginning have been more than mere social groups. Through them, students contribute to their education by joining together to pursue professional interests. With solid programming, they supplement and expand the content of their classroom experiences. By working together and engaging in social activities, they facilitate friendships that are long-lasting and often professionally beneficial. As a result, student organizations foster a better school in both professional and personal ways.

Facing page: Lasher Hall, home of the school, 1974–86. *(Photo by Ralph Izard)*

ADVERTISING CLUB

By Charles Borghese

For many of the students who join the E.W. Scripps School of Journalism's Advertising Club, one outcome seems inevitable: The club changes one's life. It has enhanced career paths of Bobcats since 1972, the year Professor Tom Peters established and began advising the club.

Along with speaker programs and visits to some of marketing communication's finest agencies and organizations in New York City, Chicago, and elsewhere, the OU Advertising Club focuses on the annual American Advertising Federation's National Student Advertising Competition (NSAC). This is where things really get interesting. The competition, involving a full year of preparation, is a real-world experience. Students at more than 150 universities compete to impress industry judges and multinational companies who provide a case study involving a particular marketing challenge they are facing.

This is exactly the kind of pitch students will face in their careers when they enter the very competitive industry of strategic communication. And it's an environment in which Ohio University has thrived. In 2008, under Professors Hong Cheng and Craig Davis, the club won the District 5 competition, ultimately going on to the national "shootout" for the AOL competition in Atlanta—a "shootout" the OU Ad Club won. Since then, the club has been a consistent regional winner and participant in national competitions involving clients such as the Century Council, JC Penney, and Nissan. The three appearances since 2008 set the high standard all current Ad Club members are working hard to maintain.

Students participating in the competition will tell you that it doesn't take a national victory to have a career-altering experience. Pete Costanzo (BSJ '77) had just one of those experiences.

"Little did I know at the time, but my foray into sales promotion for the Ad Club would correlate directly with my landing the national sales promotion manager position with Wear-Ever Aluminum just a few short months after graduating," said Costanzo. "Tom Peters inspired me to do a bunch of research, and I learned more about classic sales promotion techniques in order to produce and develop creative for the Ad Club. The experience became the most prominent part of 'my story' as I graduated and began a career in advertising."

The benefit didn't end there. After several months at his first job at Wear-Ever Aluminum, Costanzo recognized how frustrated his company was with its advertising efforts, He had the idea to show the organization the work he and the OU Ad Club had done for Toyota, the NSAC client during his senior year. "I folded over the cover of the pitch book and told my boss that this is the kind of work we should be doing," Costanzo said. His boss agreed. The fact that the work had been done by a group of creative and inventive Bobcats made it all the sweeter. The result was a redoubled effort that would lead to a great marketing communication plan that a young Costanzo was trusted to drive.

Costanzo is currently working at the highest level in the business. He is the managing partner at Marsh Brand Partners in Cincinnati. He also contributes to his alma mater as a member of the school's Professional Advisory Board.

Experience for a lifetime

Ellen Cox (BSJ '04) calls on her Ad Club experience every day at the Austin, Texas, digital communication agency T3. As a senior account director, she handles some of the agency's biggest accounts, such as Capital One, Chase Bank, and the Texas energy company NRG.

Cox came to the E.W. Scripps School of Journalism with a hard-news career in mind but was drawn to the problem-solving nature of strategic communication.

After a few classes, she discovered the Ad Club, and she knew she'd found her calling. But it was the NSAC competition that cemented the deal. "I was on the presentation team for the AOL pitch and was certainly nervous. We were well rehearsed. We really knew our stuff. And the campaign was amazing. But once we got to the question-and-answer portion of the competition with the judges, I learned something really important. You can never be too prepared. That day I learned what it means to think on your feet," Cox said. The answers must have struck a chord with the judges, because the OU Ad Club's campaign for AOL not only won the regionals that year but also went on to win the national competition. Cox heeds this lesson of preparedness every day of her career.

"I lead my team here at T3 the exact same way now," she said. "We know that when the presentation is over you're really on the spot."

When I came to Ohio University, I planned to be the next Jimmy Breslin, the legendary columnist at the *New York Daily News.* But once I found myself in an advertising class taught by the late Professor A.T. "Tom" Turnbull, I knew my goal was about to shift. Professor Turnbull quickly sent me to see Professor Peters, who sent me to my first Ad Club meeting that very week. The environment in the Ad Club was infectious, and as far as I was concerned, that was that.

Creativity is the key

The creativity happening at that club absolutely floored me, and I quickly learned what types of jobs in the real world this could lead to. I was hooked.

To me, it's almost as if it happened yesterday. I was one of the creative leaders my senior year. The competition client was Bugle Corn Chips. The campaign that followed is still fresh in my mind. The tagline was "Fun at First Sight, Love at First Bite." I have to say, I loved that work. I loved the teamwork, the collaboration. I was always envious of the folks who worked at *The Post.* They looked like they were having a blast. That was until I joined the Ad Club.

It would all lead to a long career, after my 1981 graduation, as a copywriter, then creative director at some of the country's best advertising agencies, like Ogilvy & Mather and DDB. Today I am back in Athens teaching strategic communications and advising the club I credit with launching my entire career, one that never felt like work.

My story, like those of Costanzo and Cox, is not unique. Students come to the Ad Club and find a creative spark that will create careers. The club opens up students to thinking strategically to solve real business problems. Former OU Ad Club members are employed throughout the industry in positions ranging from ad agency creative directors and account managers to public relations professionals working with some of the biggest clients in the country. They look back at their time pulling all-nighters with the NSAC pitch bearing down on them as the vital education they needed to make it in a business that is known to be highly competitive and a whole lot of fun.

—Faculty colleague Craig Davis contributed to this story.

ASSOCIATION FOR WOMEN IN COMMUNICATIONS

By Dru Riley Evarts

> In an era when women were still an oddity in the newsroom, we carried our typewriters across campus to class and believed in our abilities to become equal to any man in journalism. Being selected for membership in the School of Journalism's women's honorary, Theta Sigma Phi, gave the women a common professional bond. My first job after college was as a reporter on *The Columbus Dispatch*. I joined the local professional TSP chapter and attended its monthly meetings and its annual Matrix Table dinners, through which it honored community leaders and raised money for young women to study journalism.
>
> —*Rose Marie Peschan Thomas (BSJ '52)*

The present Association for Women in Communications has a long history, going back to 1909, when Theta Sigma Phi was founded as an honorary society for women studying journalism. It became the bedrock of succeeding organizations that, despite name changes, welcomed all women studying or practicing journalism.

In 1972, when many groups were changing from Greek to professional English names, Theta Sigma Phi became Women in Communications Inc., and the idea of its being an "honorary" society was dropped. In 1996, the final name change, to Association of Women in Communications (AWC), took place. The organization sought to unite students and professionals interested in all aspects of communication, including collegiate communicators, graduate student communicators, and young communicators on the student level. On the professional level, 10 more categories are listed in the 2015 brochure.

A major change with AWC became the admission of men to membership, so that gender equality became a reality, just as the Society of Professional Journalists had done by admitting women. But with all of the changes since this group was organized, it has been consistent in its belief that a student studying communication or a woman (later any person) recently graduated from a communications program can find help from any one of the professional groups to find a first job or to ease the transition from one communication career to another.

Opportunities for women

Because the school's first director, George Starr Lasher, and his fellow faculty members believed solidly in the importance of encouraging students to be active in and take advantage of the offerings of professional groups, Ohio University was among the first to form a chapter of Theta Sigma Phi. Because the group was an honorary society at the time, membership was selective and small.

By the time of Lasher's retirement, the Theta Sigma Phi chapter here was still relatively small (about 10–12 women initiated each spring from the junior class, with the entire group adding up to 20 or more). They met a few times a year but did not have fund-raising or community-involving activities or attend regional or national conventions. They had only a nodding relationship with the larger all-men's organization, Sigma Delta Chi (now the Society of Professional Journalists), and were much smaller because the school had many more men than women during those years.

When SPJ, in 1969, began to admit women students and professionals to membership, many women joined, and it was feared that this might weaken Women in Communications Inc. But WICI remained strong. It welcomed all women studying journalism (without regard to the applicant's grade-point average). They could be interested in writing, editing, public relations, advertising, broadcasting, whatever—as long as they were studying for a BSJ.

The Ohio University chapter became one of the strongest in the country, often being recognized with national awards such as best chapter, best adviser, best student officers, and so forth. The OU WICI chapter raised enough money each year to provide transportation to get members to the organization's national and regional conventions.

In addition, a group of members attended a WICI mid-February career weekend each year, sometimes with as many as 40 young women and an adviser setting off in an 8- or 9-car caravan for the eight-hour trip to Chicago. At the meeting, the North Shore and the Downtown professional chapter members provided home hospitality and a whiz-bang Friday evening reception. This was followed by an all-day Saturday session of professional seminars, more seminars mixed with sightseeing on Sunday, and an on-the-job experience Monday for each attendee. OU always had the largest group there, but the professionals of those two chapters took charge of seeing that everyone had a good look at possible future careers.

The largest ever regional convention

In 1977, the OU chapter hosted the largest ever WICI regional convention. UPI White House reporter Helen Thomas, NPR's top reporter, Susan Stamberg, and *Ms.* magazine's cofounder Pat Carbine were the three most prominent speakers, and the program also featured other female filmmakers and journalists. Continuing education (CE) credit was offered to both students and professionals, and the convention was attended by about 400 persons (both students and professionals of the region), as well as some national WICI personalities who enjoyed seeing what can be done at a medium-size university in a small town.

Nothing like this had happened in the School of Journalism before or since. At the time, the school had one VDT (video display terminal—the predecessor of the individual computer). It was a Wang, standing on its own legs in the school's graphics lab, and people were eager to see if a writer could really back up to correct spelling or change the order of words, if whole paragraphs could be moved, and so forth. Of course, there was no printer, but just the opportunity to see what could be done on the screen was thrilling to most visitors.

The present-day AWC defines itself as "a nonprofit, professional organization for women and men in journalism and communications." It is open to both undergraduate and graduate students in those fields. At least eight members are required to have a campus chapter, and a faculty or professional adviser is required.

The national office is in Severna Park, Maryland, and professional chapters are willing to give advice and assist with opportunities. Those in Ohio are located in Akron, Cincinnati, Cleveland, Columbus, and Toledo. Student members may find advice and other information through the group's website, *www.womcom.org,* and members may file information about themselves on the site's My Profile link. This makes job seeking more convenient and speedier than it was in the old days of letters or even emails. The information is right there permanently for professionals to find persons with the skills needed in particular situations, and that information can be updated constantly by students as well as professionals looking for a change.

TRAILBLAZERS AND MENTORS

Ann Puderbaugh. *(Photo provided by Ann Puderbaugh)*

Watching the recent *Anchorman* movies brought back painful memories of humiliations I'd endured in the sexist newsrooms of the 1970s and '80s. Some journalists have criticized the Newseum's related exhibition as trite, but it certainly resonated with me.

Gazing at the period props and polyester costumes, I was transported back to long-ago days interning in local TV news, observing the lone female show producer don high heels and tight skirts in an unsuccessful bid to project authority and earn respect from her male bosses. Later, while producing foreign news for an American network, I routinely fended off propositions from married network correspondents and watched as young female interns ruined their careers with drunken encounters with their male supervisors.

Life in small-town Ohio had done little to prepare me for this. My mother had taught elementary school until her pregnancy with my little sister began to show, and she was forced to retire. My mom had little else to share with me regarding sexism in the workplace. I wanted a bigger life—to travel the globe, to bear witness to history—but it was a terrifying prospect.

I was fortunate to find encouragement and enlightenment in the OU chapter of Women in Communications Inc. (WICI). We weren't the largest journalism group on campus, but we were pretty tight, drawn together by our fears —would we find a job, could we compete with our male peers, would we be able to land the big assignments and, if we did, could we deliver? Our uniquely female angst hung over us like a dark cloud: How the hell could we hope to live the hard-charging journalist's lifestyle and still have kids before our eggs dried up? We watched Barbara Walters' star rise and the ill-fated Jessica Savitch's struggles, and we wondered what fate had in store for us.

We took solace and wisdom from the trailblazers who generously took the time to share their stories with us. By learning about their failures and challenges—as well as successes—we gained confidence that we, too, could forge a path in this demanding profession.

Always on hand to offer advice, payment for an odd job, or a shoulder to cry on was our intrepid adviser, Dru Riley Evarts. A close personal friend of the famed Helen Thomas and numerous other journalistic luminaries, she helped us secure accomplished speakers, offered her car for trips to meetings, and taught us the finer points of grammar and AP style.

The WICI sisterhood-at-large also warmly embraced us as student members, offering discounted conference fees and opening their homes to us since we couldn't afford hotels. But most of all, they provided inspiration. They strove for excellence in their professions and wanted us all to benefit from lessons learned. They offered mentorship, career advice, and contacts that might lead to internships or even jobs. They shared tips on how to succeed at every aspect of communications—from launching ad campaigns to producing long-form stories to succeeding as a freelancer.

When I eventually landed in our nation's capital a decade after leaving the warm embrace of the Bobcat chapter, my WICI sisters again provided support, welcoming me into their offices, sharing their contacts, providing intelligence on upcoming job openings. To borrow from the old cigarette ad, "We've come a long way, baby." But with women still earning only 77 percent as much as our male counterparts, Women in Communications Inc. still has a vital role to play today.

–Ann Puderbaugh

NATIONAL ASSOCIATION OF BLACK JOURNALISTS

By Carolyn Bailey Lewis

In the early 1970s, when Ohio University and the College of Communication experienced an upsurge in the number of African American students who were interested in the broad disciplines of communication, a need was created for both personal and professional support of these students.

This resulted in the 1973 founding of what came to be called the Black Student Communication Caucus (BSCC), an organization dedicated to providing consistent dialogue and interaction among African American students. As an early adviser, I saw that, from the beginning, the organization's focus was to be on curricular issues and extracurricular services (such as media outlets) pertaining to the College of Communication and those issues that affected these students.

Pointedly, the students wrote a mission statement that said BSCC was designed to "professionally develop its membership as well as expose members to the vast array of academic, scholarship, internship, and career opportunities available in the field of communication. Members are also encouraged and are assisted in branching out into other organizations on the Ohio University campus and in the greater Athens community. Students of all backgrounds and majors are welcome."

The student-run group has operated under various names, an early version being the Association for Black Journalists, but for most of its history it was known as the BSCC. In 2007, with the leadership of two presidents—Brandi Baker and Shaylyn Cochran—it became a chapter of the National Association of Black Journalists (NABJ).

The goal: Consistent dialogue

Whatever its name, the organization has never wavered in its primary purposes: to provide consistent dialogue and interaction among black communication majors, to voice the concerns (academic, social, and psychological) of black students in various schools within the College of Communication, and to promote awareness and understanding about minorities in the communication disciplines.

Over the years, specific activities and programs have included professional development workshops that involved guest speakers and faculty who discussed, for example, ways to improve résumés, effective development of videos, examinations of how to find jobs and internships, and ways to make themselves marketable in the communication disciplines.

In some years, the students hosted an annual Jazz Festival, published a campus magazine called *The Black Pages* that included listings of minority students on campus, and shared information about minority organizations, businesses, and events on campus. The magazine/newsletter was updated and published each quarter and eventually was moved to a digital format. Among the outreach programs was the hosting of networking events during the university's annual Black Alumni Reunion.

The students are goal oriented, organized, and focused. The executive board and general body meetings are well structured, always with a slant toward professional development. The students involved are passionate about the organization and work feverishly to recruit new students to carry on the legacy.

The value of good student leadership

The success of the organization over the years resulted, in part, from the extraordinary journalism and communication students who served in the leadership positions. These include Brandi Baker (BSC'06, MFA '08), president from 2004 to 2006, who said she learned the benefits of involvement quickly when she joined BSCC as a freshman.

"Within BSCC, I found a family of upperclassmen, faculty, and staff who cared, led, guided, and mentored me through my college transition," Baker said. "They taught me about leadership, commitment, and dedication. We affirmed and supported each other on various projects and initiatives within our major. BSCC taught me the value of networking, diversifying your professional portfolio by trying new things, and utilizing the great resources that the Scripps College of Communication has to offer."

She continued, "All of these skills helped prepare me for success in graduate school and for my career pathway to education administration. I have truly utilized each and every skill developed through BSCC. OU has been a wonderful platform on which I have developed professionally and established my career. My participation in BSCC and as a student at OU has truly been marked as some of my most memorable life experiences."

Another former member, Shaylyn Cochran (BSJ '07, BA in Political Science '07), said she was a quiet freshman when she went to her first BSCC meeting in fall 2003. She was nervous about interacting with upperclassmen and reluctant to do anything that took her away from studying.

"But I soon learned that participation in the organization was, in many ways, just as valuable as some of my classwork," she said. "From invaluable advice on internships to useful writing opportunities through publications like *The Flow* and *The Black Pages* to a ready-made study group for some of my toughest journalism classes, BSCC was a constant source of support for me. A few years later, after being elected president of the organization, I was able to welcome a few new freshmen into the BSCC family at one of the first fall meetings. That transition from mentee to mentor was yet another opportunity for the personal and professional development afforded to me by BSCC. My experience at Ohio University was undoubtedly enriched by my experience with the organization."

Like Cochran, Don Jason (BSJ '10) particularly remembers the value of the student-run newsletter.

"The publication has gone from print to digital and has been renamed several times over the past few decades," he said. "However, one thing has remained constant. BSCC provides a safe forum for students to share their voices with the campus and the world. BSCC is more than a student organization. It is a support network for students of color. It is a true manifestation of the collaboration and unity that abound within OU's black student community. Serving as the president of BSCC helped me grow as a leader. I learned that in order to accomplish the goals of the organization, everyone had to be invested in a shared vision. I learned that setting clear expectations and providing constructive feedback were crucial to the success of the organization."

Kiersten Smith (BA, MDIA '12), another former president, likewise stressed the value of the group's newsletter, which she labeled "a voice for the multicultural community on campus."

Her BSCC involvement, she said, facilitated her growth during her student years.

"Being a part of BSCC changed my perspective on college," Smith said. "Not only was I more community focused, but I was also more career focused. With BSCC, I was able to engage with the students and faculty of Ohio University on a different level. We planned events that fostered community and scholarship. We were also able to help the African American Studies department promote its event for the Tuskegee Airmen. Being a member of BSCC helped me shape my professional development and I believe helped me get into the career field that I am in today."

Hugh M. Culbertson. *(Photo courtesy of the Ohio University Archives, Mahn Center for Archives and Special Collections)*

PUBLIC RELATIONS STUDENT SOCIETY OF AMERICA

By Hugh M. Culbertson

As THE PROFESSIONAL role of public relations in the mid-1960s began to expand into something more akin to the multi-functioned discipline we know today, Ohio University students enthusiastically contributed to the School of Journalism's response, a redefinition of PR education on this campus.

Professionals in PR and their campus counterparts were at the time on the cusp of a much broader set of functions. Crises stemming in part from the social and political turmoil of the period were contributing to a growing emphasis on crisis management. Two-way communication with employees was being expanded. Fundraising was emerging as a subdiscipline as nonprofit organizations sought to serve society. And many other changes were under way.

Ohio University provides a good example. Only two public relations courses were offered in the late 1960s—a number that expanded to five within a few years. But it was clear among professionals and academics that more could be done for students, and this attitude resulted in formation of student chapters by the Public Relations Society of America (PRSA), the principal national association representing the discipline. These chapters collectively came to be known as the Public Relations Student Society of America (PRSSA).

Ohio University was among the first to be called upon when its chapter was formed in 1968–69, as the third or fourth student chapter in America. By 2014, that number had grown to about 300.

The dedication and purposefulness of the Ohio University chapter have resulted in its assumption of a leading role nationally over the past 45-plus years. The chapter was part of the East Central District of PRSSA, including Ohio, Kentucky, Michigan, West Virginia, and Indiana. As districts began to hold annual conferences and to carry out programs at the national level, this district dominated to such an extent that a move developed to "break up the Yankees." Districts were redefined at that point, with the OU chapter becoming part of the Ohio Valley District. At present, PRSSA functions in 10 regions, with the state of Ohio constituting one full region.

The OU chapter grew from modest beginnings. Perhaps its first major project was to work for the congressional campaign of an OU Appalachian studies professor named Doug Arnett. He challenged long-time Congressman Clarence Miller in the 1970 election. Miller won, but the students gained a sense of accomplishment because his margin of victory was lower than in prior races. (One important note: The students worked as individuals because they felt that formal chapter support might be seen as contravening the ideal of not aligning formally with one political party.)

By around 1980, PRSSA had developed rather extensive awards programs at the national and district levels—and Ohio University students and faculty advisers distinguished themselves in all categories.

Many honors brought home

The OU School of Journalism's chapter, by then called the Hugh M. Culbertson Chapter, was named the outstanding chapter nationally in 2001, and the chapter's newsletter, *PR Press* (later renamed *profeSSional)* became a perennial all-star. It was named the top newsletter in the nation in 1998 and 2011 in addition to winning top district honors in 1983, 1988, 1995, 2000, and 2006.

Another strength of the chapter has long been its array of professional advisers, almost all from the very strong Central Ohio Chapter of PRSA in Columbus. In 1985, Richard Baker (BSJ '74), Denise Mihalko Johnson (BSJ '77), and Sue Mathie King (BSJ '83) shared the national award as outstanding professional advisers. In 1995–96, Tammy O'Neill Grimes (BSJ '87) received this title at both the national and district levels. Other professional advisers, mostly loyal alums of the chapter and school, have included Zachary Bingham (BSJ '97), Aaron Brown (BSJ '01), Andy Brussard, Mary Jane Clark (BSJ '95), Jennifer Dally (BSJ '80), Frank Deaner (BSJ '67), R. Devin Hughes, Rebecca O'Neill, Kate Simpson (BSJ '07), Gary Snyder (BSJ '86), and Zachary Wright (BSJ '09).

These folks often speak at weekly chapter meetings, participate in learning experiences on campus, help locate and define internships, and provide other valuable support.

Partly as a result of their efforts, OU took top honors nationally for PRSA-PRSSA chapter relationships in 1998, 2006, and 2012, as well as at the district level in 2002. In a related vein, Ohio was rated No. 1 for chapter development in 1994–95.

Other awards included outstanding chapter website (nationally in 1999 and 2005) and outstanding chapter agency (district level in 1994 and 1996, nationally in 1997, 2005, 2007, and 2015).

Also, School of Journalism faculty member Jerry Sloan was named the district's—and the nation's—top academic adviser in 1996, and I received the title of top OU student-organization adviser in 1985. Other academic advisers have included cofounder J. William Click (MS '59), Robert Baker, Alan Freitag (PhD '99), Tanya Morah (PhD '97), Bojinka Bishop, Diana Knott Martinelli, Mary Jane Clark (BSJ '95), and Dan Farkas (BSJ '98, MBA '14).

In the 1970s, the chapter received national recognition for its leadership in developing internships as part of a program called PRIDE (Public Relations Internships to Develop Expertise). This was done with the oversight of advisers, but a strength of these advisers was their insistence that students, not advisers, had to do the work and planning for projects.

Students were strongly encouraged to complete multiple internships. One chapter president, Rich Kammer (BSJ '89), completed no fewer than 10 internships. Brian Tedeschi (BSJ '88), another president, had nine. These résumé items helped greatly in job searches.

Student-run agency

In 1982, the chapter formed an agency, ImPRessions, which served clients in the Athens area. At the time, this was the only PR agency with offices in Athens.

In 1985, ImPRessions won a competition to gain funding for a project to promote Levi's 501 Jeans. The agency held a fashion show on the College Green with students wearing jeans appropriate for various subcultures and lifestyles. At halftime of a football game in Peden Stadium, cheerleaders tossed small footballs into the stands with gift certificates usable in obtaining jeans. Finally, a benefit for the Multiple Sclerosis Society involved a "Stitch in Time" contest. Contestants guessed the number of stitches in a jean pocket, with the most accurate estimators receiving prizes.

The ongoing contributions of ImPRessions over the years have involved a large number of clients, including a student-run TV news show, at the time called *ACTV-7 News,* in the Scripps School and a program of the Armco Steel Corporation called "Help the Elderly."

In the late 1980s, ImPRessions personnel interviewed Athens residents in a survey of how people viewed community-service activities of the Athens Police Department, then helped organize, publicize, and carry out a "Cops for Kids" program that allowed kids to meet APD officers and learn about their jobs. In the mid-1980s, the agency began preparing public-service announcements and ads for a call-in weather service run by The Scalia Laboratory for Atmospheric Analysis, conducted by the OU Department of Geography. Also in the 1980s and 1990s, ImPRessions edited a newsletter and conducted employee surveys at the Pillsbury plant that produced pizza and other food items in Wellston, Ohio, southwest of Athens.

Assorted activities

There's more.

In 1982, the chapter hosted a program called "Partners in Professional Development" jointly with Ohio State University students. Professionals interviewed students for 3–5 minutes about some issue or project that the pros' clients were dealing with. Interviews were videotaped. And all participants watched the tapes with professionals offering critiques.

In 1994, the chapter organized and ran a session at the national conference in Orlando, Florida, on maintaining strong client relationships with a student-run firm. Only three chapters among the 179 then operating were selected to conduct conference sessions.

But it's not all hard work, and students, especially those who attended district and national conferences, have their more informal stories to tell. One occurred in 1986 at the Monday night social event at the national conference in Denver. The NFL Denver Broncos played a home game that night, and the famous triumvirate of Howard Cosell, O.J. Simpson, and Don Meredith covered the contest as the Monday night game of the week. The ABC crew was staying in the hotel with PRSSA. After the game, O.J. Simpson joined the student party and had his picture taken with his arms around the two Ohio University delegates, President Stacy Waldron (BSJ '85) and President-to-be Janice Gaynor (BSJ '86). This picture surely became a valued item in the chapter files eight years later when O.J.'s world collapsed.

RADIO TELEVISION DIGITAL NEWS ASSOCIATION

By Mary T. Rogus

> To pursue the highest ideals and principles of the practice of electronic journalism; and, to foster closer cooperation and opportunity for discussion, debate and education between students of electronic journalism, journalism educators, and professional practitioners of radio and television news.
>
> —*Radio Television News Directors Association Student Affiliate Constitution, 1987*

THOSE WORDS ARE still part of the Student Affiliate Constitution for what first was the Radio Television News Directors Association (RTNDA) but what since 2010 has been the Radio Television Digital News Association (RTDNA), labeled on its website as the "world's largest organization exclusively serving the electronic news profession." And to this day, they are the best description for what OU-RTDNA is to its student members and alumni.

"OU-RTNDA was the first organization I joined at OU, and I was a member for four years and was president of the group in 1994–1995," Darrel Richter (BSJ '95) said. "OU-RTNDA introduced us to media professionals and allowed us to ask questions and understand the industry in a way that was different from classroom ties, internships, and real-world experience. I have many OU classmates and fellow OU-RTNDA members who obtained jobs during or after college as a direct result of the relationships formed through OU-RTNDA forums and seminars."

Deborah Sachar (BSJ '90, MSJ '98) lists similar advantages: "The networking, the professional advice, the critiques . . . all great things that came from that OU-RTDNA chapter. I was actually one of the founders of the OU-RTNDA chapter back in the mid-'80s. I'm still in touch with peers from those days."

Two former OU-RTDNA officers—Sara Nealeigh (BSJ '14), former president, and Bradley Parks (BSJ '14), former webmaster—take advantage of a 2011 anchor workshop sponsored by the organization. *(Photo used with permission from RTDNA)*

Chartering of the local student affiliate

On October 16, 1987, the Ohio University student affiliate of RTNDA was chartered as one of the inaugural student chapters by then-Chairman Bob Brunner. Brunner, a longtime news director at television stations in West Virginia, would proudly point to his signature on the charter certificate when he visited Ohio University for conferences. The development of student affiliate chapters was one of his major accomplishments in his year as chairman of the organization.

In addition to bringing hundreds of broadcast and digital news professionals to campus as speakers, the organization also provides workshops that offer students opportunities to improve their broadcast skills. In 1990, members put together the first OU-RTDNA Spring Conference, which has been a hallmark for the organization ever since. Most Scripps School broadcast students, even those who are not OU-RTDNA members, attend the conference for professional advice, critiques of their work, and networking, as well as mentorship throughout their careers.

"Networking through the national conference and organizational events helped me get a sense of what employers were looking for and what would be expected in my first job," said Sara Magee (BSJ '97, PhD '08). "The opportunities provided by OU-RTNDA really helped me find my place in the television world both as a student and later as a broadcast producer."

To this day Mary Ellen Hardies Smalley (BSJ '01) tells people that OU-RTNDA was instrumental in getting both her first and her second job.

"I remember dashing to the OU-RTNDA conference in April 2001 to meet a man named Marty Moran," she said. "I had interned in his newsroom at WDTN [in Dayton], and he wanted to chat. I walked in and also met a man who later in my career would be instrumental in bringing me to a large market. A few weeks after that, I got a call and was offered a job to produce the 5 p.m. news in Dayton."

Graduates return to work with students

"The OU-RTNDA conference is where I first met the person I consider to be my biggest mentor," Jennifer Tomaso Frye (BSJ '04) said. "A stand-up montage by Brian McIntyre (BSJ '91) will always be ingrained in my memory. Little did I know when I met him initially that he would go on to teach me so many valuable things about broadcast journalism over the course of my career. I credit the OU-RTNDA conference for making that important connection."

McIntyre and Sachar are just two of the many Scripps alums who come back year after year to give back to the chapter because of the many contacts and experiences they shared as members. The Scripps family was devastated to lose Brian McIntyre to cancer in 2012, just a year after his last appearance at a spring conference here. Several of his fellow broadcast and OU-RTDNA alums created a memorial fund in his honor to help urban high school students attend the summer High School Journalism Workshop.

In 2011, OU-RTDNA and Ohio University's Society of Professional Journalists chapter cosponsored one of the most impactful student journalism conferences in the state. The Ohio Sunshine Summit brought together more than 150 students, faculty advisers, and media professionals from across Ohio and surrounding states to discuss access to campus public records, spaces, and administrators. Held during the annual National Sunshine Week, the conference resulted in a resolution calling for universities across the state to abide by Ohio sunshine laws in dealing with student journalists. The resolution was endorsed by the national executive boards of both RTDNA and SPJ and was presented to the state attorney general and Ohio University's Board of Regents.

One of the leading student organizers of the event, OU-RTDNA and OU-SPJ executive board member Evan Millard (BSJ '11), was quoted in *The Ohio Journalist* about the event: "For the first time ever, students from across the state came together and spoke with one voice and told our administrators enough is enough with the culture of hostility."

But OU-RTDNA is not just about learning to be an ethical and skilled electronic journalism professional. It also provides a social outlet for broadcast students who put in lots of hours outside of classes working with WOUB Public Media, All-Campus Radio Network (ACRN) Internet radio, and Athens Video Works (AVW) student production company. The organization sponsors at least two social events a semester. A favorite is pizza and movie night to view broadcast classics such as *Broadcast News* and *Anchorman*.

"OU-RTDNA was a way to get to know my fellow Scripps people outside of class or WOUB. We were often so focused on getting the job done that it wasn't until we were in a meeting or a lecture or a conference put on by the group that I was able to kick back and talk job strategy and actually get to know my peers!" said Katie Primm (BSJ '06).

SCRIPPS HISPANIC NETWORK

By Ralph Izard

THE PROFESSIONAL DEDICATION of Hispanic students in the E.W. Scripps School of Journalism has prompted creation of a new student organization to provide an inclusive and beneficial space for anyone interested in securing a position in Hispanic and Spanish-speaking media.

The Scripps Hispanic Network is a student-run group that seeks to promote professionalism in digital media, according to the group's mission statement.

"The school has been working hard to expand student diversity, but unfortunately Hispanic journalism students have yet to identify with a specific group or news outlet on campus," junior Marisa Fernandez, the network's vice president, said. "The school has done a pretty good job bringing in speakers to talk to students about current events, the state of journalism, and ways we can market ourselves."

She added, however, that employment is ultimately what every student wants and "just from six months in this organization alone, I've met many alums and professionals who sincerely want to help me and network with me. Never have I had such an immediate support group from people I have known for only a short time. These are people I can identify with and people across the country that have experience in what I may want to do someday."

Director Robert Stewart fully agrees with the value the students receive, and he recognizes a broader benefit for the school.

"Having such an organization . . . demonstrates to our Latino and Hispanic students that we celebrate and promote diversity within the school," he said. "For prospective students who come from that background, the SHN can be a 'home' to them, to make them feel welcome in our program."

Organized initially in December 2015 with Stewart's encouragement, the group first sought to select student leadership, recruit members, and set up its programming. Its adviser is Michael Rodriguez, director of production services and student development for WOUB Public Media.

The students are looking toward possible evolution of their new organization.

"Our goal is to eventually become a local chapter for the National Association of Hispanic Journalists [like NABJ and SPJ] and to bring in speakers who can share experiences about their heritage and what they have brought to the professional world, to name an example," Fernandez said.

Among other goals are securing positive representation of Hispanic people in digital media; encouraging diversity by promoting Spanish-speaking storytelling and celebrating dialogues from the Hispanic world as necessary pieces of the cultural zeitgeist; and working toward these goals by organizing relevant and useful programming, including workshops and networking opportunities.

And these students are not modest in their ambition for their new organization, Rodriguez said. Their aim is to gain prominence that will result in selection as Scripps College's student organization of the year.

—Michael Rodriguez contributed to this story.

SOCIETY OF PROFESSIONAL JOURNALISTS

By Halina J. Czerniejewski

A LONG TIME AGO and not so far away, 10 college men initiated a mission that today, given the context, would be considered surprisingly secret. It was 1909; they were students at DePauw University in Indiana, and they met, covertly, for an ideal.

Intending to make journalism their life's work, they wanted to combat the prolific "yellow journalism" and "tabloid journalism" by a type of war of attrition—preparing honorable young journalists who would work and watch as the sordid types retired or died.

They chose the name Sigma Delta Chi (SDX) for their men's journalism fraternity. In 1910, other campus chapters formed. In 1921, five professional chapters formed. Five years later, the founders could take great pride in the organization's adoption of its first code of ethics, a major step toward emphasizing journalism as a profession.

Eventually, the secrecy and the trappings of a fraternity were discarded in favor of greater professionalism. Over time, the organization took on issues of privacy, freedom of information, freedom of the press, and ethics and professional responsibility. It initiated several steps that in 1988 resulted in adoption of its current name, the Society of Professional Journalists.

Ohio University's chapter was chartered in 1932, and it accepted both students and professionals in journalism. It began as a fraternity with 10 men. (The women's honorary society, Theta Sigma Phi, began the same year.)

"Students, then and now, clearly saw the advantage of being involved in an organization dedicated to professional programming," said Ralph Izard, who advised the chapter from 1968 to 1988. "They appreciated the classroom but sought more directed and contemporary professional knowledge and experience. The chapter, for years, has provided this through programs, special projects, and attendance at professional conventions where students could make contacts."

Professional fund-raising projects

Consistently, the chapter has sought to use its journalistic skills to raise funds to support its programs. Among the earliest of these, with L.J. Hortin as adviser, was publication of a large desk blotter that was distributed free on campus and around the community. The popular blotters carried advertisements for Athens merchants and paid for travel to SDX events.

Another project resulted when the chapter was granted the right to produce the university's basketball program to sell at home games. It "employed" an editor, copy editors, layout artists, and photographers, reporters who wrote about the game, athletes, and the prospects. And, of course, the group had to sell advertising. Hawkers at the Convocation Center, including students and advisers, sold the programs initially for a dime.

The professional focus of the organization received a boost in the 1960s. As government attempted to limit access to information, journalists invoked the Freedom of Information Act. FOI badges circulated at conventions. Members talked about freedom of the press, the Freedom of Information Act, ethics in reporting, responsibility, the use of unnamed sources, and what to do if you were called before a government body that demanded to know your sources.

At OU, as at many universities, protestors marched, shouted, and closed down buildings, and journalism students demanded the people's "right to know." When four college students were killed by National Guardsmen at Kent State University that spring of 1970, OU students, like others, rioted. Barbara Kaufmann (BSJ '72) recalled that OU journalists continued to cover the news as the campus was shut down and students awaited rides home.

The admission of women

When students returned to campus in fall 1970, the scene for chapter members was quite different. As the result of a vote at the national convention in 1969, women had been admitted into what had been an all-male domain for 60 years.

Allowing women to join had been an issue that jittered members at a number of national conventions. Naysayers argued that women had "their own organization," which would be sapped of members, as the women would obviously join SDX. Another objection was that women would not stay in journalism. They might work for a while and then they would do what they always did—look for a husband, get married, have children, and quit journalism.

Finally, the 1969 national convention accepted the obvious—if SDX was the society of journalists, it should allow all journalists to join. (And, of course, letting them join would increase membership numbers.)

OU's chapter immediately invited all people in journalism to join. The organization's membership had ebbed and flowed over the decades, but it nearly doubled when women were invited. Izard enjoys telling of how the national executive director approached him at the November 1970 convention in Chicago and said, "Is it true that you folks initiated more than 100 new members this year?" Oh, yes. The Ohio University group had become the largest campus chapter in the nation.

Women quickly became involved and led like gangbusters. There was a new benefit for joining—the social one. Kathy Lieberman (BSJ '72) reminisced that in addition to the professional benefits, "It was a great way to meet guys." And it's likely the guys felt it benefited them socially, too.

The very next year, 1971, I was elected the first female president of the largest student chapter in the country.

We women did not feel particularly honored; we were welcomed without hoopla. The guys were fine with women joining. Many women majored in journalism. And women assumed they would be treated as equals—in class, in working for the student newspaper, in chapter activities. It was later, on the job, that they found they were not always considered quite equal.

How did bringing women into the organization change things? For one, women had a new voice and power behind it.

One day, two young women approached me, as the president of SDX. They said a classroom teaching assistant was telling female students, including them, that their grades could improve if they had sex with him. I sought the advice of a professor. Did I believe them? Yes. Would they tell their stories if necessary? Yes. And by the way, the chapter's female population, if not the entire group, would likely cause a stir if this continued.

Later, the professor told me that the assistant was reprimanded and the issue was brought up at a faculty meeting, reminding all that this kind of behavior was unacceptable. The students thanked me and said the instructor never approached them again.

Many honors and much service

The value of what came to be called the Society of Professional Journalists (SPJ) has multiplied in many ways.

Katlin Hiller, chapter president for 2014–15, joined SPJ on the recommendation of a faculty member. The chapter, which had 46 members then, met every Tuesday, featuring speakers, talks on FOI and ethics and diversity, or workshops such as putting together a résumé or a how-to on a specific job. The events appeared on social media, an improvement over the old bulletin board and landline phone calls of my day. Usually the speaker comes to the campus, but sometimes the chapter uses Skype. The chapter had a "Grammar Smackdown"! Brilliant!

As a result of its continuing activities and contributions to the educational program of the school, the chapter has earned a strong national reputation for excellence. This includes selection as the nation's outstanding chapter seven times, with Ohio University bringing home the honor in 1976, 1978,

OUTSTANDING IN MANY WAYS

ALAN ADLER (BSJ '80), president of the Ohio University chapter of the Society of Professional Journalists, walked quickly to the front and stood behind the lectern before the crowd of perhaps 1,000 fellow journalists.

The occasion was the 1978 SPJ convention in Birmingham, Alabama. Adler and his colleagues were especially excited as he responded to an announcement that the OU chapter had been selected as the nation's most outstanding student chapter. The honor was enough for the students, but the selection also carried with it a $100 award.

Adler accepted the award and the check. After thanking SPJ and the members of his chapter, he then surprised almost everyone in the room by quickly endorsing the check and returning it to the master of ceremonies. The chapter wanted to contribute the money to the society's Freedom of Information Fund, he said.

Officials were surprised and confused and didn't know what to do with the check. Adler was told to take it back and turn it over later to national headquarters officials.

But the point had been made. This was the kind of action on which the OU chapter thrived, and perhaps it was symbolic of why it was judged the best in the nation that year.

—Ralph Izard

2006, 2010, 2014, 2016, and 2017, more than any other chapter in the country. It has been selected as the Region 4 outstanding chapter 24 times.

In SPJ's national journalism competition, labeled the "Mark of Excellence" awards, Ohio University consistently has done well. National winners reflected the breadth of the OU journalism program, including newswriting, television reporting, radio reporting, spot-news reporting, feature reporting, overall student-produced magazine (*Athens*), feature, news and sports photography, and nonfiction articles.

National attention also has been focused on some of the chapter's advisers. Most recently this occurred in 2015, when Nerissa Young received the David L. Shulman Outstanding Campus Adviser Award. Ralph Izard, who served as a member of the society's national board from 1975 to 1978 as vice president for campus chapter affairs, received the Distinguished Teaching in

Journalism Award in 2007 and the Wells Key (the highest honor in SPJ) in 1985. Professor Russell N. Baird received the Distinguished Teaching in Journalism Award in 1982. And Donald Lambert was selected Outstanding Campus Adviser in 1988.

Since students were first given a voice in the society's governance as members of the Board of Directors, Ohio University has had its share of representatives: Tim Smith (BSJ '80) represented District A as a student member of the board in 1978–79. Autumn Sanders (BSJ '03) was a campus representative-at-large to the board in 2002. Erin Smith (BSJ '07) was a campus representative-at-large in 2006. Taylor Mirfendereski (BSJ '14) served as the student rep on the national board for 2010–11 and 2011–12. Kate Hiller was elected one of two student representatives to the board in 2015, and Hayley Harding likewise was elected one of two student representatives in 2017.

The OU chapter joined the Columbus professional chapter as cohosts of the SPJ national convention in 1980. And the Ohio chapters of SPJ and RTDNA hosted the Ohio Sunshine Summit on campus in 2011 to educate students about public meetings and public records regarding higher-education agencies. Draft legislation for revisions came out of that conference.

A TRIFECTA OF EXCELLENCE

THE SOCIETY OF Professional Journalists—an important part of my life as a student and as a faculty member at Marshall University and later in the Scripps School—has provided me with a wonderful trifecta of sorts.

I was president of the Marshall University campus chapter when it was named national campus chapter of the year, president of the West Virginia Pro chapter when it was named small pro chapter of the year, and adviser of the Ohio University chapter when it was named national campus chapter of the year in 2014 and again in 2016.

I haven't done the research, but I don't know of any of my fellow SPJers who can lay claim to all three honors.

I was a master's student in journalism at Marshall University when that chapter received the national honor in 1993 after it joined the campus newspaper and the journalism school in their fight against a takeover bid by the university president.

The Parthenon, the campus paper, published the name of a rape complainant, and President J. Wade Gilley attempted to disband the student publication board to replace it with his own appointees.

SPJ national quickly joined the fight by writing supportive op-eds, providing interviews for the newspaper staff covering the attempted takeover, and even pledging money from the Legal Defense Fund if students wanted to sue Gilley for First Amendment violations. The MU chapter supported editors by attending faculty meetings in which the matter was discussed. Plus, many on the staff were SPJ members, too, including me.

The West Virginia Pro chapter received its honor in 1997.

That was the first year I lobbied on behalf of SPJ for the legislature to revise the Open Meetings Act. It took three years of lobbying before Governor Cecil Underwood signed the bill into law. I remember that Wyoming Senator Alan Simpson was the keynote speaker when the chapter awards were presented. I had described our chapter as either the scrappiest in the nation or just too stupid to know when to quit. Simpson took the stage and said he thought we were talking about him.

The Ohio University chapter won its awards for its overall strong programs and collaboration with other student media organizations.

There's such a great award-winning tradition in SPJ at OU. When I was a student at Marshall and later a professor there, we always competed hard against the OU chapter. It's an honor and pleasure to be part of it now.

–Nerissa Young

JOHANN
SEBASTIAN
BACH

International: The world is our stage

In these days of the emergence of new forms of communication media, it is common to hear that the world is shrinking. This may be so, but what is most obvious in Athens is that the E.W. Scripps School of Journalism has expanded its reach into that world. In the classroom, greater attention is devoted to the local impact of world events. But even more conspicuous is that the school in recent years has provided increasing opportunities for students to gain international experience as part of their OU education. In this chapter, we count some of the ways that has been accomplished.

Facing page: Students from Ohio University congregate before a statue of Johann Sebastian Bach during a visit to the Institute of Communication and Media Studies in Leipzig, Germany. *(E.W. Scripps School of Journalism photo)*

A HOME FOR INTERNATIONAL OUTREACH

By Burton Speakman and Ralph Izard

From its base in small-town Athens, Ohio, in the Appalachian foothills, the Ohio University School of Journalism over the years has developed a worldwide reach in professional and educational circles.

Some might consider this surprising. Others, knowing the university's international emphasis and the global interests of many of the school's faculty members, would more likely use the word "inevitable."

International communication has been part of the school's programming for many years, in the earlier days mostly in the hands of individual faculty members. An early example of external outreach came in 1970 with introduction of the John R. Wilhelm Foreign Correspondence Internship program. And in 1978, faculty member Ralph E. Kliesch began scheduling the Communication Capitals of the World Study Tour, a program he conducted for 13 years.

To strengthen and add to these individual contributions, the school's faculty followed the lead of then–university President Charles J. Ping, who said in his 1989 convocation address, "The ideal time to start a U.S.-based Center for International Journalism is the 1990s."

"One should not underestimate the influence Ping had on the efforts to establish a global focus in the journalism school," said Ralph Izard, former director. "He set up the model university-wide, and he took the unusual step of coming to a journalism faculty meeting to stress the importance of the school broadening its programming beyond Ohio and the United States."

Anne Cooper-Chen and Ralph Izard pose with Franco Messerli, center, a broadcast journalist from Berne, Switzerland, who visited the school in 1990 as the first visiting professional in the Institute for International Journalism. *(Photo courtesy of the Ohio University Archives, Mahn Center for Archives and Special Collections)*

Gaining formal approval

The result was approval in 1991 by the university Board of Trustees of what was first called the Center for International Journalism, later changed to Institute for International Journalism.

From the time of its founding, the center/institute has played a major role in training journalists and journalism educators from around the world and in enhancing a global focus within the school's classrooms and lecture halls. It has a broad mandate, including raising OU students' international consciousness; implementing journalism training workshops for international professionals and academics, with special focus on developing countries; fostering an international internship program for OU students; developing exchange programs with overseas institutions; and engaging in global awareness communication research among international scholars.

Over the years, leadership in the quest of these goals has been placed into the hands of four faculty members, each of whom served as institute director: Anne Cooper-Chen, Terry Anderson, Robert Stewart, and, currently, Yusuf Kalyango Jr. Each has developed both global and academic priorities, and each has expanded the role of the institute according to these priorities.

Cooper-Chen said among her goals as institute director in the early days were broadening the international internship program by expanding its footprint in Asia, solidifying the selection process, and developing more paid internships.

These efforts did indeed result in geographical expansion of what had been a predominantly European-based international internship program, she said. She was able to add a number of internship opportunities for Ohio students in Asia, including at *Nagoya Avenues,* an English-language magazine in Japan; the *Free China Journal* in Taipei, Taiwan; and the *China Post* in Taipei. Later, a student had a copy-editing internship at *The Daily Post* in Suva, Fiji.

"At that time we had a lot of students coming here from Asia, but we weren't sending many there," Cooper-Chen said.

Among specific programs during her term was a relationship with the National Chengchi University in Taiwan. The sister-school arrangement brought a graduate student to study at Scripps in 1990–91 and sent faculty member Tom Hodges to Taiwan from August 1990 to June 1991 as the first Scripps faculty member to teach at Chengchi.

In addition, five mass media practitioners from overseas—representing four countries—Switzerland, Taiwan, Argentina, and Poland—spent one or more quarters as nondegree students at the school taking courses of their choice and pursuing other activities.

An International Media 2000 program organized by Cooper-Chen, with cooperative sponsorship of the International Communication Division of

AEJMC and the College of Communication, featured participants from around the globe in research presentations and discussions of the major international issues of the day.

Anderson, the former Associated Press correspondent who achieved worldwide prominence when he was held captive in Lebanon by a group of Shiite Muslims linked to Hezbollah for nearly seven years before being released in 1991, joined the school's faculty in 1998. As director of the institute, he developed a Middle East focus and maintained the European links, primarily through continued development of foreign correspondence internships and special cooperation with AP.

The important addition of Germany

Germany became a principal institutional focus in 1992 when a partnership was formed with Leipzig University in the former East Germany, the birthplace of communication/journalism education in central Europe. At the suggestion of university Provost Jim Bruning, Izard was among those who visited the former East German nation, worked with officials there, and came home with an understanding that Ohio University would make itself available to assist in program development.

Within months of the fall of the Iron Curtain, 10 Ohio University journalism faculty—Robert Stewart, Patricia Westfall, Dru Riley Evarts, Marilyn Greenwald, Pat Washburn, Larry Levin, Mel Helitzer, Hugh Culbertson, Tom Hodges, and Anne Cooper-Chen—were scheduled for German travel. Funded by an initial $80,000 grant with a follow-up of $10,000 from the Freedom Forum, these faculty members taught students and consulted with their German counterparts.

The Leipzig program, under the direction of Robert Stewart, became one of the more prominent and long-lasting of the school's international efforts. In 1994, it became a university-wide program, and it remains to this day among the university's hallmark cooperative international efforts. The partnership has expanded from those beginnings. Importantly, Stewart says, over the years hundreds of students have crossed the Atlantic in both directions to visit and study at the two universities. Today, students can receive a double master's degree at OU and Leipzig.

An offshoot of the faculty travel to Germany was development of a working relationship with the RIAS Kommission of Berlin. This resulted in visits to Ohio University in 1994 and 1995 of two sets of four young German journalists for three weeks each.

Kalyango, who joined the faculty and institute in 2008, sees the contribution of the institute to the school and university in the use of global engagement to establish a unique branding, both professionally and academically.

Among his specific goals were to expose American students to international reporting and writing, thus giving them opportunities to experience the world through international exchanges, workshops for journalists in developing countries, and programs of international awareness.

It was not by intent, but Kalyango's background and available opportunities led him to development of a focus on Africa, through both programming and internships in African media.

Service around the world

During Kalyango's tenure as institute director, more-recent efforts under the umbrella of the institute include the following:

- SUSI (Study of the U.S. Institute on Journalism and Media), through which international media educators from more than 85 countries over six years visited Athens and other major cities in the U.S. South and West, plus Washington, D.C. The program was funded in 2010 by a $299,000 three-year grant, followed by a second three-year allocation of $289,000 from the U.S. Department of State. The purpose of SUSI is "to foster mutual understanding between the people of the United States and citizens of other countries around the world."

- The Mandela Washington Fellowship for Young African Leaders, known as YALI Connect Camps, funded through a $485,000 annual grant from the U.S. Department of State, trains more than 150 young African entrepreneurs, leaders, and professionals. The Mandela Washington Fellowship and all other YALI projects are initiatives of the Obama administration designed to invest in the next generation of African leaders. The YALI Connect Camps program was funded through December 2017.
- One of Kalyango's most recent efforts will bring three to four master's students from Kazakhstan to Southeast Ohio to study for a semester as nondegree transient students, taking two to three classes and then returning home.
- Professionally, another goal has been to increase opportunities for students to cover international events. Students have traveled to and developed news presentations about the 2012 Summer Olympics in London and the 2014 soccer World Cup in European locations and Brazil. These were designed as internship experiences for the students, said journalism faculty member Justice B. Hill, who accompanied the participants to four European nations.
- In 2014, Kalyango assumed the editorship of the International Communication Research Journal (ICRJ), a project of the Association for Education in Journalism and Mass Communication. The journal will be produced from the Athens-based institute during his five-year term.

During Kalyango's term as director, the school's international focus has turned what started out as a center to provide OU students with international learning opportunities into a global research and training institute. Two edited books were published between 2014 and 2015 showcasing SUSI scholars' research through the institute's sponsorship. Also, the institute has joined a consortium of principal investigators from more than 60 countries to produce biannual surveys of journalists to measure the state of the profession. The consortium of principal investigators works under the name Worlds of Journalism Study.

1973 intern Paul Zach (BSJ '73) covers the Yom Kippur War for the AP. In the background, Israeli soldiers round up Egyptian POWs on the shore of the Suez Canal after the final ceasefire. *(Photo provided by Ken Klein)*

WILHELM LEADS JOURNALISM SCHOOL TO THE WORLD

By Ken Klein

WORLD WAR II correspondent and international news executive John R. Wilhelm brought a novel idea to out-of-the-way Athens, Ohio, when he joined the Ohio University faculty in 1968.

Wilhelm, first as director of journalism and then as founding dean of the new College of Communication (now Scripps), launched foreign news internships in 1970, sending kids barely in their twenties to overseas bureaus to cover world events and to learn journalism from topnotch correspondents.

The concept was rooted in Wilhelm's own journalistic globetrotting. In 1944, he was in his twenties when he accompanied a landing party at Omaha Beach, covering the D-Day invasion for the Reuters news agency. After the war, he was a European correspondent for the *Chicago Sun* and chief of McGraw-Hill's news bureau in Buenos Aires and Mexico City. In 1955, Wilhelm became editor of McGraw-Hill World News Service in New York.

Soon after his move to Ohio University, Wilhelm persuaded managers of foreign news to offer internships to the school's students, vouching for their worthiness. In 1970, Wilhelm sent the first overseas intern to Westinghouse Broadcasting in Paris.

Through more than four decades, 282 Ohio University students have completed foreign internships in 32 countries, according to Yusuf Kalyango, current director of the Institute for International Journalism.

The need for scholarship support

Six separate scholarship funds—one named for Wilhelm—support a handful of annual internships. The contemporary award is typically $5,500 for 90 days. Creating foreign news scholarships illustrated Wilhelm's reach and resourcefulness, which he called the "accident of age" as his peers reached the top echelons of print and broadcast news.

Included among the scholarships were three honoring highly successful communication professionals.

To raise the initial internship funding, Wilhelm leveraged his friendship with legendary author Cornelius Ryan, who had gone on to publish several books about World War II, including the best seller *The Longest Day.* An initial $50,000 endowment was raised for the scholarship. As a result of that success, along with Wilhelm's friendship, Mrs. Ryan donated many of her husband's papers after his death to the Ohio University library, where they now reside in a special collection.

A second scholarship memorializes Bob Considine, a World War II correspondent and prolific Hearst columnist who had connections to colleges other than Ohio University. A graduate of George Washington University, Considine had given his papers to Syracuse University before he died in 1975.

After Considine's death, a group of influential friends explored ways to honor his career. Wilhelm knew the leader of the group, who suggested Ohio University to Considine's widow, Millie. The renowned *CBS Evening News* anchor Walter Cronkite, a fellow World War II correspondent, visited Ohio University at Wilhelm's invitation in 1968 and signed the fund-raising letter to launch the Considine scholarship.

In 1971, Ohio University alumnus William Fleischer and his wife, Shirley, began sponsoring Wilhelm's interns to Israel. Fleischer, a successful marketing pioneer from East Hills, New York, was grateful that OU journalism Professor and Director George Starr Lasher helped him get a job. People like Fleischer, said Senator Daniel Patrick Moynihan in a 1990 tribute, personified postwar America: innovative, ambitious, and willing to reinvest their gains for the overall good.

As noted, an additional internship award was established later in Wilhelm's name.

In more recent years, current school Director Robert Stewart and his wife, Penny Shelton, established the Maxine Stewart Foreign Correspondence Internship for Coverage of Culture and Religion. It honors Stewart's mother, a missionary in Thailand who wrote about the work of other missionaries. Student Taylor Pool (BSJ '13) completed the second Stewart internship in fall 2012 in Niger. She used her video skills to cover overseas mission work.

Further support for international internships came in 2016 when a special internship travel fund was established in honor of former faculty member Mark Leff by his sister, Judi Leff. Because of Leff's extensive international work, the school has dedicated this fund to support a foreign correspondence internship. The first award was given to Sam Howard (BSJ '16) in 2016 for an internship at CNN's Indonesia bureau.

In the program's early years, Wilhelm taught a class in foreign news reporting and hand-picked interns. Today, students must take the foreign correspondence course and then apply for the funding.

The impact on students

For interns, the trajectory from classrooms to foreign news bureaus producing headlines around the world seemed like the gap between playing pickup basketball and suiting up with pros.

"It made me realize that I wasn't as good as I thought I was and inspired me to be better," said former intern Gary Putka (BSJ '77). Assigned to The Associated Press bureau in Tel Aviv, Putka helped cover a top international news story during America's bicentennial year. On July 4, 1976, Israel Defense Force commandos carried out a successful hostage-rescue mission at Entebbe Airport in Uganda.

The internship helped launch Putka's award-winning career writing and editing for *The Wall Street Journal* and Bloomberg News.

Susan DeFord served as a 1976–77 foreign correspondence intern for The Associated Press in Cyprus and Cairo. Ken Klein was a 1976–77 AP intern in Tel Aviv. *(Photo provided by Ken Klein)*

Former intern Laura Landro (BSJ '76), another leading talent at *The Wall Street Journal* until 2016, said she "barely squeaked through Economics 101" at Ohio University. In 1976, Landro turned down a job at *The Courant* in Hartford, Connecticut, after Wilhelm awarded her an internship with McGraw-Hill World News in London, steering her career to business journalism.

"Suddenly," Landro recalled, "I found myself reporting on the oil industry, the metal trading business, nuclear power companies, and petrochemical trading." It suited her.

Michael Precker (BSJ '76) extended his 1977 Tel Aviv internship into an 11-year sojourn, reporting from Israel for The Associated Press and *The Dallas Morning News*.

Not all foreign news interns have been successful.

An early intern was assigned to a one-person news bureau in Europe. But the student never linked up with the busy, traveling correspondent. In short order, the student spent the internship money and returned with little to show. Baffled and irritated, Wilhelm pleaded for proof that the student had tried to carry out his mission. The student produced an airline napkin.

After that painful lesson, Wilhelm avoided one-person news bureaus.

Anecdotes like this earned Wilhelm the nickname "The Dizz" or "Dizzy Dean." A visionary with global contacts, Wilhelm was neither an academic nor always a faculty favorite. Students, invited to his home for meals, appreciated his robust Rolodex as a connection to potential jobs.

Epilogue

At age 78, Wilhelm died on June 6, 1994, the 50th anniversary of the D-Day landing he had covered as a young war correspondent. Eulogies at his Maryland retirement center, veering a bit into hyperbole, said Dean Wilhelm had plucked Midwestern kids from cornfields to put them in foreign news bureaus.

Wilhelm's foreign internship program validates a journalism fundamental that at times is compromised or sold short: being there.

Witnessing everyday life in Israel helped "destroy any one-dimensional view," Putka said.

As media fragmented and transformed in the digital age, American news bureaus overseas have shrunk or shut down, with more international coverage produced by foreign reporters. Bucking the long retrenchment trend, Ohio University continues to dispatch novices overseas, saluting the principle that knowledge of the world is not a luxury amid globalization.

Lindsay Boyle (BSJ '13), 2013 intern with *The Daily Graphic* in Ghana, climbs the narrow and steep stairway of the James Town Lighthouse in Accra. *(Photo provided by Lindsay Boyle)*

After her 2013 newspaper internship in Ghana, Lindsay Boyle (BSJ '13) said foreign experience helped her get a job and helps her on the job. In upstate New York, Boyle's assignments for the Utica newspaper included coverage of international refugees.

Classmate Kaylyn Hlavaty (BSJ '13) left Ohio for a 2013 internship with *The Daily Star* in Lebanon. The editor told her—after she arrived in Beirut—that the internship had been eliminated. Hlavaty stayed. A year later, she was still in Lebanon, freelancing, blogging, and learning Arabic.

In Brussels, multimedia intern Caleigh Bourgeois (BSJ '14) conducted a long-term reporting project for a bilingual newspaper, looking back to World War I. Her other accomplishments would have been hard to fathom nearly a half century earlier when Dean Wilhelm's first foreign news intern set out from Athens. Bourgeois made a video of a Flemish YouTube star, posted on social media, and helped lead the paper's conversion from print to the web.

Far from Athens, she noted that her scholarship carries the name of an old-style print correspondent who wanted Ohio University students to see the world: The John R. Wilhelm Foreign Correspondence Internship Award.

BROADENING HORIZONS THROUGH TRAVEL

By Ralph E. Kliesch

WHILE ACADEMIC attention to international dimensions of journalism dates back at least half a century in the School of Journalism, many students gained their first opportunity for firsthand experience with journalism in other lands in the late 1970s through organized tours that took them to communication capitals of the world.

At the time, I shared with others the belief that there could be more to broadening students' horizons than just lecturing and assigning readings. The answer, of course, was travel. Was there a way? A window of opportunity presented itself when the university switched from semesters to quarters, including a nearly six-week winter break.

It proved a perfect time to organize international tours of media. After one false start, the first trip was scheduled in 1978—the beginning of 13 years during which I organized tours of media in New York, London, and Paris, involving in all some 140 participants. The students saw the advantages of such international travel and the chance to talk with high-level media practitioners.

"It was an experience that I benefitted greatly from—learning foreign customs, traveling on my own, and getting along with and working with others—in addition to the vast amounts of journalistic information I accumulated," Lynn Samuels (BSJ '91) said in a letter to me following the experience.

Student Nancy Wade (BSJ '93) had a similar reaction. "Americans should be more globally aware," she said. "I'm glad I went on this trip because it helped me learn that and become more attuned to international affairs and how they affect Americans. We need to work hard to make it a global effort," she said in an article about the tour in the Spring 1992 issue of *The Ohio Journalist.*

Global news agencies a focus

Tour activity varied from place to place, but a key component involved the global news agencies. One New York session found the group facing Associated Press President Keith Fuller; another, United Press International Editor-in-Chief H.L. Stevenson. Most of the annual wire service HQ meetings were with agency foreign editors.

Early among these was AP's Nathan Polowetzky, who held that job for 13 years and, in 1987, received the school's Carr Van Anda Award. The crusty character resurfaced memorably for me years later, via trans-Atlantic phone, when he kept Paris staffer Elaine Ganley (MS '75) from leaving her desk to join me for dinner (an intended thank-you for help in Paris scheduling) un-

OU students, on a tour of communication capitals of the world, discuss operations of McGraw-Hill World News with Editor Michael Johnson. *(Photo provided by Ralph E. Kliesch)*

til she determined whether the Duchess of Windsor had died. The rumor proved unfounded, but that was a late dinner.

Another regular visit stop was at Black Star, a New York–based international photographic agency founded in 1935 by three German Jews fleeing Nazi oppression. Until his 1990 retirement, and once thereafter at his residence, its president, Howard Chapnick, hosted the visits. Students always smiled at his unfailing mention that he had started there not as the messenger boy but as the assistant messenger boy.

French and British news agencies loomed large on the tour itineraries. At an early-on Agence France-Presse (AFP) visit, students were invited to see still-in-development digital handling of photographs. (Similarly, the only computers to be seen on the earliest tours sat in business offices, but even before the last tour rolled around in 1992, everything, everywhere was digital —a revolution that occurred in little more than a decade.)

Fittingly anchored at Number 85 at the foot of London's Fleet Street (though no longer) was Reuters, the great British wire service founded in 1851, three years after the AP's beginning. Hosting the OU visitors for most years was Shahe "Gubby" Guebenlian, who had for decades headed its Cyprus bureau. He was to become a good friend of the J-School, once giving a Communication Week lecture in Athens.

During the 1985 visit, Guebenlian presented each of the group's 10 female participants with a red carnation as they entered for the afternoon meeting. The gesture triggered another memorable moment just a few hours later, when the group crossed the street to meet an indelible character, William Francis "Bill" Deedes, editor of *The Daily Telegraph,* who greeted the arrivees with, "Where'd you get the posies?" That session with Deedes, no anomaly, was frequently interrupted by staffers popping into his office for approval of a cartoon, a leader, whatever. One could not escape concluding that here was a hands-on editor fully in charge. After Deedes retired, the broadsheet moved from Fleet Street out to Canary Wharf, along the Thames.

In Paris, the usual calls on *Le Monde* proved rather less colorful. One year, though, the City of Lights perhaps decided to compensate by offering a close-up, right-out-of-the-hotel-windows look at hundreds of French university students rioting about some issue or other. Cars burned, tear gas seeped through window frames, and I was hard-pressed to dissuade any of my lot from joining the party.

In New York, *The Times* was the obvious choice of newspaper. Visits there always included a tour, personally conducted by tour head Jim Morgan, and ended down at the giant presses. At that point, Morgan and I would pop across 43rd Street to a bar popular with *Times* staffers for a tall one or two before the group taxied off for its flight to Europe.

Another regular stop, in London, was Visnews. With videotape and satellite broadcasting still in their infancy, newsfilm for television was flown in from over the world for processing and distribution to local outlets. Visnews was located in London's outskirts at a site next to the Guinness brewery and relatively close to Heathrow Airport.

The groups visited TF1, France's private television channel, and global radio was another focus. Students heard about the Voice of America from U.S. Information Agency (USIA) officers at American embassies in London or Paris. The BBC World Service, broadcasting in 29 languages globally, and Radio France International (RFI) gave generously of their time. So did BBC Television.

Former students helped out

Highlighting the list of magazines visited was *Newsweek,* with particular emphasis on its then many overseas editions, a fact of life in those days over at *Time* as well. In Paris, *Reader's Digest* occupied surprisingly non-commercial-looking quarters in a residential section of town. In London, another magazine regular was the *European Rubber Journal,* edited by Robert Grace (BSJ '79), like Ganley among my former students.

Speaking of former students, New York–based graduates of the school (and once in Paris) annually sponsored an evening get-together with the travelers, often in a convenient bar. A big surprise one year came when one of the alums brought along former OU President John C. Baker, already in his 90s. Baker systematically buttonholed each participant and took him or her aside for a friendly lecture on making the most of this opportunity. Judging by the mandatory journal participants kept, for which I provided feedback during travel between cities, most appeared to have heeded that advice.

Overall, it was an eye-opener for most students. The study tour let them see a cross section of media and get a chance to talk to practitioners and managers for insights and firsthand knowledge. For many of these people, an abstraction became real for the first time. Even the term "culture shock" took on new meaning.

RELAXED MOMENTS

TELEVISION NETWORKS, of course, were high-profile visits for students on the Communication Capitals of the World Study Tour, and occasionally these visits produced interesting —sometimes unusual—experiences.

On one occasion at the ABC bureau in Paris, correspondent Greg Dobbs waved and called from across the newsroom, "Hey, I see Ohio University is back again." On another, Pierre Salinger, former press secretary for President John F. Kennedy, subbed for the absent usual host. He held court, cigar in mouth, feet up on Bureau Chief Peter Jennings' desk. Quite a show.

When students watched live national newscasts, the participants generally were divided between the studio and the control room for half the show and switched places for the second half. In New York, when asked how many times a year ABC's *Good Morning America* did this for a visiting group, a hosting producer smiled and held up just one finger.

Students marveled at the apparent precision of New York TV operations, only to be surprised at the seeming chaos in Paris, with the director and others in the control room screaming at one another. And during one unbelievable instance at Antenne 2, the French equivalent of Diane Sawyer fought to retain her composure as the weatherman and another staffer snaked along the studio floor, out of the camera's view, to tug playfully at her mike and earpiece cords. Good luck with that in New York, or probably any other TV news studio.

–Ralph E. Kliesch

PUBLIC RELATIONS AND CULTURE

By Hugh M. Culbertson

IN MANY ASIAN societies, gift giving is an essential part of social interaction. When public relations people or their clients offer gifts, journalists there often feel compelled by the force of culture and custom to accept them.

"We feel we must accept envelopes with cash in them," one Filipina journalist said. "But we also feel we must write critical stories about the gift givers to show we have not sold our soul to the devil."

But that's not the only influence of culture. A PR campaign in Thailand to control the spread of AIDS encountered a thorny language problem because Thai people avoid the use of what they consider a racy word such as "condom." Campaign organizers decided to substitute the name of a popular government minister with the last name of Mechai. It was OK to talk and learn about using Mechais. And the campaign took off.

In China and other Asian societies influenced by the teachings of Confucius, *quanxhi* (formation and maintenance of friendly, trusting relationships) is almost everything. One can scarcely buy a cup of tea or a theater ticket without becoming a close friend of the vendor who sells it. Unfortunately, loyalty to friends can be carried too far. Corruption goes unchecked as a result and is a major concern to both foreign and domestic communicators in many places.

These examples make it clear that public relations and mass communication are shaped by the cultures in which they operate. U.S. practice and ethics don't always fit cleanly and easily in foreign contexts. Obviously, public relations practitioners must wrestle with such differences when they work abroad.

Chinese doctoral student Ni Chen (PhD '92) recognized this in the late 1980s as she tried to size up the practice and educational preparation of PR people working in her homeland. Surely, she reasoned, it was important to find out how practitioners worked in various countries around the world.

A study conducted by Chen, who now teaches at the University of Macau, found that public relations—seldom even mentioned in China prior to the 1980s—had grown into a large and respected, if somewhat controversial, occupational field. After all, *quanxhi* was a personal phenomenon. And the Chinese media, while growing and influential, had low credibility largely because the state and the Communist Party owned and controlled all indigenous stations and publications.

I had the pleasure of serving as Chen's adviser, and we began querying colleagues in the Association for Education in Journalism and Mass

Communication, the Public Relations Society of America, three different PR associations in mainland China, and other groups. We found that quite a few people had done at least exploratory research on public relations as practiced in various countries. So we pulled together the work of these scholars, along with their own research, in a book called *International Public Relations: A Comparative Analysis.*

Published in 1996, this volume helped spur interest in what one might call an emerging subdiscipline of international PR. It has helped focus on a key question that underlies much contemporary public relations scholarship: Do PR people work primarily to persuade? Or do and should they focus primarily on relationship building and maintenance?

The latter seems consistent with the Western ideal of people fostering mutual understanding and equality—as well as give-and-take—within civic society. Anthropologists say that societies have high power-distance, with certain social groups having much higher status than and power over other groups. Such inequalities are widespread, even in America. And they become particularly troublesome when based on gender.

Feminist scholars have particular concern that women tend to earn less than their male counterparts who do the same work. In China, this concern, as applied to public relations, has been called the "Miss PR" problem. Female practitioners there often work primarily as translators and hostesses. However, they have begun moving into management positions.

At least three other alumni completed dissertations designed to enhance understanding of international public relations: Ali Alanazi (PhD '93), now at King Saud University in Saudi Arabia; Ali Kanso El Ghori (PhD '86), professor at the University of Texas–San Antonio; and Alan Freitag (PhD '99), now a professor at the University of North Carolina–Charlotte.

LASTING FRIENDSHIPS ACROSS THE ATLANTIC

By Bernhard Debatin

Located in the eastern part of Germany, Leipzig is a beautiful, thriving, and popular college town with a population of more than 550,000. The longstanding partnership between Ohio University's Scripps School and Leipzig's Institute of Communication and Media Studies (KMW) is arguably the school's most important collaboration with a foreign institution. It is fair to say that the secret of its success has been the personal dedication and friendship of the participating faculty and students on both sides of the Atlantic.

Since 1996, I have been a highly involved player in this partnership. I started working as a professor at the KMW Institute in Leipzig when both the university and the city were still in the rebuilding phase following a half century of domination by the Soviet Union. These were exciting times, as the 1989 fall of the Wall and the ensuing German reunification had opened up East Germany to the West.

On a sunny day in late spring of 1997, I met Professor Robert Stewart from the E.W. Scripps School of Journalism, who was visiting Leipzig and had joined us for a faculty and staff retreat. We were fascinated with the opportunities that working together would offer. Soon thereafter, we initiated a virtual collaboration, employing web-based video technology to deliver lectures and enable real-time student discussion between the two universities.

Later, I was invited to spend fall and winter quarters of 2000–2001 as a visiting professor at Ohio University. During my stay, the School of Journalism had a job opening that was very close to my research and teaching interests. Enchanted with Athens, its friendly people, and the Scripps School, I applied, although originally I had planned to return to Germany. I was offered the position and accepted happily.

Kelly Fisher (BSJ '16) takes her place on Mephisto, the student radio station at Leipzig University, during a 2014 study-abroad program. *(E.W. Scripps School of Journalism photo)*

To some degree, it is an unlikely serendipitous coincidence that all this came about. As early as 1991, Ohio University Provost James J. Bruning started to explore partnership opportunities with the newly accessible East German universities. He found Leipzig University to be the most promising partner. At Bruning's suggestion, in 1992, the director of the school at that time, Ralph Izard, traveled to Leipzig with John Lewis Gaddis, director of the Contemporary History Institute, to establish relations with Leipzig University's newly established Institute of Communication and Media Studies. This led to the beginning of a fruitful exchange of faculty between the two institutes, supported with funding from the U.S. Information Agency (USIA) and the Freedom Forum.

Formal agreement to cooperate

The successful and growing collaboration among departments from the two universities—eventually and most prominently journalism, history, economics, and chemistry—resulted in a formal agreement of academic cooperation between Ohio University and Leipzig University. It was signed by OU President Charles Ping and Cornelius Weiss, Leipzig's rector, in June 1994. This agreement has since been renewed and expanded several times (1999, 2004, 2008, and 2012). It has made possible a number of cutting-edge collaborations, such as the Ohio-Leipzig European Center (OLEC) and the recently established joint double master's degree program between the Scripps School and KMW.

Stewart was the first Scripps School faculty member to teach in Leipzig, and he spearheaded the newly founded partnership and served as an adviser in the formation of the KMW Institute and establishment of the student-run radio station Mephisto 97.6. Over the next few years, thanks to a grant from the Freedom Forum, 10 Ohio faculty members visited Leipzig.

At the same time, faculty from Leipzig traveled to Athens to give talks and conduct research, as well; the most notable of these were Rüdiger Steinmetz and Gerhard Piskol, who would become long-lasting collaboration partners and friends. Other visiting faculty and staff from Leipzig included Günter Bentele, Michael Haller, Tilo Prase, Bernd Schorb, Heide Schochow, Jörg Land, and myself.

The partnership also opened up opportunities for Leipzig journalism students to come to Ohio: Gabriele Mäurer (MSJ '93) and Katrin Pomper (MSJ '95) were the first Leipzig students to earn Ohio master's degrees. Ine Dippmann, Sabine Witt, and Nina Schlüter were the first to complete professional internships at WOUB and on *ACTV-7 News* in 1996. The professional internship program has since been a permanent and successful fixture in the partnership. At the same time, the first Scripps School students went to Leipzig, too: Deborah Schwartz-Shaar (MSJ '98) conducted research and interviews with professors in 1996 and 1997 for her thesis on the rebuilding of journalism education at Leipzig University.

The first student groups from Leipzig to travel to Athens were members of the student radio station Mephisto, who visited in 1995, 1996, and 1997. Two additional groups visited Athens in 1998, under the guidance of Leipzig Professors Walther von LaRoche and Rüdiger Steinmetz. During the same period, several student groups from the journalism school traveled to Leipzig, led by Robert Stewart.

The Ohio-Leipzig European Center

In 1998, a video conference, organized and led by Professor Stewart and myself, brought together the new leadership of the two institutions: Robert Glidden, president of Ohio University, and Volker Bigl, rector of Leipzig University. This virtual meeting resulted in a plan to create a European studies program in Leipzig for students from Ohio. That agreement to create the Ohio-Leipzig European Center (OLEC) was formally signed in March 1999.

The program was implemented in 2000. The first Ohio student group to embark on the OLEC program, during the spring term of 2000, was led by Timothy Anderson (geography). Now an Ohio faculty member, I led the first OLEC summer school in 2002.

Over the next few years, many students from both universities were given opportunities to study at the partner institution. Funding was provided by the two universities, the Leipzig foundation Medienstiftung, and Fulbright or the German academic exchange service (DAAD).

For instance, Katie Horn, a master's student from Leipzig, spent the 2006–07 academic year at OU as a nondegree student in the journalism program. During this time, she not only worked toward and completed her master's thesis for Leipzig but also participated in a research project on Facebook and privacy and coauthored a journal article on it.

"I was stunned," she said. "So many wonderful teachers for my master's classes, such a great variety of topics and research, open doors and helpful advice by my professors at any time—what a benefit for my academic and professional career!"

Another graduate student from Leipzig, Anne Herrmann, came to Athens for fall 2013 to pursue her research on online volunteering, innovation, and social media. She conducted interviews with students from Ohio University and gave a number of classroom presentations.

"The time in Athens," she recalled, "meant for me both adventure and enrichment: it did not only immensely advance my thesis project, it also provided me with an opportunity to get to know wonderful people and a tremendously diverse country."

The program continues to expand. Over time, a number of additional collaborative research and teaching projects have been implemented, most notably the grant-funded international broadcasting LightHouse Media project, led by former Scripps School Professor Kevin Grieves and Leipzig Professor Rüdiger Steinmetz (2011–15). Recent collaborations also include newer faculty and staff from both sides. These included, from Ohio, Michael Sweeney, Aimee Edmondson, Craig Davis, Allison Hunter, and Brook Beshah (who received his PhD from Leipzig) and, from Leipzig, Ansgar Zerfaß, Sonja Ganguin, Patrick Merziger, Werner Süss, Cornelia Wolf, and Uwe Krüger.

Professor Grieves was also instrumental in developing a new form of study abroad experience for Ohio students, bringing a student group to Leipzig in the summers of 2014 and 2015 for an internship and shadowing project with Radio Mephisto and other Leipzig media. Undergraduate Kelly Fisher, who participated in the 2015 program, said that this was "one of the most unique reporting experiences" she'd had in college. She really appreciated the friendships with German students, as "they were incredibly helpful and generous with everything they provided," and she said she was "looking forward to being able to visit again and hopefully host them in the U.S. one day."

The most recent expansion of the partnership with Leipzig is the implementation of a joint double master's degree program. Funded, in part, by the German academic exchange service (DAAD), this program annually allows up to five graduate students from each side to obtain an international double master's degree from both universities. Participating students graduate with an MS in Journalism from OU and an MA in Global Mass Communication from Leipzig. The program is directed by Dr. Alexander Godulla (Leipzig) and me (Ohio).

This unique and groundbreaking double degree program was implemented in 2015 and that fall admitted its first cohort. To date, it is the only such program in both the United States and Germany, allowing for simultaneously obtaining degrees within the regular two-year period of the master's program.

Kate Hiller (BSJ '16), who as an undergraduate interned at Radio Mephisto, is among the students who are part of the new double-degree pro-

PARTICIPANT IN THE GLOBAL COMMUNITY

THE INITIAL CONVERSATION that led me to Leipzig—standing in Bob Stewart's office, sometime in 1995—went something like this:

"I'm Jeff Johnson. I'm a Scripps student. I heard that OU has a relationship with Leipzig University, and that you're the person to talk to about it."

"Yeah, wanna go?"

My interest in Leipzig started the year before in Salzburg, Austria, in an OU German Department language program.

In Salzburg, we acquired sufficient linguistic skills to get around, hoarded rolls we swiped at breakfast, and took pretty pictures on 24-exposure film rolls. I was glad I'd done it, but it left me feeling unfulfilled. It was observatory study abroad. I wanted to participate. The result? By fall 1996, I was the first OU undergraduate matriculated at Leipzig University since at least before World War II.

I received a stipend of about $450 per month from the German Academic Exchange Service (DAAD) for one semester. It was enough to cover meals and a room in a renovated concrete-slab dormitory. The building looked like the pictures they'd shown us in middle school, in San Diego in the '80s, when they wanted Cold War American youth to know what communism looked like: slab concrete, kids.

Fortunately, the Leipzig city center and the university campus were energetic and inspiring. And I already had friends there—or at least friends from there.

One friend was Sabine Witt, a Leipzig journalism student. She wasn't in Leipzig that fall: the same day I traveled to Germany, Sabine traveled to Athens to intern at WOUB. We exchanged tips by email and once by phone before we left. She needed a place to stay. I put her in touch with friends in Lakeview Apartments. We wouldn't meet in person for another two years, but we remain in contact today.

In summer 1996, WOUB had hosted another Leipzig intern, Ine Dippmann. I was the *Summer Post*'s editor and helped introduce her to Athens. In Leipzig, she lived on my street, Johannes R. Becher Strasse, named for the poet who wrote the lyrics to the East German national anthem.

gram. "I may not have otherwise decided to try to stay at my alma mater for graduate studies had I not been able to be part of this collaboration," she stated. "I am so excited to see where this program goes in the future."

Celebrating its 25th anniversary in 2017, the Ohio-Leipzig partnership is here to stay. It has brought educational enrichment, professional development, and widened horizons to the participants. At its center, however, is the unique opportunity for an encounter that transcends educational and scholarly purposes. Countless friendships have resulted from the exchange, and this personal experience is the lifeblood of the partnership.

Ine enforced linguistic tough love, refusing to speak English to me. I'm grateful for that. She also took an interest in my integration and got me into Leipzig's Vivat Akademia student choir. Her efforts were successful: in that choir, I met Ulrike Junge, a Leipzig student, whom I married in 2001. That's another story. (Yes, we're still married.)

I enrolled in two courses and had a couple of assignments for the student radio station, Mephisto.

On my suggestion, Mephisto sent me one winter evening to the Leipzig Zoo for "person-on-the-street" interviews at an after-hours indoor tour. Microphone in hand, I asked, in atrocious German, what people thought of the zoo animals at night.

Most people walked away.

Some Leipzig students kindly speculated that I'd witnessed locals' latent fear of being recorded, stemming from their fear of the Stasi, the former East German secret police. That could be, I supposed. It's equally likely that I'd just invaded their space.

Such setbacks only drove me to try harder. Partly, it was my way of understanding a changing world.

Just four years earlier, we had watched the Berlin Wall fall—on broadcast television, with rabbit-ear antennae. The networks interrupted scheduled programming for that breaking news. Demonstrations had been going on for weeks in places like Leipzig's St. Nicholas Church. The government relented. President Ronald Reagan had demanded that Mr. Gorbachev "tear down this wall," but in the end, it was the people who had done so.

I felt lost in those years. It was hard to imagine a direction. The Internet was fueling a U.S. economic miracle, but the print journalism jobs I had trained for already looked threatened. Moving toward disruption was a way of coping, the way a surfer rides a wave.

I wouldn't say I gained one particular skill in Leipzig that made me successful. I learned German fluently and a lot of history and culture. I didn't stay in journalism. My career took a different path—not as exciting as I'd hoped but a respectable path. Mostly, Leipzig made me a participant in the global community, not just an observer. That was the point.

–Jeff Johnson

THE MALAYSIAN CONNECTION

By Ralph E. Kliesch

It was an uneventful spring afternoon in 1971 when my phone rang. A visitor from abroad was on campus, and the caller wondered if I, as the school's assistant director, could give the man a tour of the J-School's facilities in Copeland Hall. Of course, no problem.

Arshad bin Ayub was the director of the Mara Institute of Technology (ITM, for Institut Teknologi Mara), located in suburban Petaling Jaya, just outside Malaysia's capital of Kuala Lumpur. That program was established in 1967 in "response to a crucial need in the country for trained manpower at professional and semi-professional levels, especially among *bumiputras,*" the Malay word for the county's indigenous Malay population.

ITM already had an ongoing, successful relationship with OU's College of Business, through which Malaysian students earned Bachelor of Business Administration degrees, coordinated by and largely taught by visiting OU faculty. Director Arshad—energetic, liberal minded and forward thinking—was acutely aware of the need for something better than Malaysia's existing mode of journalism education. Perhaps, he believed, his institution could lend a helping hand. He had gotten word of the Ohio J-School's reputation and inquired if he might have a look around, hence the call for a tour guide.

When my phone rang that day, I knew very little about Malaysia—and had no inkling whatsoever of how it would change my life. I was aware that journalism "education" there was but a hand-me-down from its British Colonial heritage of on-the-job, apprenticeship training. Beyond that, I knew little.

The tour, largely of journalism and radio-television facilities, was the usual, with conversations about how the professional components were supported by a solid base of liberal studies—the usual, that is, to us but not to Arshad. At one point, while passing Radio-TV's third-floor windowed radio studio where a student was reading the WOUB news, Arshad looked concerned. "But who's watching him?" he asked. He was surprised to hear that there was no need, that students were taught what to do and simply did it.

Recommendation for an OU connection

Then he surprised me. "Would it be possible," he asked, "for you to come to Malaysia and do a feasibility study for us, about setting up a mass-comm program at ITM?" As it turned out, I was eligible for a sabbatical leave the following year, so, yes, it was.

When spring quarter ended, my family and I were off to Kuala Lumpur. For the next six months, ITM arranged for me to visit a cross section of Malaysian media. Among others, I interviewed editors of *The Straits Times* and *The Malay Mail,* respectively the nation's leading broadsheet and tabloid. I spoke with numerous advertising and public relations executives, discovering that many were either British or American, either expats or assigned there from overseas headquarters. I learned that commercials and public relations spots were produced without sound, with audience-specific audio tracks in Bahasa Malaysia (the national language), Chinese, Tamil, or English to be added later.

When I submitted my report, it included the recommendation that ITM establish a program paralleling the one in business, with students taught by visiting OU faculty as well as OU-trained local teachers, coordinated by a resident Ohio faculty member. Although not very realistic about its chances, I nevertheless included a recommendation that since the Malaysian mass media served all races, the new program should be available to Chinese and Indian students as well as *bumiputras.* That would be a problem, Arshad said, explaining that ITM's charter, targeted exclusively for *bumiputra* uplift, left no room for such consideration.

But my report was accepted and implemented, in 1972, despite shortsightedly, in my mind, excluding its multiethnic component.

Years later, in January 1982, I returned to Malaysia to fill in when the resident coordinator of OU's College of Business BBA program in Malaysia accepted another position. During the next 18 months, that proximity gave me the opportunity to observe the progress of the ITM mass communication program. It seemed a good time to start graduate-level instruction in Malaysia. Accordingly, I drafted a proposal for a joint OU/ITM master's degree and submitted it to ITM's then-Director Nik Rashid, who wasn't interested. Dead, the proposal was buried.

A short-lived program

But another surprise would provide the last word, so to speak. In 1995 or so, Sankaran Ramanathan, an ethnic Indian Malaysian and 1974 Scripps School grad who'd been on ITM's mass-comm faculty since its beginning, got into the act. (The *bumiputra*-only proviso at ITM applied only to the student body, not to faculty, administrators, or staff.) He resurrected my proposal, and this time it would bear fruit, and the master's degree program was established at ITM.

Ohio's involvement in this master's degree program lasted for only a short time, however, and ended when ITM was authorized by the government to grant degrees and become a full-fledged university (UiTM). During the five quarters of the program's existence, Professor Drew McDaniel of OU's Radio-Television faculty served as resident coordinator. Instruction was provided by a group of rotating Ohio faculty members, including two from the School of Journalism: Dru Riley Evarts and Patricia Cambridge.

Fast-forward to today. ITM has grown to university status. The department has become the Faculty of Communication and Media Studies, numbering some 20 to 30 instructional staff. Degrees are offered up to and including the doctoral level. Although much has changed, ITM faculty generally acknowledge that the current curriculum has evolved from that established in the original "feasibility study" and by Ohio University's partnership with ITM back in the 1970s.

EXPERIENCING MIDDLE EAST CULTURE

By Abhinav Kaul Aima

Scripps Howard Visiting Professional Terry Anderson wanted his Ohio University students to understand Lebanon and how to cover the complex culture of the country in which he had been kidnapped and held captive for nearly seven years.

"I have always felt, since my return from Lebanon, that American perceptions of that country and its people were distorted," he said, "that there was little recognition that the radicals who kidnapped me were a minority, and that most Lebanese, like most people everywhere, are decent, ordinary people trying to live their lives in the midst of chaos."

Anderson was Middle East bureau chief for The Associated Press at the time of his 1985 kidnapping by a group of Shiite Muslims linked to Hezbollah. He was released in 1991 and joined the Scripps School of Journalism faculty in 1998.

As a faculty member and director of the Institute for International Journalism, Anderson created the Middle East Studies Program to provide students the opportunity to travel to Lebanon for cultural and journalism study. He organized the tours in the summers of 1999, 2000, and 2001.

His goal was clear.

"I also believe that few Americans really understand the complexity of the Middle East and that we have a simplistic and distorted perception of the people and problems there," Anderson added. "Taking journalism students to Lebanon seemed to me a very good way not only to give them a better understanding but to help them explain to their future readers/viewers those complexities."

The student travelers spent five weeks in Lebanon, staying at the American University of Beirut, attending lectures on political science and history from the AUB faculty, visiting local news organizations, and conducting their own research projects on topics relevant to Lebanon and the Middle East. The program was supported financially through grants from the Fares Foundation and the Earhart Foundation, which covered most of the costs of the trip.

Field trips to meet locals

Students participated in group field trips to visit other areas of Lebanon, usually driving out from Beirut heading east to Baalbek for an overnight stay and then taking a northwesterly route back to Beirut, passing through diverse Lebanese towns. On other days, students made individual or group trips to visit different Lebanese constituencies around Beirut or within a few hours of driving distance.

"The highlight for me was getting to interview a warlord in his mountain palace," said Michael Bellart (BSJ '01), copy editor for the *Global Times* (China), who participated in the trip to Lebanon in 2000. "It was a surreal experience for a suburban kid who had never been abroad before. The AUB trip still stands out for the breadth of experiences we had. We visited almost every part of Lebanon over those weeks and met so many people."

As a part of the trip, students visited different sites of political and social activity in Beirut and heard about the experiences of those who were involved in issues of national and international impact. These lessons often were put into perspective by the time students spent with local journalists from news organizations such as *The Daily Star,* Lebanon's leading English-language newspaper, and *An Nahar,* one of the most prominent Arabic-language newspapers.

"The studies program gave me an opportunity to see things from different perspectives," said Ayako Hirayama (MSJ '02), *The Japan News* staff writer, who participated in 2001. "The Middle East had never felt close to my life before taking part in the program. I only knew about the region through stories in the media."

Hirayama continued, "When I was in Lebanon, I had chances to meet people from different backgrounds, including politicians, journalists, Palestinian refugees, and Hezbollah representatives, and directly talk and listen to them. These firsthand accounts raised my awareness of the complexity of the world and helped me better understand, for example, the meaning of the aphorism 'one person's terrorist is another person's freedom fighter.'"

Diverse people, contrasting views

Bellart also speaks of the diversity of people he met in Lebanon and the contrasting political views they represented.

"I remember the Palestinian refugee who said he threw away his son's college admission letter because he didn't want the next generation to abandon the struggle," he said. "I remember the Hezbollah fighter turned prison tour guide who never stopped smiling as he described how his captors once forced him to lick the floor while he was incarcerated there. I had never heard anything like it before."

Bellart said, "We also had great access to the country's leadership at the time, thanks to our contacts at *The Daily Star.* With a phone call, I was able to get interviews with government ministers and members of parliament, which turned out to be important for the project I was working on. As far as university experiences go, it was an eye-opening one. I'll never forget it."

For many students who participated in the program, as was Terry Anderson's goal, the experiences continue to inform and influence their professional lives.

"My experiences in the program also made me feel closer to international news," Hirayama said. "In 2005, when I was checking stories from wire services at the office in Tokyo, the news that Gebran Tueni, a Lebanese politician and publisher of *An-Nahar,* an influential daily in that country, had been killed by a car bomb, came in. During the program, we visited the newspaper. The news that someone I had met had been the target of an assassination sent a shiver down my spine."

However, students also remember the cultural and social aspects of the trip, which provided experiences of a diverse and buoyant Lebanon. "The program was educational and also fun, as we visited a winery and other tourist attractions," Hirayama recalled.

"Learning about the culture of Lebanon and the complexities of the country's political structure and media was hands down one of the most profound experiences of my life," said Emily Swartzlander (BSJ '01), who was part of the 2001 trip. "I think about the trip with great fondness. More importantly, I believe that the lessons I learned about Beirut and the region have had tremendous impact on the person I am today. I would go again in a heartbeat."

Looking back, Anderson, who left OU in 2002 and now teaches in Florida, expressed the belief that the students benefited as he hoped. "I think it worked very well," he said. "I continue to hear from the students who went on those trips about how much it changed their lives and their outlook."

SING TAO CENTER

By Dwight M. Woodward and Ralph Izard

It may have been one of Ohio University's most entertaining building dedications in 1997 when lion dancing and Chinese zither music highlighted the formal opening of Sing Tao Center on Court Street across from Scripps Hall.

The building, the initial home of the Institute for International Journalism, stands as a monument to the contributions to the E.W. Scripps School of Journalism by former faculty member Chang Kuo-sin and noted Hong Kong newspaper publisher Sally Aw Sian.

Chang joined the Ohio University faculty in 1985 as part of an exchange that sent faculty member Sandra Haggerty to Hong Kong Baptist College. A former United Press journalist, who is credited with being the first to report the victory in China by Communist forces, he stayed in Athens for three years before retiring and moving to Portland, Oregon. Before coming to Athens, he had worked in Hong Kong as head of the Department of Communication at Hong Kong Baptist College.

"Chang was highly respected by his students, his colleagues and particularly the professional community in Hong Kong and in Mainland China," Haggerty said in the summer 1988 issue of *The Ohio Journalist*. "Most of the major media facilities were peopled by Hong Kong Baptist students. The graduates of the Department of Communication were considered to be the best in Hong Kong."

Most important, however, it was in Hong Kong that he became a trusted adviser to Sally Aw. It was through his introduction and influence that she donated $150,000 to buy the former Sigma Nu fraternity house in 1993. On the Ohio University campus, that site became the location of the namesake building of Aw's company, Sing Tao Center.

Aw is the adopted daughter of the late Aw Boon-Haw, who, with his brother, created a successful business empire in Burma selling Tiger Balm medicinal ointment. The story is that he entered the newspaper business when he grew weary of paying to advertise his product.

Sally Aw inherited the publishing company and expanded it into a worldwide enterprise, publishing both English- and Chinese-language newspapers on three continents. Sing Tao, the name of her company, is a nickname for Hong Kong. Aw sold the company in 1998.

Aw also gave $500,000 to support a chaired professor of international journalism at Ohio University. In 1988, she became the first international journalist to be awarded the school's Carr Van Anda Award, and in 1997 she received an honorary degree from Ohio University.

"Sally Aw Sian has seen momentous times . . . from her early childhood in Burma to her stewardship of the Sing Tao newspaper empire to the handover of Hong Kong to mainland China in 1997," said Anne Cooper-Chen, former director of the school's Institute for International Journalism. "We were lucky to have UP's Chang Kuo-sin link her to the J-School," and the institute was also fortunate "that she attended the dedication of Sing Tao Center. She was one of Asia's most prominent businesswomen."

Facing page: OU President Robert Glidden and Hong Kong–based newspaper publisher Sally Aw Sian participate in the dedication of Sing Tao Center, initial home of the Institute for International Journalism. *(Photo provided by Anne Cooper-Chen)*

Sing Tao
Center
College
Green

INTERTYPE
ALL IN RACKS 10¢

The practice of journalism

Given a positive slant, the old axiom "Them that can, do" may be construed as part of the foundation of the E.W. Scripps School of Journalism. It applies to faculty, to students, and to working journalists. Without denying the importance of formal instruction, it may be said with certainty that those in the school understand that education involves more than what happens in the classroom. The school encourages—sometimes requires—students to take advantage of opportunities to gain professional experience. These are some of the ways through which that has occurred.

Facing page: A group of 1968 *Post* staffers pose at *The Athens Messenger.* Among those included are Mark Roth (BSJ '69), Cathy Martindale (BSJ '69), Andy Alexander (BSJ '72), Cynthia Boal Janssens (BSJ '69), Clarence Page (BSJ '69), Tom Hodson (BSJ '70), Bruce Jorgensen, Carol Towarnicky (AB '69), John Felton (BSJ '75), Gary Rings (BFA '69), Ken Steinhoff (BFA '70), Ann Ford (BSJ '69), Jane Navid (BSJ '69), Leslie Bonar (BSJ '69), and Don Hudson. *(© Ken Steinhoff, all rights reserved, reproduced with permission)*

SIX HOURS OF NONSTOP POLITICAL COVERAGE ON WOUB

By Henry Heilbrunn

Politics pulled people left and right.

The unrest of the 1960s—rooted in disputes over civil rights, the Vietnam War, and concern for the future environment of the world—intensified in the early '70s as a Baby Boom generation, growing with discontent, was graduated from high school.

These new college students couldn't drink legally in Ohio until they turned 21. They were prevented from voting until the state's constitution was changed in 1971. A reestablished national lottery assigned a random number to each male signifying the likelihood of being drafted into combat. And the draftees could be killed in an ideological war in a sliver of a distant country fighting an enemy whose culture, language, and motivation they didn't comprehend.

This was the volatile environment of the early '70s: What unfolded halfway around the world was as close as Court and Union streets for the students. Their future in Athens—whether Democrat or Republican, liberal or conservative, pro- or antiwar—was directly linked to politics, those of Vietnam, in Washington, D.C., and in the state capital of Columbus, Ohio.

For teething journalists eager to learn their print or broadcast profession, Athens was a petri dish of opportunities to practice the coverage of politics, an experience that would resonate through their careers.

The university-owned radio and television station, WOUB AM-FM-TV, was an 18-hour, seven-day learning lab, overseen by a handful of full-time professionals and operated hands-on primarily by a small group of paid and a large group of highly committed volunteer students.

Politics coalesced these people.

Henry Heilbrunn anchors live election results in May 1972 during the Ohio primary from the radio studio at WOUB AM-FM. *(Photo provided by Henry Heilbrunn)*

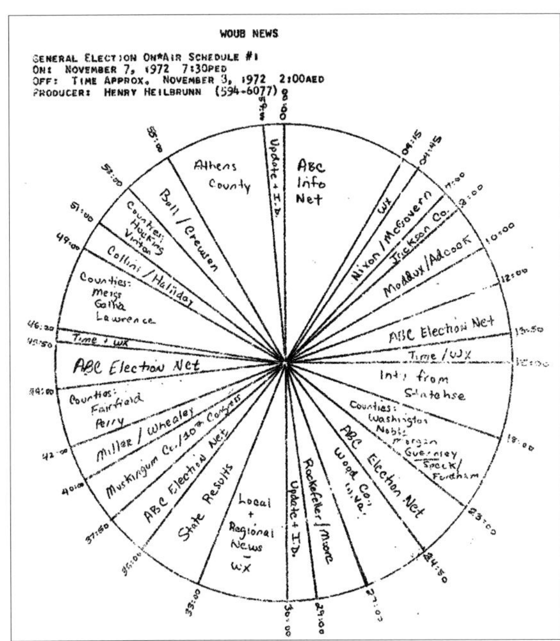

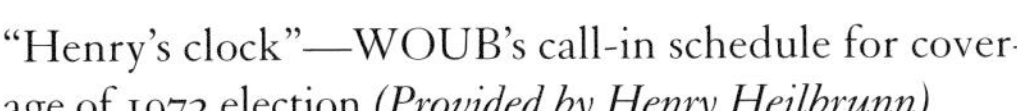
"Henry's clock"—WOUB's call-in schedule for coverage of 1972 election *(Provided by Henry Heilbrunn)*

When George McGovern, a U.S. senator and opponent of the war in Vietnam, opposed incumbent Richard Nixon for president in November 1972, an army of student journalists assembled to report the results of the race at the top of the ticket—and to uniquely cover every other contest from the 18 counties in Southeast Ohio that constituted the primary coverage area for WOUB. For most of this army, it was also the first time that they cast their own vote.

An ambitious project

"This was the most ambitious election coverage I may have ever been a part of," said Frank Robertson, who spent 40 years in front of a TV camera after he graduated from OU in 1973. "I was never involved in something that was both radio and television."

More than a hundred students volunteered on November 7, 1972, driving to county boards of elections, local cable TV headquarters, or nearby radio newsrooms in the 18 counties during these pre–cell phone times, to beg, borrow, or steal telephones to report the latest results back to Athens. These results were broadcast instantaneously on WOUB AM-FM and separately on WOUB TV.

It was the biggest, most comprehensive, continuous live coverage that WOUB radio and television had ever undertaken for any local news event—brought to life by student journalists, producers, bookers, assistants, engineers, camera operators, lighting and sound engineers, and directors, who for six hours sustained live election results coverage that could not be rehearsed in advance.

They reported extemporaneously on the winners and the losers, for many the first time they would ad-lib, explaining in unscripted reportage history in the making to which they were bearing witness. They stuck microphones in front of happy victors willing to speak and tracked down the tearful defeated. In one night, they learned, practiced, and perfected the craft of a practice that occurs every four years.

A time of career development

"It was a very important seminal moment in my career development," said Eric S. Land, who upon graduation in 1973 went to WCPO TV in Cincinnati as a reporter and eventually ran TV stations as president and general manager at WTLV/WJXX, Jacksonville, Florida; WFLA, Tampa, Florida; WIAT, Birmingham, Alabama; and WGRZ, Buffalo, New York.

In 1972, Land led a team of student reporters inside the Ohio Statehouse all election night, alternating between twice-an-hour audio reports telephoned to WOUB radio and standups before a remote WOUB TV crew broadcasting the first live, in-color origination from outside of Athens.

The general election two years earlier and the primary election six months before were trial runs for the students, with reporting of each election becoming more complex as confidence grew. The general election of 1970 was the first time students had worked side by side in the statehouse with members of commercial statewide media outlets. The students elbowed their way to outhustle professional reporters gathered in the secretary of state's office to get the story first rather than to rely on the slow-clacking teletype.

On radio in 1972, Land's live twice-an-hour, two-minute audio reports were collated into a hand-drawn 60-minute on-air clock that would be followed precisely for six hours.

Much planning, precise scheduling

Land kindly credits me, as WOUB's student news director, with much of the election night coverage success: "[Henry] was not only our executive producer and radio anchor but developed a 60-minute 'clock' that was mimeographed for every reporter's call-in assignment with a specific time to call and length of the report. We referred to it as 'Henry's clock.' That clock, on a single sheet of paper, was the roadmap for success that evening and served many of us well in future coverage plans with which we were involved after college."

I anchored WOUB radio continuously from 7 p.m. until 1 a.m., when the results of most races were known. We squeezed 30 unique segments into each 60 minutes—ABC News reported 5 times an hour from New York and Washington. Student reporters in 18 counties each telephoned in once an hour with live results.

I joined The Associated Press after I graduated in 1973 and was one of the founding executives of the early pre-Internet online service Prodigy, started by CBS, IBM, and Sears.

Don Benson, who spent three decades as an editor and supervisor at the Voice of America in Washington, D.C., following graduation in 1973, covered the mayor's race in Athens.

"We were there all night awaiting the results," Benson remembered. The race was heated and controversial. The winner, Donald Barrett, was an Air Force colonel who commanded the Reserve Officers Training Corps, an irony for town/gown relations two years after the university was closed by rioting following the 1970 shooting deaths of four students at Kent State University. Barrett served as mayor for the next 12 years.

While radio hummed for six hours of nonstop local and national coverage, Douglas Caldwell, the full-time professional news director at WOUB who had attended Ohio University in the 1960s, began a three-hour marathon under the hot lights in the TV studio at 8 p.m. He was supported by a cast of dozens who were handwriting numbers on blackboards to update the latest results for the nation, state, and nearby counties.

He pivoted among narrating the latest results, calling for the remote feed from the statehouse, introducing the live national summary from PBS, sitting with political professors who were providing instant analysis, and adlibbing interviews with local winners and losers.

It was produced to imitate the news networks—just with a hundred-plus volunteers—all of whom would return to their classrooms and homework the next day with a unique experience that they could describe in job interviews and would propel them in their careers.

"What I remembered over the decades since," Caldwell said, was that "while there was competition in individual markets from radio stations for these results, no one that day—or perhaps since—had better coverage of the election. Comprehensive and interesting because our reporters had prepped so well, and energized as everyone began to realize that this team effort was unmatched anywhere by anyone."

Land said he incorporated this model into his career.

"This was the bedrock of how we would attack elections and how we would approach any long-form TV coverage," he explained. "The planning and execution of what we did for election coverage was instrumental in guiding how I led our coverage for hurricanes. It taught my team and me how to prepare and execute major breaking news coverage over a long period of time and remain organized."

Caldwell, who ran news departments at TV stations and is now editor and publisher of the *Central Valley Business Times* in California, said, "These were the smartest, most driven people I had ever worked with up to that point. I've since met many more, but keep in mind these young men and women were 'students' and were not supposed to have that level of professionalism."

One of those students, Robertson, who anchored at WTVT, in Tampa, puts the experience into context: "My university launched me. It gave me my start. WOUB gave me that real-life experience every day. I got the chance to immerse myself. All of us who went through were much better prepared to get into the industry."

When the radio and TV transmitters were silenced for the night, the result was as everyone expected—a landslide victory for Nixon, with 61 percent of the popular vote. The surprise followed in less than two years. After the Watergate scandal—revealed by persistence of two reporters—Nixon became the only president to resign in disgrace.

ELECTION UPSET: A LESSON ABOUT DEADLINES

By Howard Wilkinson and Ken Klein

In hindsight, *The Post*'s award-winning election coverage in 1974 foreshadowed a hard truth for print journalism: Publishing news every 24 hours for home delivery seems eerily like the horse and buggy as the car goes by, honking.

Once-a-day deadlines can be killers, especially when the unexpected occurs on deadline, or worse, immediately afterward. In the 1974 Ohio gubernatorial election, *The Post* benefited from this unforgiving reality.

When James Rhodes upset incumbent Governor John Gilligan (D-OH), we got it right because *The Post*'s deadline was the latest in the state. Bigger morning dailies, trapped by deadlines, hedged wrong. In the end, Republican Rhodes, who had been governor for two terms in the 1960s, defeated Gilligan by 11,488 votes out of nearly three million votes cast—less than one vote per precinct statewide.

With more luck than experience, we learned an important lifelong lesson: whoever has the latest deadline wins, or at least has significant advantages. Print journalism, painfully, is still trying to figure out this lesson.

The context

The 1974 Rhodes-beats-Gilligan election was so confounding that pundits like Larry J. Sabato still refer to it as a baseline for upsets. That midterm vote was a perfect storm for Democrats. President Richard Nixon had resigned in disgrace, and the economy was sputtering. Republicans lost 48 House seats and five governorships. John Glenn (D-OH) won his first term in the U.S. Senate.

"Governor John J. Gilligan will win re-election in Tuesday's voting," said the *News-Journal* in Mansfield on Saturday, November 2, 1974, three days before the election, citing polling.

Gilligan, had he won, would have been a presidential contender in 1976.

On election day, we drove from Athens to Columbus, settling in for a long night at the downtown office of Ohio's Secretary of State, which certifies elections.

Victory cake as metaphor

Both candidates for governor hosted election-night parties in separate ballrooms in the now-demolished Neil House hotel across from the statehouse. At the time, the Neil House—with a popular ground-floor bar—was an epicenter of Ohio politics.

About midnight, as the Democratic incumbent outpaced Rhodes, Gilligan's supporters wheeled a giant cake into his "victory party," a hopeful symbol in the shape of the White House. Trailing, Rhodes had conceded and gone to bed in a Neil House suite. Aides later roused him as he pulled ahead. After returning to his ballroom, Rhodes delivered a second speech to a handful of supporters, proclaiming he never had any doubt he would win the election.

Meanwhile, in the somber Gilligan ballroom, the White House cake began to wilt and fall apart as the governor's supporters stumbled out of the room.

Definition of "deadline" evolves

Most reporters covering this story had already filed, saying Gilligan had a small lead. *The Post* was able to keep working the story. We filed the last lead about 6 a.m., via telephone, reporting the information to John Kiesewetter, *Post* editor.

Our we-got-it-right front-page triumph was made possible by an extremely generous deadline. *The Post* was printed by *The Athens Messenger;* we didn't have to get our pages to the press room until 6:30 a.m.

Later that school year, we would win a deadline-news award from the Society of Professional Journalists' Region 4 Mark of Excellence competition.

Six years later, as the definition of "deadline" evolved, risk-taker Ted Turner started Cable News Network, a precursor to the Internet and social media.

Deadlines are to journalism as gravity is to physics. They're always there, but now more often.

ON THE OTHER HAND . . .

WHEN *THE POST* makes a mistake, it can be a big one. And years ago, corrections were more complicated.

Like at the start of Daylight Savings Time in February 1975, when I was editor. *Post* staffers forgot the old adage "Spring forward, fall back."

Working in the Pilcher House first-floor newsroom and pasting up pages in the adjacent production room, staffers were chanting "Turn Back Time" all night . . . so that was the headline on our Page 1 story the morning of Friday, February 21, 1975.

Instead of "springing forward," *The Post* told readers, "Don't forget to turn your clocks back one hour at 2 a.m. Sunday morning in a return to Daylight Savings Time."

After realizing our mistake that Friday morning—decades before cell phones, text messages, emails, push alerts, Facebook, Instagram, or the Internet —*The Post* diligently corrected the inaccuracy as soon as we could: 72 hours later, in Monday's paper.

A front-page story titled "Behind the times" read, "*The Post* offers its apologies to those readers who followed its Friday advice, and reported for classes two hours late. PST (Post Standard Time) resumes in October. This, of course, is in reference to *The Post*'s admonition to turn clocks back rather than forward, as most of the nation did over the weekend. We hope you enjoyed the extra sleep."

–John Kiesewetter

A MODEL OF EDUCATIONAL COOPERATION

By Roger Bennett

Young journalists-to-be are told to get all the experience they can, but then they often have problems finding a job because they don't have experience.

For many years, the School of Journalism sought to help deal with this dilemma through what at the time was a one-of-a-kind program designed to give students on-the-street assignments in a real-world newspaper setting.

It began in 1925, when the director of the journalism program, George Starr Lasher, and Frederick W. Bush, publisher of *The Athens Messenger,* developed reporting practice and editing practice courses at the newspaper. The courses were reported to be the first of their kind in the United States.

For at least 25 years, the school's advertising students had the same opportunity. The advertising practice class involved students assuming responsibility, under faculty supervision, for clients and meeting their needs for *Messenger* ads.

Connecting *The Messenger* to the university's education system must have been a dream of Frederick Bush's because he was a teacher before becoming editor. Bush, who graduated from Ohio University with a bachelor of pedagogy degree in 1892, purchased the paper in 1895 and became publisher. The courses continued to be offered throughout the years that the newspaper was owned by the Bush family. Frederick's son, Gordon—who received an AB degree from OU in 1924, the same year he received a journalism degree from the University of Missouri—directed the newspaper until his son, G. Kenner Bush, took over. Kenner continued the student practice program until the business was sold to the Brown Publishing Company in 1997.

Staff members at *The Messenger,* including Charles Reamer (BSJ '33) and Roger Bennett, consult as part of the newspaper's practice program. *(Photo provided by Roger Bennett)*

G. Kenner Bush, in retirement, exhibits his photography at Ohio University's Kennedy Museum of Art. *(Photo by Chris Eaton)*

Bush family ownership

Over three generations, the Bush family had owned *The Messenger,* covering 102 years, with Kenner, as the last family member in the position, serving for 32 years. He sold the paper to the Brown Publishing Company, which in 2007 sold it to American Consolidated Media. The current owner, Adams Publishing Group, bought the paper in 2014. The reporting and editing practice courses ended during the Brown ownership.

One of the last editors to be involved in the reporting and editing practicum courses was Karl Runser, now residing in Athens. He served as editor and was also involved in the program as an adjunct professor from 1973 until

1998; Editors at the paper served as adjunct faculty for their work handling the student reporters and editors.

"I really enjoyed serving in the adjunct position. It was rewarding for me to be able to work with the students and try to instill an interest in news in young people," Runser said. "I think the program made a real contribution to the journalism school because students learned a lot."

Kenner Bush, as a young man, actually was a participant in the program. He worked two summers in the newsroom as a student reporter when he was home from college.

"My first job at the paper was rewriting the local copy sent in by correspondents from the small surrounding communities," he said. "These were stories of people 'shopping in Columbus' or of people having guests. The staff made me jump through the hoops, and it was good for me."

He said the hardest part was deciphering the handwritten copy.

"I gained essentially the same experience that journalism students received in their reporting and editing practices courses," Bush said. "The experience was so important that the program continued to be of special interest to me during my years at *The Messenger.*" He continued, "I remember instances when news would break, and there was no staff available. We would send student reporters. The program gave students a small-town experience covering service clubs, such as Rotary and Kiwanis."

Bush said, "I always felt the program was a great plus for the university and *The Messenger.* The program was in our own self-interest. One of the real benefits was having a regularly changing cadre of talented young students in and around the newsroom. That helped make us a better, livelier community newspaper."

"Talented young students"

One of those "talented young students" was a student reporter named Halina Czerniejewski (BSJ '72).

"Working at *The Messenger* meant you were dealing with professionals. They were more demanding," she said. Czerniejewski said writing stories in a classroom "was completely different from writing for an audience." While the classroom was great, she said, it "was harder writing for publication."

Upon graduation, Czerniejewski went to work for the *Toledo Blade,* where that local grounding paid off. She suggested a story idea that necessitated a trip to Pennsylvania with a *Toledo Blade* photographer. They went to Wilkes-Barre to report on a devastating flood. There was a local angle for Toledo—Wilkes-Barre was a sister city, and Toledo residents had sent loads of material to help the Pennsylvania victims.

From Toledo, she went to Columbus with The Associated Press bureau. From there she took a copy editing job with *The Quill,* the publication for the Society of Professional Journalists. While pursuing an MBA in Chicago, she worked as a copy editor for the *Chicago Sun-Times.*

Czerniejewski was nominated for a Pulitzer Prize for a story she wrote for the (Cleveland) *Plain Dealer.* The story was about her family's Polish heritage and the problems the family faced in the post–World War II era. She now does freelance writing from her home in Scottsdale, Arizona.

Residents of Athens may not have known that students worked at *The Messenger,* but some city officials, such as long-time Fire Chief Charles Dalton, did. Dalton, chief in the 1960s and early '70s, prior to the current 911 system, often knew when a new student was assigned to his beat, because the emergency fire alarm would sound. It didn't take him long to teach the students that when they called the station for any overnight news to not use the emergency phone number, which set off an alarm. The students had to call the nonemergency number.

In all those years there have been memorable moments for students, including coverage of the phantom Point Pleasant "Mothman" in 1966 and the Silver Bridge collapse in 1967.

The late George Lovell, photographer for *The Messenger,* took a group of reporting practice students to Point Pleasant to gather information on the "Mothman." After arriving in Point Pleasant, however, they discovered a problem: No one had remembered to bring a flashlight. Stumbling around in a darkened rural area looking for the monster was bad enough. It became more difficult as Lovell would blind everyone trying to provide light by flashing his camera's strobe unit.

The end of *The Messenger* practice program, Kenner Bush said, was foreshadowed when the newspaper moved from its location on Union Street in what is now Lasher Hall to new facilities outside of town on US33. That made it much more difficult for students to get to the newsroom. With the growing reputation of the school, he added, students had many more opportunities for internships around the state and nation.

But it was a program remembered fondly by many students for the real-world experience it gave them. And it was a program that highlighted a strong relationship between the newspaper and the school, one that continues in a modified form today. Monica Nieporte (BSJ '93), *The Messenger*'s current publisher, said even though the practice courses ended a few years ago she still hires Ohio University students as interns and as full-time employees.

ALTERNATIVE EXPERIENCE

By Terry Smith

The Athens News, a twice-weekly alternative/community newspaper in Athens, had a tight, if not always tightly organized, relationship with Ohio University's journalism school long before the school acquired the E.W. Scripps imprimatur.

Founded as a '60s-style "underground" newspaper in the spring of 1977, *The Athens News*—then called the *Athens "A" News* ("for alternative")—from the start was heavily staffed with OU journalism graduates and undergraduates. This pervasive Bobcat influence hasn't changed in the 38 years of the newspaper's existence.

Bruce Mitchell, the paper's founder and majority owner until September 2014, when he sold the paper, gave props to three Scripps faculty members in particular—Byron Scott, Ralph Izard, and the late Bob Baker—for the early development of the newspaper. All three had "a profound impact on the success of *The Athens News,*" said Mitchell (BGS '75).

Of the three, Baker had the biggest impact, and early in the paper's existence he became a part owner. Baker, who taught advertising in the School of Journalism when the paper was founded, helped develop a focused advertising sales team from the inexperienced staff of the barely surviving weekly free-distribution paper.

"He helped us create marketing plans for local businesses and built sales material," Mitchell said. "His expertise and advice became the foundation for the business's future success, and he was my own mentor for nearly 20 years, until his death."

Terry Smith. *(*Athens News *photo by Dennis E. Powell)*

Scott used the *News* as a case study when the paper was considering how many days a week to publish. At the end of the quarter, the class gave its report and specific recommendations.

"To my extreme disappointment, and complete surprise," Mitchell said, "the class recommended the paper *not* increase to a three-day-a-week publication but concentrate on building up our twice-weekly product. It was a recommendation that stopped *The Athens News* from making a catastrophically bad business decision. Sometimes, learning what not to do is critically important."

Izard also served as an important adviser to the newspaper in its early years, according to Mitchell. "Reviewing our news coverage and our market position with Izard gave us critical information in shaping our development," he said. "Finding a professional sounding board to review ideas and share observations with is helpful for any organization."

A staff of OU journalism graduates

The newsroom staff's ties to the Scripps School were obvious to me when I took over as editor in 1986. All of the full-time writers had attended and/or graduated from the J-School, as had nearly all of the freelance reporters. Other departments at the paper, including the ad sales staff, usually had Scripps representation as well. For example, David DeWitt, longtime associate editor and reporter, graduated from Scripps in 2007, and general-assignment reporter Conor Morris received his BSJ in 2014.

A particularly fertile period for the Scripps–*Athens News* relationship came during my 10-year stint as an adjunct instructor teaching newswriting at Scripps, from 2000 to 2010. During this decade, I recruited several promising student writer/reporters from my classes every year.

For a period of about a dozen years in the 1990s and 2000s, the *News* also kept a stable of student journalists, the *Athens News* Campus Bureau, supervised by a student editor. This bureau supplied a steady stream of campus-related stories.

Chelsea Toy (BSJ '10) served as a freelance reporter for *The Athens News* during her last two years before graduating. Now managing editor of *Spin to Win Rodeo,* the largest magazine in the sport of rodeo, Toy recalled the valuable learning experience she received both at *The Athens News* and in Scripps Hall.

"I really count *The A-News* as the core of my journalism training and education," she said. "I had a lot of great classes at Scripps, of course, but I think I took advantage of the need for editing at *The A-News* and took just about every assignment I could get. . . . I learned to write quickly and efficiently and to create complimentary web packages to go with my stories."

By the time she started working at *The A-News,* Toy said, she had taken a computer-assisted reporting class and learned how to dig through numbers and find relevant statistics. In addition, the community journalism classes taught by Professor Bill Reader "were outstanding in giving me pretty much the exact skill set I needed to be pretty helpful on a few different fronts at *The A-News.* We learned to think critically about important issues in small towns, and we learned how to use multimedia to tell those stories," she said.

Another former *Athens News* freelance reporter, Lindsay Boyle (BSJ '13), said that mixing her Scripps School education with front-line work reporting for the paper helped set her up for success in the news business.

A supplement to college classes

"Working for *The Athens News* was a great supplement to what I was learning in Scripps," said Boyle, who currently works as a reporter for *The Day,* a daily paper in New London, Connecticut. "Even midway through my junior year, I often found myself yearning for a more hands-on aspect to the things my professors were saying. Part of what makes Scripps a great school is that there are so many opportunities to get involved outside the classroom."

Another alum, Megan Workman (BSJ '11), got involved with *The Athens News* in September 2010. She had taken my sophomore-level newswriting class in Scripps, and I remember thinking she showed promise.

"*The A-News* is the sole reason I applied for only newspaper positions when I graduated college," Workman noted, "what led me to serve as the business reporter for the *Charleston Gazette* for two years, and what helped me to crave that daily news, that daily adventure out into the city."

She said the Scripps School played an essential role as well. "After years of talking my education over with my peers, I realized how special the program is and how much it truly involves its students. Scripps pushes you to think outside the box, to be well-rounded and try when others might not think it's possible," she said. "To hear my peers on the radio, to watch their videos of hard work on the Internet, and to read their stories in print and hear them live on TV—all of that happened while I was still enrolled at OU."

Workman recalled my newswriting class "as one of the first classes in Scripps where I started to see the stars align in journalism. Mark Tatge's classes also did this for me. (As an example, Tatge required his students to request public records—from the clerk's office, gasp!—and other tasks that he knew one day would be a reality.)"

The benefits of the Scripps pipeline don't stop at cheap, raw talent, however. Having student reporters and photographers acting as our eyes and ears has helped the *News* maintain its OU coverage and its important student readership.

The only downside to the close relationship between the journalism school and newspaper is the same bummer that anyone who staffs or teaches at a college feels. You get to know some great young people for a few years, benefit from their energy and talent, and then, poof, they're gone.

That is, unless they, like a lot of other people, end up staying in Athens.

A FUNNY THING HAPPENED . . .

By Van Gordon Sauter and Ralph Izard

For several years, Professor Mel Helitzer's humor-writing class was among the most popular in the E.W. Scripps School of Journalism. Perhaps its most memorable element was its final examination, which required each student to perform a stand-up routine with an audience. But it wasn't the only role of humor among students. From time to time, satirical publications emerged. Perhaps there were many, but two in particular—*The Green Goat* and *The Hocking River Valley Silt*—are mentioned here. What they had in common was their lack of formal association with the school, their tendency to irritate university administrators, and the delight they stimulated among students and perhaps even some faculty.

The Green Goat

As a business major who failed pathetically the mandatory pass of classes in statistics and accounting for a business degree, Van Gordon Sauter crumpled into a terrified academic refugee and sought haven on the beguiling, welcoming shores of L.J. Hortin's "you'll-find-a-home-here" journalism school. It housed the most interesting students on the campus, he said, and the classes were unfailingly interesting or diverting. Well, most of the classes.

Sauter described his experience with *The Green Goat* this way:

"At some point in the mid-'50s, I, along with two other guys desperate for ways to underwrite beer, pizza, and carnal aspiration, somehow became responsible for publishing the college humor magazine, *The Green Goat.* In effect, I think we owned *The Goat.* I was the journalism major and thus the content guy. Our business chief brought the discipline and congeniality of a Cleveland mafia don to our bottom line. And a really nice guy took over advertising and distribution and brought in money. We adored him. (Frankly, my memory of all this is tenuous, so excuse mistakes and the absence of details.)

"*The Goat* actually dated back to 1913, when it started off as a quasi-university-sanctioned publication mainly dedicated to literary aspirations. It folded in the Depression and occasionally returned over the years as whatever kind of magazine someone thought might make a payroll.

"Our *Green Goat* was neither sanctioned nor literary. We were, for the time, too often gross and contemptuous and were thoroughly (and, one must concede, justly) abhorred by the university management. But the university, home to an esteemed journalism school and celebrating the First Amendment, found it awkward to deal as it wished with 'a publication.'

"We found housing in a large office on the second floor above the legendary Tavern, a bar on North Court (later the Blue Gator and now known as The Overhang), at the time haunted by the louche, aspiring elements of the fraternity and sorority assemblage. It was owned by a delightful first-generation Greek, James Anastas.

"The exact nature of our agreement with Jim was known only to The Don, who considered journalistic and advertising people inherently unfit to know, let alone deal with the realities of business. Across the hall were the living quarters of an advanced music student, his walls lined with those big old long-play records. One of his favorites was calliope music from Paris—which at times became the sound track for *The Goat*.

"We lifted about 60 percent of our content from other college humor magazines. There were a lot of them, and that was a commonly accepted practice. We created the other 40 percent. The local product was surprisingly good. Well, not to the university's dean of men and all Hocking River valley enthusiasts of decorum and chaste behavior. They were aghast. Justifiably.

"At one time, the university had a very simple black-and-white parking permit for faculty and administrators. Parking was a nightmare, and a permit was treasured. Well, we published an exact copy of that permit in our magazine. Suddenly, for a mere pittance, you could buy our mag and get your own thoroughly credible parking permit . . . and access to the most treasured real estate in Athens.

"The university seethed. On another occasion, and here we went so far over the top that I cringe when even thinking of it today, we found (i.e., lifted) a collection of photos depicting haughty Nazi generals and administrators, —maybe even the Führer,—traveling about Germany inspecting the Third Reich. We, of course, translated all this in our pages to depicting the OU dean of men and his factotums swaggering about the campus, lording over the groveling students. Our readers seemingly loved it. We should have been flogged.

"The university then began talking behind closed doors of ways to stifle the magazine and to dispatch the three *Goat* owners to a mechanical arts trade school in Steubenville.

"I was then enthralled with a young woman taking her junior year in Paris. Her landlord apparently agreed to assume, if necessary, ownership of the magazine, thus supposedly diminishing our vulnerability to some but not all university retribution.

"But through it all *The Goat* facilitated laughs, beer, and unrelenting expressions of abhorrent taste. And a lot of good, clean, middle American fun, too. The university shook its head in resignation and accepted the horror of it all. And life on the second level of The Tavern was, for a bunch of callow youth, addled by calliope music and beer, resplendent. We had folding money.

"A few days before graduating in '57, our favorite *Goat* artist dropped by with a gift for me. It was Jim Dine, who went on from *The Goat* and Ohio University to become a distinguished American artist and poet. Indeed, *The Goat* had a lot of contributors (most of them quite rational and decent), including more than a few from the journalism school (somewhat less rational and decent).

"I do retain a lasting mortification about how we treated the dean of men. With all our accumulated (thimble-sized) wisdom, we considered him a troll. Unbeknownst to us, Maurel Hunkins was a man of accomplishment. He was a graduate of UC Berkeley, one of the nation's most esteemed universities. A Phi Beta Kappa, no less. And a credible musician who founded a highly regarded string quartet. A thoroughly civilized and benevolent influence in the society. But it's far too late to apologize.

"In those years, the McCann Erickson advertising agency (the country's second largest) every spring hired five MBAs and five supposedly creative types from colleges across the country. Because of *The Goat* and some columns for *The Post,* McCann invited me into the Mad Men world of New York City. I eventually opted out for journalism, but I consider the happy trifecta—OU, *The Post,* and *The Green Goat*—as the benefactors of my career. Maybe I should have added the dean to that list. I fear he would not be pleased."

HOCKING RIVER VALLEY SILT

The following is reprinted with permission from *The Ohio Journalist,* July 16, 2015:

BETWEEN 1969 and 1970, Rudy Maxa (BSJ '71) was editor of the *Hocking River Valley Silt,* a student-run satirical magazine.

"I made a lot of money with it," Maxa said of the magazine, which was unaffiliated with the university. "It helped me pay some of my way through college."

Maxa said he sold all the ads for *Silt,* which was published every couple months and distributed for a quarter on the streets by people wearing white gloves. Thus the publication's catchphrase: "Untouched by Human Hands."

After he became editor of *The Post* his senior year, Maxa said *Silt* stopped publication because "there was nobody to take it over."

EXPERIENCING THE HECTIC LIFE OF BROADCASTING

By Sara Magee

CLASSROOMS PROVIDE the needed foundation for any college student, but it's the experience that counts when you go for your first job. Students are told, and we knew it to be true, that the more internships and hands-on work you do, the better.

This was classic advice, and the E.W. Scripps School certainly delivered on providing opportunities for experience to a young woman who wanted nothing more than to be a journalist. One of the culminating moments for any Scripps broadcast sequence major at OU was the semester (or two, or even three) in which the *ACTV-7 News* class was taken.

During my time, under the watchful eye of then-Professor Larry Levin or Professor Eddith Dashiell, students worked on developing storytelling skills through reporting, editing, anchoring, and producing the daily 5:30 p.m. newscast, which aired live over the Athens cable network. It was not an uncommon sight to see numerous students, myself included, running from an edit bay to master control (a short distance of not more than 14 or 15 steps), VHS tape clutched in a death grip, dodging people and backpacks that littered the control room floor in hopes of getting the tape in the machine and cued up—often just moments before it went on air.

I'll never forget the time I walked into the studio fresh off a 6 a.m. morning shift at WOUB followed by three hours of class and was told to go interview a local Athens official and put together a story on community development—and have a package edited and put together by show time three hours later. A show that I also happened to be anchoring. I can still feel the ¾-inch camera, lighting kit, tripod, and edit deck weighing down my short figure as I trotted up Court Street, got the story, then made it back to Scripps and into an edit bay to whip something together, and somehow made it to the anchor desk for the show with minutes to spare.

Students saw ACTV-7 News as a job

Experiences such as these made *ACTV-7 News* so much more than just a class. It was a job. Not many college broadcast programs at the time provided the "live-newscast" experience, much less a daily live broadcast. But in the Scripps School, *ACTV-7 News* was, for a broadcast student, the summit reached after three or four years of climbing. "It truly was one of the most memorable experiences I've ever had—and it's served me well in my producing career," said fellow graduate Carrie Mertes-Nagorka (BSJ '97).

Recently, the group of women I went through Scripps with ended up chatting on Facebook and remembering a seminal Scripps experience that came during our senior year. Mertes-Nagorka, Alisa Reich Walsh (BSJ '97), Laura Yunghans Patrone (BSJ '97), Kirsten Rechenbach Matyiaski (BSJ '97), and I attended the 1996 Radio Television News Directors Association annual conference in Los Angeles in October 1996. We pointedly remembered the valuable chance we had to connect with industry personnel and show off our Scripps education to prospective employers, as well as our unsuccessful effort, billing ourselves as the "Scripps Girls," to gain selection for the TV show *The Price Is Right.*

Seven years after graduating, with years of television news producing and reporting and an Emmy award under my belt, I came back to pursue a PhD in mass communication at Scripps and was asked to teach what was once *ACTV-7 News,* renamed *Athens MidDay.* It was produced in a brand-new newsroom, with digital editing and the actual ability to go "live." Seven years might have brought major technology changes and moved the television studio from the Scripps building to the RTV building, but the students hadn't changed. Under the guidance of Professor Mary Rogus, they were producing even more professional pieces, including live sports and weather broadcasts.

But one can't talk about the *ACTV-7 News/Athens MidDay* experience without talking about the WOUB Public Radio and Television experience. Students, most of them broadcast, volunteered to work in the newsroom, writing, reporting, and delivering newscasts on television and radio.

The WOUB experience

The WOUB experience started, usually with a 6 a.m. shift, learning the ropes from Assistant News Director Fred Kight. This included learning the correct pronunciations of Southeast Ohio counties before one could go live on air. To this day, many WOUB alumni still get into arguments over the correct way to pronounce "Albany" and "Chauncey." And of course, who could forget the experience of working the newsroom the morning after the annual Saturday Halloween party? For all four of my undergraduate years, I had the joy of the 6 a.m. news shift the Sunday after. It got so the police knew I would be calling and had all the arrests (hundreds of them) and information ready for me.

Once radio was mastered, if we were lucky, we got to work for *Newswatch,* the 11 p.m. TV newscast. Working with main anchor and producer Darren Toms (BSJ '89), we learned very quickly what worked, what didn't, and when it was absolutely essential to call CNN (from which we received video) and ask then-reporter Wolf Blitzer to do a "custom WOUB tag out" for a television story.

I vividly remember the day when First Lady Hillary Clinton was on campus as the afternoon commencement speaker (June 14, 1997). It was also the day that OU graduate and *Today* show anchor Matt Lauer was giving the morning commencement address. Not only was I graduating that day, but I was covering both Lauer's and Clinton's visit for the WOUB newscast that would air the following Monday. I'm not sure how I managed it, but somehow I managed to graduate, have lunch with my family, then head back and finish interviewing people for my stories. I'm pretty sure I was on an adrenaline high—that didn't end until *Newswatch* went on air the following Monday.

These experiences, and many others, are what I believe many other broadcast graduates cherish about our Scripps experience. As Rechenbach Matyiaski said, "My Scripps experience was the perfect blend of learning, laughter, and friendship, and it also gave us some really valuable insight about our future careers."

My first boss told me I was hired heavily based on the résumé reel and experience I'd received working at both ACTV-7 and WOUB. My current career in college teaching sees me using the lessons learned from my career and Scripps students and faculty on a daily basis as I guide another generation of students into broadcasting careers.

But most important, I have found that I can always come home to my Scripps and WOUB families, current students and alumni alike. No matter how far you stray, it still challenges and awes me with what it was, what it is, and what it no doubt will become.

MISS AMERICA AND PRESS FREEDOM

By Bill Choyke

When an idea becomes reality and survives into its fifth decade, it can be called an institution.

It's a pleasure to say that in 1972, as editor of *The Post* and with the help of several others, I helped craft an institution at Ohio University: the Post Publishing Board. It wasn't easy. And in the process, *The Post* and I took a few lumps during a tumultuous time for journalism independence on the OU campus.

Laurel Lea Schaefer's name has faded from most memories except, perhaps, those of a few old-timers in Bexley, Ohio, and Miss America aficionados. Schaefer (BFA '71), an OU alumna from that Columbus suburb, became the dream of America's mothers when she was crowned Miss America on September 7, 1971, by emcee Bert Parks.

The new Miss America was the honored guest for homecoming festivities in Athens the last weekend of October 1971. *The Post,* which was on summer-quarter break when she won her crown, welcomed Schaefer back to campus with a profile written by Campus Editor Susan Reimer. The story noted that Schaefer was well liked in her Alpha Xi sorority house and that sorority sisters remembered her as thoughtful, extremely good-natured, and well-mannered.

The article also examined Schaefer's postcoronation public comments deploring premarital sex and the drug habits of America's youth. Reimer's reporting suggested that Schaefer's own behavior in college was inconsistent with her public persona. A firestorm quickly erupted, centered in Columbus, with outrage directed not at Schaefer but at *The Post,* its editor, and the writer of the story.

Reimer (BSJ '73) received threatening mail, including a handwritten note on Ohio University Inn stationery and mailed with an eight-cent Eisenhower stamp that read, "Even if true, freedom of speech does not permit those of good breeding to be so mean, low and dastardly in their thinking and expression." It was signed, "C.U. Soon."

State legislators called for my firing. *Chicago Sun-Times* columnist Bob Greene, a Bexley native who earlier wrote that no one there seemed to remember the new Miss America from her high school days, summed up the reaction to Reimer's story in the Columbus area with the headline "Nobody laughed in Bexley, Ohio."

"Choyke assigned reporter Susan Reimer to find out what Laurel Lea had been like when she was at Ohio U.," Greene wrote. "The result of Miss Reimer's reporting was a fascinating story that indicated Miss Schaefer may have gone for some of the same kicks that just about everyone else in college enjoys."

While independent in spirit, *The Post* at the time answered to the 20-member Student Activities Board and its Publications Subcommittee. Through its power of the purse—the board doled out $97,500 to more than 120 recognized campus organizations—the SAB exercised considerable power and was a rival of the separate Student Government Board, which recommended policy for campus life, among other things. *The Post* received a lion's share of SAB allocations that year—$39,700, or about a third of the newspaper's total $118,000 budget.

For *The Post* staff, the paper was more than a student newspaper; it was a professional newspaper staffed by students. The editors enjoyed a solid working relationship with SAB's Publications Subcommittee, which included among its 11 members persons with journalism backgrounds not on the SAB. After the Miss America story appeared, the subcommittee expressed regret but took no other action.

The climate changed, however, on December 1, 1971, when, after lengthy discussions, the SAB adopted a resolution that required the editor of *The*

Post to abide by the board's interpretation of *Post* policy. The resolution also suggested that if I disagreed, I should step down. I opposed the proposal on the grounds that it amounted to intimidation of *The Post,* that it was identical to a resolution rejected by the Publications Subcommittee two weeks earlier, and that it violated *The Post*'s rights under the First Amendment through a "chilling effect."

In short, the resolution set the stage for prepublication censorship by a group of special-interest students and administrators who knew little about journalism or its standards. Former *Post* Editor Rudy Maxa (BSJ '71) was quoted afterward (in a *Post* examination of the SAB) that he saw the SAB as a "hot bed" of political activity involving a lot of ego and little desire to help student groups.

Fortunately, Maxa was not the only one to think that. Shortly after the brouhaha erupted, I began seeking out smart, experienced minds to develop an alternative *Post* governance structure. *Post* adviser Ralph Izard provided his usual keen insight in a steady, rational way. So did one of Izard's faculty colleagues, Roger Bennett. Most important, we found an ally in then–OU President Claude Sowle, who privately told me that he thought Reimer's profile of Miss America was a decent piece of journalism that had triggered an unwarranted reaction.

Creation of the Post Publishing Board

On March 7, 1972, during his weekly press conference, Sowle announced the creation of the Post Publishing Board, which would assume the responsibilities of the SAB's Publications Subcommittee on April 1. The mission of the new board would be to appoint the editor of *The Post,* informally review his or her recommendations of other top staff members, and meet at least twice a month to discuss *Post* policies and review editions.

The new board, Sowle said, was created after he had "talked with people with concerns on all sides of the spectrum, ranging from *Post* editor Bill Choyke to the University Board of Trustees." He added that he believed the new board would lessen the threat of intimidation and prepublication censorship of the newspaper.

To his great credit, the OU president stood up to Ohio Board of Regents Chancellor John Millett, who a day earlier had called for an end of support of campus newspapers through student fees. "I totally disagree with that viewpoint," Sowle said. "A campus with as much activity as we have needs a daily link of communications, and the excellent job *The Post* is doing, in my mind, is a far better alternative than an official university newspaper or a School of Journalism laboratory newspaper."

The structure, size, and mission of the Post Publishing Board have remained largely intact since Sowle's actions long ago. It functions in an advisory capacity only, except for its singular formal responsibility of naming *The Post*'s editor.

The pursuit of good journalism and spirit of postpublication oversight are what we contemplated in establishing the Post Publishing Board. Then and now, it makes sense for student professionals to practice journalism that reflects time-tested standards as set forth by respected journalism groups, such as the Society of Professional Journalists.

Appropriately, the Miss America controversy has long been forgotten. Fortunately, the spirit and letter of the Post Publishing Board have not.

DID "THE BOSS" COME TO TOWN?

By Dan Sewell and Mary Beth Sofranec Bardin

By spring 1976, Bruce Springsteen was the hottest sensation in American music. His "Born to Run" album had vaulted him into what would be lasting stardom, and he was such a phenomenon that both *Time* and *Newsweek* made him their cover story in the same week of late October 1975.

Renowned performer Bruce Springsteen (most likely) enjoys a beer at Swanky's, a popular Athens bar. That's *Post* reporter Mary Beth Sofranec Bardin in the background. *(Photo by Joe Vitti/OU* Post, *reprinted with permission)*

Springsteen had a dedicated following in Athens, but his emergence as a best-selling artist able to pack large venues gave to rise to speculation that he would skip his scheduled April 1 concert at the War Memorial on campus. *The Post,* in its April Fool's edition, fueled the rumors with a fake story about how Springsteen had canceled, to be replaced by "The Lame Excuses." It was accompanied by a photo that appeared to show a student setting his Springsteen ticket on fire.

Springsteen, of course, didn't cancel his performance. And that April Fool's spoof wouldn't be the only Springsteen story in the April 1 *Post.*

Mary Beth (Sofranec) Bardin (BSJ '77) was a junior and a *Post* staff writer. Here she recounts her most-unexpected interview—and a most-memorable photo—in an uptown bar the night of March 31:

> "We were working on the April Fool's edition when someone ran into *The Post* offices and said Bruce Springsteen was in Swanky's [on Court Street near the current CVS], drinking a beer. [*Post* staff photographer] Joe Vitti grabbed his camera, I grabbed my notebook, and we raced around the corner to the popular student hangout on Court Street. It was sparsely crowded on a Wednesday night.
>
> "We spotted a guy with shoulder-length, curly dark hair standing near the bar. Even though I was a huge fan, I wasn't *exactly* sure it was him. I approached him anyway and asked if we could talk. He was uncomfortable but gracious. My one and only question was something like, 'You write about being an outsider, from the wrong side of the tracks. Now that you're famous and kind of rich, is it harder for you to write those kinds of songs?' He mumbled a reply in between sips of his Heineken: 'Being famous in itself means nothing. I just do what I do and don't worry about being famous. I don't analyze what I do—I couldn't.'
>
> "As [Springsteen] spoke, Vitti snapped as many pictures as he could without being intrusive. We hurried back to *The Post,* where I wrote an extended cutline for the photo. It would run on the 'real' front page of our April Fool's edition. The next day, my world turned upside down. A rumor circulated that *The Post* had been duped. That was not Springsteen, but a lookalike. It was an April Fool's joke on us. I was mortified. Keep in mind—there was no Internet with countless images of our rock heroes to verify his image. Die-hard Springsteen fans assured us we had the real deal, as did Swanky's employees. His concert that night was a sellout, and Springsteen veterans said he and his band played longer than usual for the Athens crowd.
>
> "Even so, it was years before I was able to look at that photo and know for certain it was The Boss. And then realize, he was smiling at *me.*"

FROM *APPALACHIA 70* TO *SOUTHEAST OHIO*

By Ellen Gerl

"We should call it Stormy Sees," says the student who wrote the article about a young girl's bond with her blind horse, Stormy. "Get it?"

The small group of students erupts in laughter.

"Corny," groans a classmate.

"No way," says a second.

It's headline writing day in the *Southeast Ohio* magazine classroom, a favorite session when alliteration abounds, wordplay reigns, and eventually, the perfect headline emerges. On this particular day, the class selected "Blind Devotion" and moved on to argue the next headline.

Since 1970, Scripps School students have produced a magazine for Athens and Southeast Ohio residents. When the magazine's mission expanded in 1988 to reach readers beyond the campus town, *Southeast Ohio* became the nation's first student-produced regional magazine.

The senior-level class—for years the crown of the magazine sequence and since 2012 a capstone course in the News and Information track—sends students out of basement labs into the community. As Patricia Westfall, now professor emerita, who advised the magazine, says, "You aren't a student in the class until you've gotten lost on a back road."

From pitching stories to proofing final layouts, students face the same deadline pressures that magazine editors do. However, in this classroom-turned-magazine, student editors manage peers and must create a harmonious team in the short timeframe of a quarter or semester. Personalities clash and computers crash; however, by term's end, the magazine is ready to print. In the process, all learn that editing a magazine requires creativity *and* collaboration.

Southeast Ohio magazine staff members prepare the next issue. Included, from the left, are Lizzie Settineri (BSVC '15), Andie Danesi (BSVC '16), Sarah Erickson (BSVC '16), and Kayla Breeden (BSVC '16). *(Photo provided by Elizabeth Meyers Hendrickson)*

Changes of name and focus

Over the years, the magazine's name and its look changed. The first magazine came out in winter 1970. Called *Appalachia 70,* the black-and-white publication was the brainchild of faculty member Fred Paine. The next magazine appeared as *Reach Out,* a name that lasted just one issue. By spring 1971, the magazine had gained the more permanent title *Athens,* which stuck for 17 years. The 36-page, premiere issue of *Athens* cost 65 cents at the newsstand or $2 for a year's subscription. Its articles described Athens sculptor John Spofforth, the boom-and-bust history of the Hocking Canal, and Mount Nebo —haunted landmarks are always among students' favorite topics.

Amid upbeat stories of people, places, and history, *Athens* writers tackled serious issues. The covers of two 1980 issues, with faculty member Robert Baker as the adviser, teased these stories: "The Teen Parent Problem" and "Can You Afford to Die?" The fall 1981 issue featured the youngest judge ever elected in Ohio, Tom Hodson (BSJ '70), who would later become the Scripps School director and now is director and general manager of the WOUB Center for Public Media. Readers learned of physicians who still made house calls, the infamous Swanky's bar on Court Street in Athens, and the decline of outdoor movie theaters. The magazine started as a vehicle for student experience. However, it evolved into a warehouse of local and regional history.

Athens became *Southeast Ohio* with the spring 1988 issue. Showcasing a local wine on its cover, the 48-page publication listed a $1.50 newsstand price and a two-year subscription rate of $7. Magazine staff traveled farther afield to find stories that would interest readers in 23 Appalachian Ohio counties. The new regional focus, motivated by Westfall, gave students the opportunity to cover an area underserved by traditional media and to write for an older, nonuniversity audience.

Students took to the backroads with enthusiasm—and some trepidation. Carisa Reeves (BSJ '99) traveled to places with funny names like Pee Pee Creek, Fly, and Knockemstiff for her winter 1999 story. Not all destinations were so whimsical. Writer Andy Cluxton (BSJ '12) milled about Lucasville for a sense of what it was like to live in the shadow of the Ohio prison that housed death-row inmates. Cary Roberts Frith (BSJ '92, MSJ '98) recalls that visiting the river town of Ironton on assignment was well outside her comfort zone. The magazine's editor her senior year, Frith would return to the front of its classroom in 2005, this time as faculty adviser.

Advisers and students who crafted the magazine before the digital age remember the frustration of pasting up layouts by hand: cutting long strips of text with X-ACTO knives, piecing waxed copy into columns, and sizing photos with a proportion wheel. Miscounting the number of lines to fill a column required trimming one line and repasting it, or starting all over. For bigger production crises, they sought the help of Dick Bean, who presided over the school's graphics lab for 19 years before retiring in 1997.

Digital technology changed just about everything, from font choices to deadlines. Today the magazine staff edits copy and fine-tunes layouts until the very last minute. The winter 2012 issue marked the first full-color issue of *Southeast Ohio.* Magazine staff, ecstatic about adding color to their layouts, used it well with Audrey Rabalais Carson's (BSJ '12) feature "Hell on Wheels." From the cover image of a red-costumed skater caught in midair to the inside photo showing her roller derby teammate dabbing a nosebleed, color pops off the pages.

Besides technological advances, collaboration with students in the School of Visual Communication aided *Southeast Ohio*'s print magazine and website. In the mid-2000s, magazine design and photography students took on the roles of art or photography editors. "Break the book" sessions in which editorial and design teams meet to determine how words and art will mesh into the finished product often resulted in lively "creative debate," Frith recalled. Just as in a real magazine, word and visual people have to talk.

Deep in the digital sandbox

Students and advisers found themselves deep in the digital sandbox, playing with html and content management systems, when they added a *Southeast Ohio* website; the position of web editor first appeared on the winter 1999 issue's masthead. Since then, students have created several iterations of *http://southeastohiomagazine.com/seo/* and now they manage multiple social media platforms promoting *Southeast Ohio.* Student writers tweet about upcoming stories, post comments for the magazine's 900 Facebook friends, and create original content for the website—all while producing a 48- to 56-page print magazine.

It's all good fun and even better portfolio building. One-time *Southeast Ohio* students can be found on the editorial and digital staffs of national consumer magazines, including *Women's Health, Real Simple, Reader's Digest, Parents, Billboard, Paste, International Business Times, Vice,* and *Elle Décor.* They edit city and regional magazines like *Cincinnati* and *Louisville.* And their names appear on the mastheads of business-to-business publications serving industries from hospitality to aeronautics.

Many former *Southeast Ohio* staffers experienced their first magazine bylines after toiling in the damp basement labs of Lasher or Scripps Hall or, since 2015, in a capstone classroom of Scripps Hall or computer lab in RTV. A few met future spouses. Others, on their way to find the refuge for feral pigs, the lady named Gus, or the tracks of Bigfoot, got lost. So far, it seems all found their way back.

THE POST GOES DIGITAL

By Emma Ockerman

For more than a century*, The Post* has served as a skeleton for the untamed ideas of thousands of college-aged journalists.

Its newsroom—whether that be in "Old Baker," Pilcher House, or Baker University Center—has been a place of word-bending, boundary-pushing, and utterly manic students. Many of them came to Ohio University to make a newspaper, and many left *The Post*'s newsroom feeling as though it had surely meant a lot more than a fistful of ink and paper on stands each morning.

To be a journalist is to be innately curious and driven. To be a Postie is to be almost insanely averse to doing what's considered "average."

That's one of the reasons why *The Post* reinvented itself as a weekly tabloid in fall 2016, redesigned its website completely, and shifted its focus to being digital-first. It was a momentous switch, but it paralleled our can-do attitudes.

We're not an average newsroom, but we had started to become a bit tired of the daily six-page broadsheet we had been married to for decades. We didn't look like our student readers thought we should, and we had started to think of *The Post* as something that should not divest from its traditions.

During Jim Ryan's tenure as editor-in-chief for the 2014–15 academic year, a task force was created that included several former *Post* editors, Ohio University faculty, and current Posties. The objective was to predict the future of *The Post.*

The result was that group—which I served as a part of for a brief time—realized that there was no safe path to a guaranteed future as *The Post* we had all come to know. There were risks that had to be taken, and we had to put our curiosity and boundless energy toward becoming what we hadn't been in years: innovative.

Emma Ockerman. (The Post *photo by Arielle Berger)*

The Post's mission has never been to be the traditional, dull news outlet on Ohio University's campus. We wouldn't have more than 100 journalists in our newsroom grinding away if that were the case. Even in 1939—when the campus newspaper changed its name from *The Green & White* to *The Ohio University Post*—readers found dozens of 150-word news briefs on the front page. Editors argued that students didn't want to have to spend hours reading a story. They wanted and deserved the news in the amount of time it took to pick up a copy of the newspaper and glance at its front page while walking to class.

Sound familiar? Currently, more than 50 percent of *The Post*'s readers view its stories on a mobile or tablet device. Those readers want to find their news conveniently. They want it to look attractive and compelling.

So we shift with the tides. We accept what has become modern journalism.

"Change can be incredibly challenging," Anna Sudar Jeffries (BSJ '09), *Post* Alumni Society president, wrote after *The Post* announced its transition. "It isn't easy to try something new, and it's definitely difficult to be the first group of student editors to explore uncharted territory. But I applaud the *Post*'s staff for being proactive in embracing change, taking charge of the paper's future as opposed to waiting, then trying to catch up."

The real final exam: Employment

In this final chapter, we yield to the practical. Students appreciate education, but they—and their parents, of course—yearn ultimately for employment. In these days in which "get a job" has achieved political prominence, students set their goals and dedicate themselves to the task just as their predecessors did. It's a process that challenges them in new ways but also, as does everything else in the E.W. Scripps School of Journalism, creates friendships and memories.

Facing page: Columbus Dispatch Editor Alan Miller (BSJ '78), left, speaks with Assistant City Editor Paul Souhrada (BSJ '86), Assistant Public Affairs Editor Michelle Everhart (BSJ '02), and Copy Desk Manager Jenny Applegate (BSJ '01) in the news conference room on May 7, 2015. *(*The Columbus Dispatch *photo by Craig Holman)*

THE SCHOOL HELPS IN THE JOB SEARCH

By Debbie DePeel

The E.W. Scripps School of Journalism and its faculty members understand the intense student interest in getting a good job. That's why they dedicate a lot of time and effort, institutionally and individually, to trying to help.

But the key word is "help."

One of the basic premises in the school's philosophy over the years has been that we tell students we aren't going to find them a job or an internship. That's their task, We will provide resources. Faculty will give input, critique résumés, and share contacts. We'll tell students about the opportunities, but taking advantage of those opportunities is up to them.

I like to summarize how the school has done this over the years this way: bulletin board → mail a job notice → email a job notice → various print publications including *Scripps Notes* → everything on the website as well as social media. Most recently, a new resource is the Scripps College internship coordinator, a position now held by Karen Peters, who coordinates Scripps College internships and is building an internship data base.

In the Scripps School, "Senior Saturday," sponsored by the Society of Alumni and Friends, plays an important role. It was developed in 2003 as a one-day event that brings two dozen or more alumni to campus to discuss employment trends and job-seeking strategies and to meet with graduating seniors to critique résumés and portfolios.

Faculty members often are the best resources for students. They provide advice and critiques of résumés, cover letters, and portfolios, as well as letters of reference (hundreds each year within the school).

In addition, individual faculty members are regularly contacted by professionals—often their own former students—about job opportunities.

These faculty then recruit students who match the employers' needs. The success of faculty assistance is evident in the university's alumni survey, in which 10 to 15 percent of alumni over the past six years report that they got their first jobs as a direct result of recruitment via a faculty member.

So sometimes—just sometimes—faculty members happily violate the policy of just providing help, by actually getting a job for a student. That's just part of the special relationship the school seeks to foster with its students.

BULL MARKET

By Dick Carelli

It's not always the case, I know, but 1968 was a bull market for young job hunters in the E.W. Scripps School of Journalism.

As we returned from winter break, the bulletin boards on the ground floor of Copeland Hall began to fill with notices inviting soon-to-be graduates to interview sessions with prospective employers. Even a kid with middling grades and no relevant summer internships under his belt had little trouble getting face time with the visiting recruiters.

The guy from Gannett seemed to like the few clips from *The Post* and *The Athens Messenger* I had brought along. And much to my surprise and delight, the *Akron Beacon Journal* guy was impressed enough to invite me to visit his city for a second interview.

They and what seemed like a large number of other recruiters had set up shop in one of Copeland's rooms for a day or longer, seemingly willing to talk to any J-School student interested in learning more. I remember the sessions as low-pressure, friendly chats.

In the end, I opted to return to my home state of New York and take a reporting job with Gannett's White Plains *Reporter Dispatch*. It was a difficult choice. The *Beacon Journal,* a fine newspaper, had offered me $120 a week—$10 a week more than the job I took.

That was the beginning of a rewarding journalism career that ultimately resulted in 24 years covering the U.S. Supreme Court for The Associated Press, followed by 12 years as senior public affairs specialist for the Administrative Office of the U.S. Courts.

Clearly, as a young high school graduate, I had picked the right place for my college education.

BOBCAT NATION, FROM PIQUA TO PARIS

By Dan Sewell

When Ed Miller (BSJ '75) visited the Foreign Correspondents Club in Tokyo, his host immediately recognized his roots when he introduced himself as a journalism grad of Ohio University.

"Oh, yes, Athens," the Japanese executive said, smiling and nodding in approval.

It's a familiar reaction for journalism alums who find that leaving the little city nestled in the hills of Southeast Ohio for the wide world of media careers means they join a Journalism Nation, a network of connections that stretches through newsrooms around the globe from Columbus to Kenya, Willoughby to Washington, D.C., Piqua to Paris.

They also inherit a reputation built over generations, one of journalists who have already mastered the basics and have the dedication and drive to do the news professionally.

Since June 2016, Miller has been director of the Office of Public Information for the Supreme Court of Ohio. His career has included stops at The

Associated Press, *The Detroit News,* Ford Motor Company, and Honda. Whether hanging out with reporters in a press room or getting grilled in a job interview, playing the Ohio University card has always been a good deal, he said.

"My Scripps credentials elicited affirmation of competence, and acceptance," Miller said. "I've worked at a lot of places, and my OU credentials always came up in interviews that led to my hiring."

The Associated Press has long tapped into the talent pipeline from Athens, and this was particularly a hallmark of Andrew Lippman, the Cincinnati AP correspondent in the late 1970s and '80s. Every summer intern or temporary staffer he hired for Cincinnati was from Athens, all having worked for *The Post.* Lippman wasn't a Bobcat, but his Ohio AP news editor, Henry Heilbrunn (BSJ '73), was, and after his first Ohio hire, Lippman simplified his recruiting: hire Bobcats, then ask them who to hire next.

Dan Sewell (note Bobcat in background). *(Photo provided by Dan Sewell)*

"All of you knew how to write a basic story, and each of you had your own styles and strengths that made you stand above the average intern," Lippman recalled decades later. "It was obvious to me . . . that you were well grounded in the basics of journalism and eager to learn." Lippman asked his former interns for advice on new prospects—and always followed their recommendations.

They included Michael Precker (BSJ '76), who also interned for AP in Jerusalem through the Fleischer scholarship in Dean John Wilhelm's foreign correspondence program, for two summers, followed by your scribe for this story, Dan Sewell (BSJ '78). Then, in succession, came Mark Brunswick

(BSJ '14; it's a long story); Brian Friedman (BSJ '78), an Amsterdam AP intern through the Wilhelm program); and Peter King (BSJ '78).

The Scripps School's attention to the need for more overseas-based correspondents to bring international events home, a push led by Dean Wilhelm and Professor Ralph Kliesch, produced Precker (Israel bureau chief for *The Dallas Morning News*); Brunswick (a reporter in Iraq, Afghanistan, and Kosovo for the *Star-Tribune* in Minneapolis); Friedman (Moscow correspondent for the AP and later working on special assignment in Japan and Egypt); and the writer of this article (Caribbean news editor for the AP).

Among a long list of Bobcats who worked for the AP in Paris, Elaine Ganley (BSJ '75) stands as the longest tenured. And Elizabeth Kliesch (BSJ '93) served as an AP intern in Paris in the fall following her graduation.

King stayed stateside to become one of the nation's best-known sportswriters, leading *Sports Illustrated*'s NFL coverage.

Before moving on to the first of a series of AP chief of state bureau roles capped by California, Lippman also plucked Joe Kay (BSJ '77) from rival UPI. More than three decades later, Kay was still reporting on Reds, Bengals, Bearcats, Musketeers, and a variety of other sports and major events as the dean of sportswriters in Cincinnati.

While Lippman may have taken AP-OU connections to a new level, they were already something of a tradition.

Journalism Professor Ralph Izard recharged his news-gathering batteries with a series of temporary stints in AP bureaus such as Charleston (West Virginia), Miami, Columbus, and Honolulu, and it was rare in any era to find AP's Ohio operations without a Bobcat or three.

Covering Ohio politics

When swing-state Ohio became a heavily campaigned and covered presidential battleground in the 2008 and 2012 elections, Scripps grads were on the front lines for AP: Liz Sidoti (BSJ '99) was an AP national politics writer in

2008 and by 2012 was the national politics editor; Phil Elliott (BSJ '03) was based in Ohio as a politics writer in 2008, then went on to cover the White House before returning to the campaign trail in 2012. Sewell, and Columbus-based news staffers Rose Hanson Schilling (BSJ '98) and Kantele Franko (BSJ '08), who got her AP start as an intern in the Cincinnati bureau led by former intern Sewell, also were involved in the AP political coverage as Barack Obama twice carried the hotly contested state on his way to the White House.

The success of AP Bobcats begat more AP Bobcats.

By the time AP Executive Editor Kathleen Carroll visited Athens in 2013 to receive the Scripps School's Carr Van Anda Award, nearly two dozen Bobcat journalism grads labored in her company's employ, including East Africa bureau chief Jason Straziuso (BSJ '97), AP auto writer Tom Krisher (BSJ '80), and AP Radio anchor/producer Sandy Kozel (BSJ '74).

In her campus speech, Carroll quoted the observation of AP Chicago sportswriter Jay Cohen (BSJ '99): "Lots of proud OU alums at AP. I think we believe our school produces the type of people and journalists that thrive at places like our fine outlet."

Whether it's covering Cubs, cars, or crises, Bobcat journalists are known in the AP and elsewhere for keeping the work fun while coming through without a lot of drama.

P.J. Bednarski, *Post* editor in '74–75, who became a national television columnist and then editor of *Broadcasting & Cable Magazine,* described the Bobcat journo style this way: "We're light on thumb-sucking, big on producing. I'm proud of that."

Brooke LaValley (BSVC '11), photographer.
(The Columbus Dispatch photo)

Lisa Abraham (BSJ '85), food editor.
(The Columbus Dispatch photo)

THE COLUMBUS DISPATCH—A CLOWDER OF BOBCATS

By Dru Riley Evarts and Dan Sewell

George Starr Lasher was respected by professional journalists because they knew that the newly minted journalists they might hire from Ohio University would be capable of good reporting and well backgrounded in the principles of editing.

It was said that his visits to *The Columbus Dispatch* newsroom occasioned a scene in which everyone there would rise and applaud, whether he or she had graduated from Ohio University or not.

Tom Baker (BSJ '62) and Gina Ranalli (BSVC '13, MA '15), graphic artists. (The Columbus Dispatch *photo by Eric Albrecht)*

Former faculty member Norman Dohn remembered Lasher's relationship with the *Dispatch.* "My recollection of Professor Lasher is limited largely to his periodic visits to *The Columbus Dispatch,* where at one time nearly one-half of its newsroom employees who held college degrees had earned them under his tutelage at Ohio University," he said. "In fact, when a job opening occurred, Professor Lasher's recommendation was the first sought. Being an Ohio State University graduate, I found this a bit hard to take."

In recent years, now with Alan Miller (BSJ '78) as editor, the *Dispatch* has stocked its newsroom with a steady stream of Bobcats while repeatedly winning honors in the 21st century as one of the Midwest's best newspapers. In 2015, Miller said about one-fifth of the news staff was from Ohio University.

"The Scripps School of Journalism attracts star students and turns out star talent," Miller said. "We don't hire them because they're Bobcats. We hire them because they are students of the game—strong players who keep

Dispatch Art Director Todd Bayha (BFA '94) shares his thoughts during a meeting with the business section redesign/review team. *(*The Columbus Dispatch *photo by Shari Lewis)*

Ken Gordon (BSJ '90), reporter. *(*The Columbus Dispatch *photo)*

Charlie Zimkus (MA '09), info graphic artist, and Jennifer Smith Richards (BSJ '83), reporter. *(*The Columbus Dispatch *photo)*

readers front-of-mind and make this newsroom the best news organization in Ohio year after year."

And these days, for precisely the same reasons, the *Dispatch* team is just as likely to include graduates of Ohio University's School of Visual Communication.

CARS, CONGRESS, OR CORPORATIONS?

By Dan Sewell

MANY OHIO UNIVERSITY journalism graduates have found success in unexpected worlds, becoming experts on subjects they never thought much about while in Athens.

Journalists might jokingly call it "going over to the dark side," but some grads will tell you that going into public relations or corporate communications, for example, was a fulfilling move that allowed them to hone their communication skills, play an important part in a major mission, and, often, have better hours and better pay. Such crossing over in the communications industries demonstrates the truth of advice given by public relations faculty member Hugh M. Culbertson, now retired, when he repeatedly stressed the benefit of journalism skills for public relations professionals.

"Journalism was fantastic training for the job I never knew I wanted," said Mary Beth (Sofranec) Bardin (BSJ '77). A *Post* associate editor at Ohio University, she worked for a few years at a newspaper and then a short time with The Associated Press before building a career with communications provider Verizon.

"The key skills were listening, speaking, and writing, as well as an ability to translate complicated or technical information for the public," Bardin said. "The CEO used to joke that I was the editor of the company. My team and I saw everything the company or its leaders said before it went out the door, and of course we helped shape it on the front end, too."

Corporate communication

She called it "a fabulous career for a communicator," and she retired early as executive vice president after 16 years with Verizon.

Former *Post* editor Lisa Popyk (BSJ '89) was a leading reporter for *The Cincinnati Post* before the afternoon newspaper's demise, and after going into media relations, she became part of the communications team of Procter & Gamble Co., the world's largest consumer products maker and advertiser.

There she worked for P&G Communications Director Paul Fox, a former British journalist who liked to call his career transition "going from poacher to gamekeeper."

Often the transition has been into politics. Ken Klein (BSJ '84) went from covering Florida's government and politics for the AP to serving as campaign press secretary for Florida Governor Bob Graham when he ran for the U.S. Senate. Klein became Graham's Senate press secretary and later chief of staff in Washington. He said he enjoyed the move from reporting about what was going on to being on the inside.

Later, journalism grad Cory Fritz (BSJ '07) also moved into politics, serving first as a campaign press aide for House Speaker John Boehner and later as the Ohio Republican's national press secretary in Washington.

"Auto-cats"

Some journalism grads have found a fast lane to success from Athens to Detroit. Let's just say they became "auto-cats."

"It's easy for young Scripps grads to think they must move to New York or Washington to cover a big-time beat with national reach and implications," said Mike Colias (BSJ '96), reporter for *Automotive News.* "I thought the same but eventually stumbled onto the richest, most competitive business beat there is—with global reach—just one state away."

Colias and Mike Ramsey (BSJ '96), for Bloomberg News and then *The Wall Street Journal,* were among several Bobcats involved in covering the dramatic restructuring of the major U.S. automakers in the 21st century while others covered the earlier rise in Japan, Germany, and elsewhere of international automotive competitors to challenge the iconic American auto companies.

Ed Miller (BSJ '76) took over the high-profile Associated Press auto-writer role in 1980, then a few years later went to *The Detroit News* to become auto beat reporter. Miller later moved into corporate media relations, first with Ford Motor and then for Honda. He is now with the Office of Public Information, Ohio Supreme Court. Ron Iori, from the same class, left journalism after stints at *The Wall Street Journal* and the *Los Angeles Times* to serve as Ford Motor's director of communications for nearly a decade.

Another OU graduate, Alan Adler (BSJ '80), was an AP auto writer, then covered the industry for the *Detroit Free Press.* He at one point shadowed Miller for a week for a Page 1 story on preparing for the 1996 Detroit Auto Show.

Tom Krisher (BSJ '80) became an AP auto writer early in the 21st century and found that even though the beat hadn't been on his mind back in Athens, he had gotten a lot of preparation back then.

"As a skinny 17-year-old freshman at OU, I hadn't the slightest clue where I would wind up or that I would be covering the auto industry," Krisher recalled. "What OU did for me was show me that my knowledge base (at that time) was far too narrow to be a journalist. Before every Journalism 231 class, the prof had a general knowledge quiz, which at the time seemed irrelevant to me. But he showed me I knew very little about anything and that I would have to write on just about everything if I were to become a journalist."

Krisher took a lot of business and economic classes besides journalism that prepared him to move from general news to business reporting. Also, for reasons that are lost to his memory, he also took a basic circuits course at Ohio University—which proved helpful years later as he covered auto recalls related to electronic issues.

A LEGAL OPTION

By Ralph Izard

An increasingly attractive route for journalism students over the years has been to tuck away the journalism degree, sometimes temporarily, while attending law school. Some seek new career paths, and others consider this a route to improved journalism skills. Or both.

The results have varied. Some have gained success in the professional media, some have moved into teaching, and others have taken different paths. Here is a small sample from among the many impressive careers put together by Scripps School graduates who moved on to a law degree and beyond.

Dick Carelli (BSJ '68) received his JD from George Washington University in 1984, 16 years after his BSJ and after four years of night classes—two hours a night, five nights a week. At the time, he was working full time for the AP, covering the U.S. Supreme Court and other law-related news, a job he held for 24 years.

"At first I thought I would practice law," he said, "but my first semester of law school convinced me such work wouldn't be as fascinating as what I was doing. I decided to get the law degree so someday I could teach, combining journalism and law. That was my master plan until in 2000 a great job with the federal courts fell from the sky."

He became senior public affairs specialist and worked for the Administrative Office of the U.S. Courts.

"Since very few federal courts have their own 'spokespersons,' news reporters nationwide ended up talking to me," he said. "Reporters didn't care that I had a law degree, but judges and court executives seemed comforted by that fact. I had the job for 12 years, until I retired in 2012 to become a golf bum."

Years later, Jonathan Peters (BSJ '07) sought to integrate law and education fully into his career, earning a JD from Ohio State University in 2010

Jonathan Peters poses with radio host Ira Glass in the New York City studios of *Serial* and *This American Life,* broadcast on hundreds of public radio stations to millions of listeners. Peters conducted a 2016 media law training session for the shows' staff members. *(Photo provided by Jonathan Peters)*

and a PhD in journalism (with a focus in constitutional law) from the University of Missouri in 2013. Currently at the University of Georgia as an assistant professor in the Grady College of Journalism and Mass Communication and an affiliated assistant professor in the School of Law, he has been a practicing media attorney since 2010. He frequently conducts training sessions and has speaking engagements about issues in media law.

Previously a faculty member at the University of Kansas, Peters has served as press freedom correspondent for the *Columbia Journalism Review* and blogged about free expression for the *Harvard Law & Policy Review.* He has written on legal issues for *Esquire, The Atlantic, Slate, Wired, The Nation,* and PBS. He also has written about the NHL for *Sports Illustrated.*

He has served as First Amendment chair of the American Bar Association's Civil Rights Litigation Committee and as teaching chair of the Law and Policy Division of the Association for Education in Journalism and Mass Communication. He practices law during his time off-campus as a volunteer attorney for the Online Media Legal Network at Harvard's Berkman Center, the Student Press Law Center, and the ACLU.

Back in Athens, the current director and general manager of the WOUB Center for Public Media and former director of journalism, Thomas Hodson (BSJ '70), received his law degree from Ohio State University in 1973. Before returning to education, he worked as an attorney in Athens for a few years and then, at 31, became the youngest judge in Ohio. In 1986 he served as a clerk for U.S. Supreme Court Chief Justice William Rehnquist.

But he never quite left education, writing and lecturing around the country on court, community, and media relations, even as he continued teaching as an adjunct faculty member in the Scripps School. He returned to campus in 2003, this time as an administrator, a set of responsibilities he has continued since that date,

A similar career combination put together by Laralyn Sasaki Dearing (BSJ '86) demonstrates some of the alternative directions the law-school decision provides. She received her law degree from the University of Michigan in 1991 and currently is president and senior strategist of Laralyn and Associates LLC, a strategic consulting firm in Columbus.

Before earning her JD degree, she was a staff reporter for *The Cincinnati Enquirer* and worked for the federal court in Columbus, Bricker & Eckler law firm, the Supreme Court of Ohio, and the Ohio State Bar Foundation.

Sasaki Dearing's classmate Marlon Primes (BSJ '86) received his law degree from Georgetown University's Law Center in 1989. He now has law licenses in Ohio and the District of Columbia.

By 2015, Primes had worked as an assistant U.S. attorney in Cleveland for 24 years and was active in a number of legal associations. In 2016, he completed his second term as chairman of the Litigation Section of the Ohio State Bar Association and was inducted into that group's 2016 Fellows Class. He will be the first government lawyer to lead the Cleveland Metropolitan Bar Association, which is the largest metropolitan legal association in Ohio. Currently serving as that organization's vice president, he is to be officially sworn in as president in June 2018.

Sasaki Dearing provided her assessment of the journalism-law combination. "Journalism school taught me to communicate. Law school taught me to solve problems," she said. "My journalism degree opened the door to law school. My law degree opened countless doors in business. Being a journalist equipped me to question and explore the world. Being a lawyer gave me the tools—and duty—to engage and serve my community."

An Epilogue

THE NEXT 100 YEARS

By Robert Stewart

When I finished reading the stories in this volume, which together weave the history of the E.W. Scripps School of Journalism, I realized that a forward-looking epilogue was needed, to answer the question "What's next?"

We are releasing this volume roughly five years before the centennial of the Scripps School, as a way to raise scholarship funds for future journalism students. This very act is one of faith in the future role of journalism, as well as our commitment to helping prepare future journalists to take up the gauntlet before them. We believe in the future of journalism, regardless of what format it will take, whether it be delivered on paper or via mobile apps. Or by some method that can't yet be imagined.

In the last days before going to press, we learned that our venerable student newspaper, *The Post,* was named top (non-daily) student newspaper in the nation in the Society of Professional Journalists' 2017 "Mark of Excellence" award program. Another campus publication, *The New Political,* similarly was recognized by SPJ in 2016 as the nation's top online outlet. The school is very proud of the work all of our students produce and wants to support them and students like them in the coming decades through the centennial scholarship program.

We look forward to a new partnership with the Kiplinger Program for Public Affairs journalism, which has been located at Ohio State University since 1972 but now is joining hands with the E.W. Scripps School of Journalism. This partnership, when realized, will bring to campus 20–25 journalists for one week each year, to learn the latest storytelling techniques and technologies, so that they can produce public affairs journalism for a contemporary audience. Those journalists will engage with our faculty and students and carry their experiences from the Athens campus back to their newsrooms. They will, in effect, be Bobcats in their own right, further enhancing the school's reputation around the country and around the world.

The addition of the Kiplinger program represents the remarkable evolution of the Scripps School, making it relevant not only to the undergraduates and graduate students enrolled in our program but also to the scores of journalists who will take part in the program in the coming decades, journalists who already will have reported for major news outlets. This union stands as a symbol of a very bright future, putting into motion what no doubt will make for an amazing second century and beyond for the E.W. Scripps School of Journalism.

RECIPIENTS OF THE CARR VAN ANDA AWARD

"... for enduring contributions to journalism"

Shana Alexander (1974)
Christiane Amanpour (2001)
Terry Anderson (1992)
Peter Arnett (1992)
William Attwood (1973)
Marty Baron (2016)
Edward W. Barrett (1968)
Rod Beaton (1980)
Alton Blakeslee (1978)
Margaret Bourke-White (1969)
Hal Buell (1983)
Richard Campbell (1982)
Pat Carbine (1976)
Kathleen Carroll (2013)
Hodding Carter III (2002)
John Mack Carter (1996)
Turner Catledge (1968)
Jerry Ceppos (2006)
Otis Chandler (1974)
Howard Chapnick (1992)
Norman Cousins (1971)
Walter Cronkite (1968)
Charlotte Curtis (1978)
Hugh Downs (1982)
Osborn Elliott (1969)
Katherine Fanning (1986)
Pauline Frederick (1972)
Dorothy Fuldheim (1985)
Wes Gallagher (1969)
Robert Gilka (1979)
Ellen Goodman (1991)
Katharine Graham (1975)
Seymour Hersh (1999)
Don Hewitt (2001)
Lee W. Huebner (1989)
Charlayne Hunter-Gault (2015)
Gwen Ifill (2013)
James Jackson Kilpatrick (1987)
John S. Knight (1970)
Elizabeth Kolbert (2018)
Richard Leonard (1972)
Flora Lewis (1981)
Philip Meyer (1975)
Paul Miller (1979)
Jack Nelson (1995)
Allen H. Neuharth (1991)
Charles Osgood (1985)
Gordon Parks (1970)
Charles Peters (2003)
Warren H. Phillips (1989)
Robert Pierpoint (1983)
Bill Plante (1988)
Nate Polowetzky (1987)
Dith Pran (2007)
William Raspberry (1994)
Harry Reasoner (1973)
James Reston (1971)
A.M. Rosenthal (1976)
Pierre Salinger (1990)
Van Gordon Sauter (1981)
Daniel Schorr (1984)
Albert J. Schottelkotte (1996)
John H. Sengstacke (1985)
John Seigenthaler (1990)
Eric Sevareid (1975)
Sally Aw Sian (1988)
Howard K. Smith (1970)
W.A. Swanberg (1990)
David Talbot (2004)
Helen Thomas (1977)
Nina Totenberg (2005)
Ted Turner (1982)
Garrick Utley (1998)
Sander Vanocur (2000)
Mike Wallace (1977)
Judy Woodruff (2017)
Bob Woodward (2007)

A bust of E.W. Scripps, a gift to the school from the E.W. Scripps Company, occupies a prominent position in the school's Schoonover Center quarters. *(Photo by Ralph Izard)*

MAKING HISTORY

E.W. Scripps School of Journalism Highlights

1923

- Raymond M. Slutz offers first journalism course in English Department, with frequent visits in class from *Athens Messenger* personnel (Frederick W. Bush, publisher; Charles Harris, managing editor; and P.O. Nichols, advertising manager). Thirty-two students take first class.
- OU President E.B. Bryan gains Board of Trustees' approval for a Department of Journalism.

1924

- George Starr Lasher hired by President Bryan to establish Department of Journalism in College of Liberal Arts, with home in Ellis Hall. News Reporting and Magazine programs established.

1925

- Lasher arranges with Frederick W. Bush for students to enroll in Reporting Practice and Editing Practice at the *Messenger,* first association of this type known in the country. Wesley Maurer becomes first *Messenger* staff member to be appointed adjunct faculty member.

1926

- First graduates of new journalism program include Clarence Bolen, president of Press Club.

1927

- Ludel Sauvageot is first woman graduate of journalism program.

1930

- News-Editorial program added to News Reporting and Magazine programs.

1932

- Student chapter of Sigma Delta Chi, men's journalism fraternity (now Society of Professional Journalists), is organized.

1936

- OU President Herman G. James reorganizes university, creating School of Journalism, placing it in College of Commerce and moving it to ground floor of Ewing Hall.
- Bachelor of Science in Journalism degree created.

1937

- First graduating class to receive BSJ degree. First graduate is John L. Weber.

1938

- Broadcast course added to curriculum.

1941

- Journalism programs formalized into sequences: General Writing and Editing, Feature and Magazine Writing, Advertising, and Business Management.
- Mary Elizabeth Lasher named first woman editor of *The Post*.
- Ohio University chapter of Theta Sigma Phi (later Women in Communication Inc., now Association for Women in Communications) organized.

1946

- School sponsors its first High School Publications Workshop.

1947

- Seven sequences defined: News Writing and Editing, Feature and Magazine Writing, News Advertising, Business Management, Radio Journalism, Pictorial Journalism, and Public Relations.

1948

- Master's degree added to school's curriculum.

1949

- Ohio Legislature passes resolution honoring Lasher's contributions to journalism education upon occasion of program's 25th anniversary at Ohio University.

1950

- George Starr Lasher and L.J. Hortin plan to apply for accreditation.

1951

- Hortin becomes director as Lasher retires from directorship and continues to teach.

1952

- First accreditation received and sequences consolidated and trimmed to five: News Writing and Editing, Feature and Pictorial Journalism, Advertising Management, Radio Journalism, and Public Relations.
- School's first external internship awarded to Carol Tyler of Willoughby, who worked at *Painesville Telegraph*.

1954

- Radio Journalism sequence name changed to Radio-TV Journalism.

1955

- School of Journalism moves with rest of College of Commerce to Copeland Hall, where it occupies ground floor.

1962

- College of Commerce name changed to College of Business Administration, with School of Journalism remaining as a major component.

1967

- Ohio Newspaper Association recognizes L.J. Hortin with its Distinguished Service to Journalism Award as he retires from directorship. J. William Click named acting director.
- School stages its first Journalism Banquet in recognition of Hortin's retirement.

1968

- John R. Wilhelm leaves position as director of McGraw-Hill World News to become director of the school January 1; he later becomes dean of College of Communication when it is created that spring.
- Journalism remains in Copeland Hall, with Ralph E. Kliesch, as assistant director, managing the school.
- Board of Regents approves PhD in Mass Communication degree to be administered jointly by School of Journalism and School of Radio-Television (renamed School of Media Arts & Studies in 2008).
- New College of Communication dean's office opens in Pilcher House.
- Faculty holds first Bush Seminar (weekend planning retreat), financed by Gordon K. Bush Memorial Fund.
- First Journalism Week held during first week of May.
- Carr Van Anda Award "for enduring contributions to journalism" initiated, with the first going to Turner Catledge of *The New York Times,* Edward W. Barrett of Columbia University, and Walter Cronkite of CBS News.
- Ohio University chapter of Public Relations Student Society of America organized.

1969

- School of Journalism moves into new Radio-Television Building, along with School of Radio-Television. Some journalism faculty offices and classes occupy rooms in Haning Hall.

1970

- Journalism Week name changed to Communication Week to incorporate entire college.
- Ralph E. Kliesch appointed associate director.
- School of Journalism retains five sequences but changes Radio-TV Journalism sequence name to Radio-TV News.
- What eventually is to become *Athens* magazine (later *Southeast Ohio*) is first published as *Appalachia 70*.
- First foreign-correspondence intern, Jeffrey Smith, sent abroad.

1971

- Ralph Izard becomes assistant director.
- Birthney Ardoin awarded first PhD given by the school.

1972

- Two full-time administrative positions created. Wilhelm becomes full-time dean of College of Communication; Guido H. Stempel III becomes full-time director of school.
- Advertising Club is founded.

1973

- Student chapter of Black Students Communication Caucus (now National Association of Black Journalists) is organized.
- The school's first university professorship awarded to Robert E. Baker.

1974

- School of Journalism moves to Lasher Hall (formerly *Athens Messenger* building), with faculty, staff, and classrooms under one roof.

1975

- Lasher Hall dedicated.
- University's first Fulbright professorship awarded to Ralph E. Kliesch.

1976

- School receives $50,000 grant from Gannett Foundation to install electronic news processing system in Lasher Hall.

1977

- School accredited for first time in all sequences individually, making it second only to University of Missouri in number accredited.

1978

- School establishes its first computer lab in basement of Lasher Hall.
- School of Journalism cooperates with College of Fine Arts to launch Institute for Visual Communication.

1979

- Stempel resigns as director of school, becomes director of Bush Research Center.
- Robert Baker appointed acting director.

- School cooperates with other academic units to establish Center for Communication Management.

1980

- Kliesch becomes acting director.
- Charles Scripps, chairman of E.W. Scripps Company, attends Journalism Banquet for first time.

1981

- Cortland Anderson resigns as vice president of corporate affairs for Washington Post Co. to become director of school.
- Thomas Peters appointed associate director.
- Wilhelm retires as dean of College of Communication but continues teaching courses.
- *ACTV-7 News* begins televising 15-minute news program five nights per week.
- New sequence in Communication Management established.

1982

- School formally named E.W. Scripps School of Journalism to honor E.W. Scripps, a penny press pioneer who founded a newspaper group that eventually included almost 40 newspapers, including three in Ohio's principal cities.
- Scripps Howard Foundation gives $1.5 million endowment with portion designated for architectural study to remodel and expand Carnegie Hall into E.W. Scripps Hall.
- Stempel becomes first Ohio University distinguished professor from College of Communication.

1983

- Associated Press Managing Editors Association names school as one of 10 outstanding journalism programs in the country.
- Six sequences and professional master's degree accredited.
- Byron White (BSJ '84) named first African American editor of *The Post.*
- School receives $10,000 grant from Gannett Foundation to sponsor First Amendment Congress.

1984

- Groundbreaking for E.W. Scripps Hall held. Scripps Howard Foundation gives additional $250,000 to equip new building.

1985

- Anderson dies on Christmas Eve. Stempel becomes acting director during period of search for new director. School of Journalism News Bureau, directed by Sally Walters, is established to provide news to state newspapers.

1986

- School moves into E.W. Scripps Hall. Dedication of Scripps Hall held May 2.
- Ralph Izard becomes director.
- Auditorium in Scripps Hall named in honor of Cortland Anderson.
- Premiere of "March E.W. Scripps" by Richard Wetzel of the OU music faculty presented during dedication of Scripps Hall.
- Bush Research Center named in honor of Gordon K. Bush.
- Lasher Learning Center named in honor of George Starr Lasher.
- Ohio Board of Regents awards school $152,000 Program Excellence Award.

1987

- Ohio University's student affiliate Radio Television News Directors Association (now Radio Television Digital News Association) is chartered in the first year the national professional organization accepted student chapters.
- Faculty creates L.J. Hortin Distinguished Alumni Award.

1988

- School of Journalism Advisory Board established with appointees from school and Scripps Howard Foundation.
- *Athens* magazine name changed to *Southeast Ohio*.
- School establishes Midwest Newspaper Workshop for Minorities.

1989

- School accredited in five sequences.
- 1804 Grant of $25,000 received to internationalize school's curriculum.
- Special master's degree cooperative program established with Ford Motor Co.

1990

- Scripps Howard Foundation approves $1 million endowment for Scripps Howard Visiting Professional Chair to bring noted working journalists to school as resources for students and faculty.

1991

- Center for International Journalism (later renamed Institute for International Journalism) approved by OU Board of Trustees. Anne Cooper-Chen named director.
- School receives $150,405 Program Excellence Award from Ohio Board of Regents.
- Joan Herrold Wood pledges $1 million to endow faculty chair.

1992

- School receives $80,000 grant from Freedom Forum to send 10 journalism faculty members as consultants to Leipzig University in former East Germany.
- Graphics facility in Scripps Hall named for Russell N. Baird.
- Funding completed by Jerry L. Sloan (BSJ '59) and Ford Motor Co. for establishment of Jerry L. Sloan Professorship in Public Relations (converted into Jerry L. Sloan Visiting Professional in Public Relations in 2014).

1993

- School receives Third Century Campaign pledge from Sally Aw Sian, chairwoman of Sing Tao Holdings Ltd., a Hong Kong–based newspaper group, that resulted in a $500,000 contribution, the proceeds of which provide a budget for Institute for International Journalism.
- Russell N. Baird Graphics Lab dedicated.
- Rufus Putnam Visiting Professional Program commences.
- Walter Friedenberg, *Santa Fe New Mexican* and former Scripps Howard journalist, joins faculty as first Scripps Howard Visiting Professional. He serves for three years.

1994

- John Wilhelm Amphitheatre at Scripps Hall is dedicated.

1996

- Graduate program named one of ten best in the country by *U.S. News & World Report.*

1997

- Sing Tao Center dedicated as the home of the school's international programs.
- Helen Thomas of United Press International serves as Scripps Howard Visiting Professional.

1998

- Ralph Izard retires as director; Daniel Riffe named interim director.
- Terry Anderson of Associated Press appointed Scripps Howard Visiting Professional.
- Society of Alumni and Friends organized.

1999

- Kevin Noblet of Associated Press appointed Scripps Howard Visiting Professional.

2000

- Michael Real appointed director.
- Doug Poling of CBS News appointed Scripps Howard Visiting Professional.
- Terry Anderson named director of Institute for International Journalism.

2001

- Kenneth Freed of *Los Angeles Times* appointed Scripps Howard Visiting Professional.
- Robert Stewart named director of Institute for International Journalism.

2002

- Bradley Martin of *Asia Financial Intelligence* and *Asia Times* Online appointed Scripps Howard Visiting Professional.

2003

- Thomas Hodson appointed director.
- John Brady of *Artist's Magazine* appointed Scripps Howard Visiting Professional
- Online Journalism added as new sequence.

2004

- Kate Webb of Agence France-Presse appointed Scripps Howard Visiting Professional.
- Student travel fund established by Martha and Ed Towns.

2005

- Leonard Pitts Jr. of *Miami Herald* appointed Scripps Howard Visiting Professional.

2006

- School accredited in six sequences.
- Mark Prendergast of *New York Times* appointed Scripps Howard Visiting Professional.

2007

- Mark Tatge of *Forbes* appointed Scripps Howard Visiting Professional. He serves for four years.

2008

- Yusuf Kalyango named director of Institute for International Journalism.

2009

- School stages first Schuneman Symposium on Photojournalism and New Media with funding from 15-year pledge by R. Smith and Patricia Schuneman.

2010

- Robert Stewart appointed director.

2011

- Andrew Alexander of *Washington Post* appointed Scripps Howard Visiting Professional.
- With financial assistance from Scripps Howard Foundation, school launches E.W. Scripps School of Journalism Statehouse News Bureau.

2012

- Julia Keller of *Chicago Tribune* appointed Scripps Howard Visiting Professional.
- School initiates Scripps Innovation Challenge under supervision of Andrew Alexander.

- As part of Ohio University's change to semesters (from quarters), faculty revises curriculum, dropping the six sequences and creating two "tracks": News and Information and Strategic Communication.

2013

- School moves into Schoonover Center for Communication, home of all programs in Scripps College of Communication.
- Julia Keller reappointed Scripps Howard Visiting Professional.

2014

- Bob Benz of Hanley Wood & Ledge Solutions appointed Scripps Howard Visiting Professional.
- Pamela Shoemaker of Syracuse University receives first Guido H. Stempel III Award for Research in Journalism and Mass Communication.

2015

- Scripps Hispanic Network organized.
- Clifford Christians of University of Illinois receives Guido H. Stempel III Award for Research in Journalism and Mass Communication.

2016

- Julie Agnone of *National Geographic* appointed Scripps Howard Visiting Professional.
- Victoria LaPoe joins the school as its first American Indian faculty member.
- Sue Morrow of *Sacramento Bee* appointed Scripps Howard Visiting Professional.
- In partnership with School of Visual Communication, Scripps Semester in D.C. program is established, offering academic courses and internships for fall and spring semesters.

2018

- Kiplinger Program for Public Affairs Journalism transfers from Ohio State University to E.W. Scripps School of Journalism.
- Julie Agnone reappointed Scripps Howard Visiting Professional.

Sing Tao Center, supplemental home of the school, 1997–present. *(Photo by Ralph Izard)*

CONTRIBUTORS

A personal note: Among the significant joys of producing this book has been the renewed contact with former students, faculty colleagues, and friends. I gained special pleasure from their words of encouragement and from the number of those who enthusiastically agreed to participate in this project. This book is not a formal history. Rather, it is a series of experiences written about by those who fondly remembered their time and the learning they accomplished at Ohio University and in the School of Journalism. This is their book, and they have my heartfelt thanks for their kind words and hard work, as well as the descriptions they provide of their memories.

Abhinav Kaul Aima is an instructor of communications at Penn State University New Kensington. He was a graduate teaching assistant for the Scripps School's Middle East Studies Program.

Andrew Alexander (BSJ '72) is a visiting professional at the Scripps College of Communication. He was the longtime Washington bureau chief for Cox Newspapers before serving as ombudsman for *The Washington Post.*

Stan Alost (MSJ '00) is an associate professor in the School of Visual Communication. He is a consultant and picture editor for the ongoing project and recent book *Delta Jewels.* Previously, Alost worked at *The St. Petersburg Times,* the *State Times* and *The Advocate* (Baton Rouge, La.), *The* (Shreveport) *Times,* and the *Natchitoches Times,* as well as being a freelance photojournalist and editor for The Associated Press and United Press International.

Mary Beth Sofranec Bardin (BSJ '77) worked in journalism for a few years, then spent the next 20 years in corporate communications, retiring from Verizon in 2004 as executive vice president–public affairs and communications.

P.J. Bednarski (BSJ '90 but should have been Class of '74) was editor of *The Post* in 1973–74. He has been a TV critic at *The Journal Herald* in Dayton, *The Cincinnati Post, USA Today,* and the *Chicago Sun-Times.* He also has been editor of *Electronic Media* and executive editor of *Broadcasting & Cable* magazine. He currently writes and curates the *Online Video Daily* newsletter for MediaPost.com.

Roger Bennett (BSJ '69, MS '70) taught at OU from 1970 to 1979. He retired in 1995 as chairman of Mass Communication at Texas State University. He had 10 years of practical experience as a reporter and editor and taught aboard Semester-at-Sea in fall 2001 and fall 2006. He retired in 2013 after serving seven years as mayor of Briny Breezes, Florida.

Maggie Scaggs Bonecutter (BSJ '94) is owner of Maggie Bonecutter Marketing Communications in Pinehurst, North Carolina. Previously, she was a marketing executive at Bank of America. She and her husband, Dustin (BA '95), have two daughters, Lydia and Sophia.

Charles "Chuck" Borghese (BSJ '81) is a lecturer in journalism, teaching creativity and strategic communications capstone classes. He is the current adviser of the Advertising Club and advises the student-run marketing communication firm, 1804 Communication. He has worked in some of advertising's most awarded creative departments. First as a copywriter and then as a creative director, Chuck has managed creative teams at Ogilvy & Mather, Merkley + Partners, and DDB.

Brendon Butler has worked as a copy editor, page designer, and reporter. He double majored in French and journalism at Utah State University and completed master's coursework at Ohio University in 2012. He now lives North Carolina, where he works for Apple Computer and supports his wife's communications studies at UNC Chapel Hill.

Dick Carelli (BSJ '68) is a retired journalist who for 24 years covered the U.S. Supreme Court for The Associated Press. For 12 years he was senior public affairs specialist for the Administrative Office of the U.S. Courts. He was inducted into Scripps College's Ohio Communication Hall of Fame in 1993.

Michael Clay Carey (MS '12, PhD '14) is an assistant professor of journalism and mass communication at Samford University, where he teaches newswriting and publication design. His scholarship focuses on community journalism. Before moving to academia, he worked for 10 years as a reporter and editor at several newspapers in Tennessee.

Virginia "Ginger" Hall Carnes (BSJ '73, MS '77) recently retired after 22 years as public relations director at Palo Alto College, one of the Alamo Colleges in San Antonio, Texas. She previously taught high school in Cincinnati and was a reporter for *The* (Huntington, W. Va.) *Herald-Dispatch* and the *San Antonio Express-News.*

Bill Choyke (BSJ '72) was editor of *The Post* from 1971 to 1972. He was a reporter and editor for more than three decades for a range of newspapers, including the Washington bureau of *The Dallas Morning News* and assistant managing editor for business at *The Tennessean* in Nashville. Most recently, he has worked as a communication strategist in Washington, D.C., for a professional association.

J. William Click (MS '59) retired in 2014 after 27 years as chair of the Department of Mass Communication at Winthrop University. He taught journalism at Ohio University between 1965 and 1983 and was director of the School of Journalism at Louisiana State University from 1983 to 1987.

Hugh M. Culbertson taught in the Ohio University School of Journalism from 1966 to 2003. He served as coordinator of graduate programs in 1972–80 and was named the university's outstanding graduate-faculty member in 1975–76. He was chosen as Educator of the Year in 1990 by the Public Relations Society of America.

Halina J. Czerniejewski (BSJ '72), now a freelance writer and editor, was nominated for a Pulitzer Prize in 1978 and received the Press Club of Cleveland's Excellence in Journalism Award for Human Interest in 1978. She worked for The Associated Press, the *Toledo Blade,* the *Chicago Sun-Times,* and SDX/SPJ national headquarters.

Sid Davis (BSJ '52) is a former White House correspondent for Westinghouse Broadcasting, a former vice president and Washington Bureau chief for NBC News, news director of WKBN-TV in Youngstown, and a former guest scholar at The Brookings Institution. He received the L.J. Hortin Distinguished Alumnus Award in 1995, was inducted into the Scripps College of Communication Hall of Fame in 2004, and received Ohio University's Medal of Merit Award in 2012.

Frank Deaner (BSJ '67) is a consultant in association management and public relations. He retired after 20 years as executive director and lobbyist for the Ohio Newspaper Association. His career includes more than 15 years in broadcast news and management. For more than 30 years he has been a senior adviser to the OU chapter of PRSSA. He currently serves on the Professional Advisory Board of the Scripps School of Journalism and annually sponsors the Deaner Journalism Scholarship.

Bernhard Debatin is professor for multimedia policy, director of the Institute for Applied and Professional Ethics, and director of Honors Tutorial Studies in Journalism at the E.W. Scripps School of Journalism. He is also director of the newly implemented double master's degree program with Leipzig University's KMW Institute. He came to Ohio University in 2000, after having taught at Leipzig University and various universities in Berlin.

Susan DeFord (BSJ '76) is a paraeducator for Montgomery County Schools in Maryland. She retired from *The Washington Post*'s Metro reporting staff in 2008 and previously reported for *The News-Press* in Fort Myers, Florida, and the *Tallahassee Democrat.*

Debbie DePeel joined the School of Journalism in 1977, a year after her graduation from high school. She was an important contributor in the school's front office for 39 years until her 2016 retirement.

Jack G. Ellis (BSC '57, ME [hon.] '97) is vice president for development emeritus. He served as CEO of the Ohio University Foundation from 1972 to 1997 and was cofounder of the Manasseh Cutler Scholars program with President Emeritus Charles Ping and Dr. W.R. Konneker.

Dru Riley Evarts (BSJ '51, MSJ '73, PhD '77) is professor emerita in the School of Journalism, having retired in 2007 after 42 years of service to Ohio University. She is well remembered for developing and teaching the school's Precision Language course. Evarts began her professional career with the *Akron Beacon Journal* and worked during sabbatical leaves and vacation times at the *Chicago Tribune,* the *Miami Herald,* the Reporters Committee for Freedom of the Press, the Scripps Howard News Service's Washington, D.C., bureau, and the U.S. Supreme Court.

Marisa Fernandez is a senior with plans for 2018 graduation. She was one of the Scripps School's three 2017 recipients of the White House Correspondents' Association scholarship. The award includes a $5,000 scholarship and an invitation to the White House Correspondents' Dinner.

Leah Fightmaster (BSJ '11) is communications associate for The Summit Country Day School and a freelance reporter for WCPO-TV in Cincinnati. Previously, she was a reporter with Enquirer Media. While at Ohio University, she worked for *The Post.*

Walter Friedenberg, the school's first Scripps Howard Visiting Professional, got his start in journalism as a sophomore at Wake Forest College when the editor of the student magazine asked him to "write a funny piece" on deadline. After Athens, he was a Fulbright lecturer in Beijing and Shanghai and, after inaugurating a new journalism chair at the University of Northern Colorado, finally successfully retired.

Lindsay Friedman (BSJ'14) is a digital and data journalist attending the Columbia School of Journalism's Lede Program. Her work has been published in the *Chicago Tribune, USA Today,* and *The Columbus Dispatch.* She was president of OU's 2014 SPJ national campus chapter of the year, a managing editor for the *Water Project,* and an editor and writer for *The Post.*

Chip Gamertsfelder (BFA '84) spent 16 years as photographer and photo editor for the *Kettering-Oakwood Times* and the *Centerville Bellbrook Times.* He has won awards from the Ohio Newspaper Association, the Ohio News Photographers Association, and the National Press Photographers Association. His work was included in a photojournalism textbook by Kenneth Kobre.

Ellen Gerl (MSJ '75), an associate professor in the E.W. Scripps School of Journalism, shot photos for *Southeast Ohio* as a student and now teaches the capstone course. She served as associate director for undergraduate studies in 2012–13.

Paul Hagen (BSJ '73) is a national reporter and columnist for *MLB.com.* He previously covered baseball for the *San Bernardino* (California) *Sun,* the *Dallas Times Herald,* the *Fort Worth Star-Telegram,* and the *Philadelphia Daily News.* In 2013 he received the J.G. Taylor Spink Award for "meritorious contributions to baseball writing."

Billy Hartman (BSJ '15) is a basketball communications assistant for the Cleveland Cavaliers. Previously, he served as an intern with the Cavaliers and the National Soccer Coaches Association of America and did freelance work with the public relations firm CMP Communications. As a student, he was a sports reporter and anchor for WOUB, worked at the Ohio Athletics Media Relations Department, and was an account executive for ImPRessions.

Henry Heilbrunn (BSJ with Honors '73) began his career at The Associated Press; moved to pre-Internet startups including Prodigy, owned by CBS, IBM, and Sears; and concluded as a strategic management consultant. He taught at OU and served on the Board of Trustees of Ohio University for three years.

Megan Henry is a senior with plans for 2018 graduation. She was one of the Scripps School's three 2017 recipients of the White House Correspondents' Association scholarship. The award includes a $5,000 scholarship and an invitation to the White House Correspondents' Dinner.

Nicholas Hirshon (PhD '16) is an assistant professor at William Paterson University in Wayne, New Jersey. He has published books and academic journal articles about sports and journalism in and around New York City. While at OU, he won top student paper honors at the 2015 national conference of the American Journalism Historians Association. Along with fellow Scripps School alum Pamela Walck (PhD '15), he coordinates the annual Joint Journalism and Communication History Conference at New York University.

Cat Hofacker is a senior with plans for 2018 graduation. She was one of the Scripps School's three 2017 recipients of the White House Correspondents' Association scholarship. The award includes a $5,000 scholarship and an invitation to the White House Correspondents' Dinner.

Ron Iori (BSJ '76) is a senior executive who has led teams of communicators at Ford, H&R Block, DeVry Education Group, and Kaplan. He started his career in newspapers (*The Wall Street Journal, Los Angeles Times*) with the help of Ohio University.

Ralph Izard, now professor emeritus, joined the School of Journalism faculty in 1966, serving as director from 1986 to 1998. After retiring from OU, he spent 11 years with the Manship School of Mass Communication at Louisiana State University, where he was interim dean in 2010–11.

Jeff Johnson (BSJ '97) is a research project manager at Educational Testing Service in Princeton, New Jersey. His wife, Ulrike, is a 2003 graduate of Leipzig University. They have two sons.

Beverly Jones (BSJ '69, MBA '75), a retired attorney and corporate executive, is now a leadership and career coach, as well as a speaker, facilitator, and writer. Based in Washington, D.C., she works with leaders in federal agencies, Congress, NGOs, companies, and academia. She is the author of a book on career resilience, *Think Like an Entrepreneur, Act Like a CEO,* and her blogs and podcasts appear on WOUB Public Media.

John Kiesewetter (BSJ '75) was editor of *The Post* in 1975. He parlayed a 13-week summer internship at *The Cincinnati Enquirer* into a 39½-year career as a reporter, assistant metro editor, and features editor, as well as 29 years as a TV critic.

Peter King (BSJ '79) is the editor-in-chief of *The MMQB,* an independent microsite covering the National Football League under the Time Inc./Sports Illustrated umbrella. He also is a football analyst for NBC Sports. He previously worked at *The Cincinnati Enquirer* and *Newsday.*

Ken Klein (BSJ '84) is executive vice president of the Outdoor Advertising Association of America. He previously worked for U.S. Senator Bob Graham, The Associated Press, and the Gannett-owned daily in Fort Myers, Florida.

Ralph E. Kliesch (BSJ '56, MS '61) is professor emeritus in the School of Journalism. He taught full time from 1965 to 1985 and as an early retiree until he fully retired in 2000. He was the school's assistant director from 1968 to 1971.

Kyle Kondik (BSJ '06) is managing editor of *Sabato's Crystal Ball,* a nonpartisan newsletter on American campaigns and elections from the University of Virginia's Center for Politics. He is based in Washington, where he manages the center's D.C. office. His book on Ohio's presidential voting history, *The Bellwether,* was released in June 2016 by Ohio University Press.

Gregory Korte (BSJ '94, BA in political science '94) is White House correspondent for *USA Today.*

Carolyn Bailey Lewis (PhD, COMS '07) is director and general manager emerita of WOUB Center for Public Media. She was the first African American woman in the continental United States to serve as GM of a public TV station. Currently, she is a faculty member in the Scripps College of Communication.

Ray Locker (MSJ '84) is Washington enterprise editor of *USA Today.* Previously, he worked for The Associated Press, the *Los Angeles Times, The Tampa Tribune,* and the *Montgomery* (Ala.) *Advertiser.* He's also author of the upcoming history book *Nixon's Gamble.*

Sara Magee (BSJ '97, PhD '08) is an associate professor of communication at Loyola University Maryland. Previously, she taught at West Virginia University, and before that, she was an Emmy Award–winning television news producer. In 2017, she became chair of the Communication Department at Loyola.

Laura McMullen (BSJ '11) is a section editor at *US News & World Report.* In Scripps journalism classes, she enjoyed covering the prevalence of bingo in the Athens area and the adventures of Grandma Gatewood, the first woman to hike the Appalachian Trail.

Isaac Noland (BSJ '14, MSJ '16) lives in Columbus, where he works as a freelance digital marketer with local chambers of commerce, small businesses, and nonprofit organizations to help improve social media and web presence. He also serves as marketing director of Ohio Brew Week. While at Ohio University, Isaac was editor-in-chief of *Speakeasy Magazine* and worked with WOUB Center for Public Media, the Ohio Pawpaw Festival, and Jackie O's Pub & Brewery.

Emma Ockerman (BSJ '17) served for two years as editor-in-chief of *The Post.* She is a financial reporter for *Bloomberg News* and has interned for the *Detroit Free Press, The Columbus Dispatch, Time* magazine, and *The Washington Post.*

Clarence Page (BSJ '69) is a Washington-based nationally syndicated columnist for the *Chicago Tribune.* He received Pulitzer Prizes for local general or spot news reporting in 1973 and for commentary in 1989. He has been a regular commentator on *The McLaughlin Group,* the *PBS NewsHour,* and other news-panel television programs.

Colette Jenkins Parker is codirector of associates for the Dominican Sisters of Peace. She worked as a staff writer at the *Akron Beacon Journal,* where she was a member of a Pulitzer Prize–winning team and earned honors from the Ohio Society of Professional Journalists and the National Association of Black Journalists. She earned an undergraduate degree in psychology at Indiana University and an associate degree in liberal arts at Holy Cross College.

Ted Pease (PhD '91) was a doctoral student and founding director of the Midwest Newspaper Workshop for Minorities at OU from 1987 to 1991. He recently has completed a 20-year stint at Utah State University, including 15 as department head, and now is a freelance writer, photographer, and salmon fisherman on the Northern California coast.

Katie Pittman plans to graduate in 2019 with degrees in journalism (News and Information) and Spanish. She is editor-in-chief of *Thread* magazine, a student-produced fashion publication.

B. DaVida Plummer (BSJ '84, MAC '86) is assistant vice president for marketing/media at Hampton University. Plummer is a six-time Emmy Award–winning writer/producer who has launched television newscasts in several media markets including Los Angeles, Chicago, and San Diego.

Sue Porter joined The E.W. Scripps Company in 1976 and was a Scripps Howard Foundation trustee from 1985 to 2005, when she became vice president of programs for the foundation. She has made more than 100 trips to campus during the past 30 years.

Michael Precker (BSJ '76) earned an MSJ from Columbia University in 1977, then went to the AP Tel Aviv bureau on the William and Shirley Fleischer Scholarship and stayed for 11 years. He became the Middle East correspondent for *The Dallas Morning News,* part of a 25-year career at the newspaper as a reporter, editor, and columnist. He now works in marketing and public relations in Dallas and can sing the OU fight song in Hebrew.

Susan Crites Price (BSJ '72, MAIA '73) is an award-winning author and a national expert on family philanthropy. Her most recent book—*Generous Genes: Raising Caring Kids in a Digital Age*—was published by Majestic Oak Press in 2015.

Tom Price (BSJ '68) is a Washington-based freelance journalist. Previously, he was editor of *The OU Post,* city editor of *The Athens Messenger,* chief politics writer for *The* (Dayton) *Journal Herald* and *Dayton Daily News,* and correspondent in the Cox Newspapers Washington Bureau.

Ann Puderbaugh (BSJ '82) is communications director of the Fogarty International Center at the National Institutes of Health in Bethesda, Maryland. Previously, she spent a decade based in London, producing foreign coverage for ABC News.

Randy Rieland (BSJ '73), after 22 years as a newspaper and magazine writer and editor, made the switch to digital media in 1995 to become part of the team that launched *Discovery.com.* He now is digital editorial director of Remedy Health Media.

Mary T. Rogus has been a faculty member in the E.W. Scripps School of Journalism since September 1999 and has been faculty adviser for OU-RTDNA since 2000. Prior to coming to Scripps, she spent 20 years as an award-winning broadcast journalist working in local television markets ranging from Dayton to Minneapolis and Pittsburgh.

Mohamed Najib El Sarayrah (MSJ, PhD '87) is professor of mass communication at Sultan Qaboos University, Oman, where he is editor-in-chief of the SQU *Journal of Arts and Social Sciences.* Previously, he was dean of the College of Arts and Social Sciences at SQU and secretary general of the Higher Population Council and the Higher Council of Media in Jordan.

Laralyn Sasaki Dearing (BSJ '86) is president and senior strategist of Laralyn and Associates LLC in Columbus. She was a staff reporter for *The Cincinnati Enquirer* before earning her JD from the University of Michigan and working for the federal court in Columbus, Bricker & Eckler law firm, the Supreme Court of Ohio, and the Ohio State Bar Foundation.

Van Gordon Sauter (BSJ '57) was a reporter for the *Detroit Free Press* and *Chicago Daily News,* anchorman in Chicago, TV station manager in Los Angeles, and censor for the CBS Television Network. He was also Paris bureau chief for CBS News, president of CBS News and CBS Sports, executive vice president of CBS, and author of four books.

Dan Sewell (BSJ '78) is Cincinnati correspondent for The Associated Press. Previously, he was the AP's Southeast Regional writer, Caribbean news editor, Florida news editor, and Chicago assistant chief of bureau, with assignments as sportswriter, business reporter, and political correspondent. He also was at *The Cincinnati Enquirer* as suburban editor.

Jerry L. Sloan (BSJ '59) is a professor emeritus of the School of Journalism. Previously, he was executive director of public affairs for Ford Motor Company. He was selected as University Professor in 1996–97, voted outstanding professor by the Greek Community Council in 1996, and named the nation's top PRSSA adviser in 1996.

Terry Smith (BSJ '77) has been editor of *The Athens News* since 1986 and added the title of publisher in 2016. Before returning to Athens, he worked as a reporter for newspapers in Ohio, Arizona, Idaho, Colorado, and West Virginia. Smith served as an adjunct instructor in Scripps from 2000 to 2010.

Burton Speakman completed his PhD at Ohio University in 2017 and currently is a part-time instructor at the University of Georgia. His 13 years in the newspaper industry included the (Bowling Green) *Sentinel-Tribune, The Madisonville Meteor, The Courier* of Montgomery County, *The Vindicator* in Youngstown, the *Bowling Green Daily News,* and the *Glasgow Daily Times.* He received his bachelor's degree from Bowling Green State University and master's degree from the University of Nebraska.

Ken Steinhoff bounced from newspaper to newspaper in Missouri, Ohio, North Carolina, and Florida, carrying business cards that called him a reporter, staff photographer, photo editor, director of photography, editorial operations manager, and telecommunications manager. When he took a buyout from *The Palm Beach Post* in 2008, he started digitizing his work, finding that the photographs he had taken since 1963 had grown enough gray whiskers to be considered history by museums today.

Guido H. Stempel III, distinguished professor emeritus, taught in the School of Journalism for 31 years—serving as director from 1972 to 1979 and in 1986—before retiring in 1996. He was editor of *Journalism Quarterly* for 17 years. Among other OU duties, he served as director of the Scripps Survey Research Center from 2002 to 2009.

Robert Stewart joined the faculty in 1987 as an assistant professor, teaching primarily broadcast journalism, media history, and international media. He served as associate director from 2006 until 2010, when he was named director. During his time on the faculty, Stewart helped develop the program with Leipzig University and was awarded Leipzig's medal of honor in 2014.

Thomas Suddes (MS '02, PhD '09) is assistant professor and coordinator of the school's Statehouse News Bureau fellowships. He also is a political columnist and editorial writer for *The* (Cleveland) *Plain Dealer* and Northeast Ohio Media Group. He worked at newspapers in Illinois, Iowa, New Hampshire, and Mississippi before joining *The Plain Dealer,* primarily as statehouse correspondent.

Michael S. Sweeney (PhD '96) is a professor and associate director for graduate studies in the School of Journalism. Previously, he filled various roles at the (Fort Worth) *Star-Telegram* and headed the department of journalism and communication at Utah State University.

Martha Cordes Towns (BSJ '60) worked for many years at the *Chagrin Valley Herald* and later at the *Chagrin Valley Times*. In 1966, she was voted best weekly newspaper columnist in Ohio. In 1985, she helped found and was the first editor of a monthly Cleveland paper called *Currents*. After 18 years, she returned to feature writing and the column she had written since 1963. Currently she is on temporary sabbatical.

Joe Vitti, born and raised in Connecticut, attended Ohio University from 1974 to 1977. In the spring of 1977, an internship at the *Arizona Daily Star* in Tucson, Arizona, working for Jack Dykinga, who had worked with Chuck Scott in Chicago, turned into a full-time job. This led to a 37-year career as a photojournalism and photo editor at newspapers in Tucson; Charleston, West Virginia; and Los Angeles. He finished his career in 2014 as a photographer and photo editor at *The Indianapolis Star*.

Patrick S. Washburn retired from the E.W. Scripps School of Journalism in 2012 after teaching for 28 years, including more than 13 years as assistant director for graduate studies. Before joining the OU faculty, he worked 10½ years on newspapers in Texas, Virginia, Georgia, and New York and spent four years in college sports information at Harvard and Louisville.

Howard Wilkinson is the politics reporter for 91.7 WVXU, Cincinnati Public Radio. For nearly 30 years prior to that, he was politics writer for *The Cincinnati Enquirer* and spent five years at the *Troy Daily News*. In 2012, Wilkinson was inducted into the Queen City Society of Professional Journalists' Greater Cincinnati Journalism Hall of Fame.

Steve Woo (BSJ '99) has worked at newspapers across the country. Most recently, he was the associate editor of *The New Physician* magazine covering medical education.

Dwight M. Woodward (BAIS '81, MSJ '89, MAIA '89) is a former newsman with The Associated Press. He worked for 10 years as senior writer/national media liaison at Ohio University News Services and as assistant director for communication at the Center for International Studies. His work at OU received awards from the National Council for Advancement of Science and Education.

Nerissa Young, associate lecturer in the E.W. Scripps School of Journalism, each year serves on the committee that plans the Schuneman Symposium on Photojournalism and New Media. She conducts summer orientation for the school, advises each year's freshman class, and advises the student SPJ chapter. In 2015, she was named the nation's top SPJ adviser, being presented the David L. Shulman Outstanding Campus Adviser Award.

INDEX